THE LION IN THE SAND

The British in the Middle East

GERALD BUTT

BLOOMSBURY

First published in 1995

Bloomsbury Publishing Plc, 2 Soho Square, London W1V 6HB

Copyright © 1995 Gerald Butt

The moral right of the author has been asserted

The publishers have made every effort to contact all holders of
copyright work. All copyright holders who have not for any reason
been contacted are invited to write to the publishers so that a full
acknowledgement may be made in subsequent editions of this work

A CIP catalogue record for this book is available from the
British Library

10 9 8 7 6 5 4 3 2 1

ISBN 0 7475 2015 1

Typeset by Hewer Text Composition Services, Edinburgh
Printed in Great Britain by Clays Ltd, St Ives plc

CONTENTS

INTRODUCTION

A mid the fog of my very earliest childhood memories at the start of the 1950s in Jordan is the clear image of a goat munching a Kit-Kat wrapper. I was watching it grazing on rocky scrubland next to our house on Jebel Webdeh, one of the hills over which the Jordanian capital, Amman, is built.

The setting was unmistakably Middle Eastern, biblical one might say, with goats and donkeys wandering over the hills. Yet the presence of the Kit-Kat paper, discarded most probably by the author, injects a discordant image of the modern West. In my subsequent memories of childhood there is often this juxtaposition of Middle Eastern and Western images, though the former are far outnumbered by the latter. I remember, for example, as a very small boy eating and enjoying tabbouleh, an Arab salad made with cracked wheat, tomatoes, mint and onion. I remember how our Arab servant, Saleh, answering the telephone, would address the caller with a loud and intimidating interrogatory 'Na'am?' meaning 'Yes?'. But these images are set alongside memories of going to Amman airport to watch my father play cricket; of being taught how to hold a cricket bat; of the news from London or of the football results coming out of the big brown radio; of hanging up my stocking on Christmas Eve ('Gerald was eager to go to bed early for once,' my father's diary of 24 December 1954 records, 'to see in the morning what Father Christmas had brought'); of having ballet lessons at the British Community School; and – in later years – of tearful airport farewells at the end of holidays from boarding school in England. In other words, like hundreds of thousands of other Britons before and since, I lived part of my life in the Middle East, but in an environment that was influenced only marginally by the world around me. It was a colonial lifestyle, and much of what the following chapters contain is a saga of expatriate life, set in the cities, villages, mountains and deserts of the Middle East.

By the early 1950s, when I was a small child, many of the great events of the century which touched the life of the Middle East had happened. Two world wars had been fought, most Arab states had won their independence from Britain and France, Israel had been created, and the Arabs had fought and lost the first of their wars against the Jewish state. Still to come were the Suez crisis and more Middle East wars. These events, though I had only the barest understanding of them at the time, touched upon my life and the lives of other Britons associated with the Middle East.

The early part of this book contains a number of historical signposts which indicate the background of some of the political and diplomatic events against which the lives of the British expatriates were lived. It is not a comprehensive history of the Middle East, nor even of Britain's role in the region. The time limit of the BBC Radio Four programmes which this book accompanies necessitated a focus on only a selection of countries where Britons were based. So the historical survey concentrates, in the main, on developments affecting these particular countries. In the later chapters, the great moments of history are described only inasmuch as they were part of the personal experience of Britons living in the region at the time. This is a collection of personal experiences, a social rather than a political history.

Although as a child in Jordan I was not aware of it, by the early 1950s most of the maps had been drawn, and the great British adventurers had hung up their topis, if they had not already gone to their graves, their memories and journals published and received with acclaim. T.E. Lawrence ('Lawrence of Arabia'), author of *Seven Pillars of Wisdom*, was one of the last and most famous of the men associated with the romantic belief that there is some mystical affinity between the British and the desert Arabs. Lawrence was realistic enough to recognize that the novelty of the descriptions contained in the early travellers' tales was enough to make their books popular. 'Our predecessors' was a larger day,' he wrote in 1938, 'in which the seeing Arabia was an end in itself. They just wrote a wander-book and the great peninsula made their prose significant.'

In the wake of the famous travellers and explorers came ordinary people leading what seemed in their day to be ordinary lives, not necessarily the stuff of significant prose. Now, with the passing of time and the phenomenal technological and social changes that the twentieth century has witnessed, the lives of the British in the Middle

INTRODUCTION

East in past eras – but in eras still well within living memory –
frequently seem quite extraordinary. The purpose of this book is
to chronicle some of the experiences and thoughts of the Britons,
including my mother and father, who lived in the Middle East for
one reason or another in the decades up to the late 1960s, and to
suggest that in many respects they have good reason to qualify as
adventurers in their own right.

Part 1

ASPECTS OF HISTORY

1

THE 'SPELL OF FAR ARABIA'?

'A respect for the rule of law and a passion for football.' The sum, in a nutshell, of Britain's legacy after many decades of British colonial rule in the Middle East – or so a retired British diplomat, Glencairn Balfour-Paul, and an Arab government minister concluded after a light-hearted discussion of the subject in the 1990s.

'It doesn't sound a very monumental legacy,' the former diplomat agreed, smiling, as he told me later about their discussion. But trying to quantify Britain's legacy is not easy. Mr Balfour-Paul related another anecdote to try to shed light on the subject. 'I was in Aden on holiday seven years ago. At the time you couldn't talk to Adenis or they would be interrogated by the police afterwards. We were on our way back from the beach, and we were in a taxi. The taxi driver suddenly said – we were talking Arabic of course – "Ah, I wish you British were back. You taught us everything of any use that we've got." "What sort of things do you mean?" I asked, out of interest. And he said: "Walking on the pavements and ironing your trousers." That was a different sort of legacy, but one could see faintly what he meant. In a sophisticated way it was probably to our credit that we didn't leave more obviously British elements behind. You see we taught them football. We never taught any Arabs cricket. Now there would be a subject for a PhD. Why among all our imperial subjects did we never get the Arabs interested in cricket? I can't answer the question.'

The tone of Mr Balfour-Paul's remarks characterizes in many ways the spirit of the complex relationship which developed during the twentieth century between the British and the Arabs. At the official level there has been much bitterness and resentment expressed by the Arabs. Blame for past actions continues to be laid at the door of succeeding British governments. Britain was the dominant colonial

3

power in the Middle East. Britain was a major exploiter of Arab oil resources. Britain was the country which played a key role in the creation of the state of Israel. Britain was one of the countries which connived with Israel at the time of Suez to try to topple President Nasser of Egypt. And so on. But at the same time, many Arabs are prepared to admit that British rule meant the imposition of order: 'a respect for the rule of law', symbolized in the words of the taxi driver in Aden as 'walking on the pavements'.

This is not to say that there is a movement in the Arab world calling for the clock to be put back and for Britain to resume its colonial role in the Middle East. Far from it. But it is interesting that even in some of the most difficult days for Britain in the region, Arabs have respected the sense of order inherent in the British presence. Abla Odell, a Palestinian lady married to a Briton, remembers the comments of her mother during one of the most traumatic moments in the life of their family. The scene was the eastern Mediterranean port city of Haifa in the closing days of the British Mandate, just before the creation of the state of Israel in 1948. Abla's family were preparing to leave their homeland of Palestine, never to go back as it turned out. 'My mother saw the British police guarding us on the way to the harbour and she said: "What a pity we are going to lose the British." We learned a lot from the British – especially their organization.'

The governments in London in the first half of the century may have mistaken respect for the order of British rule for a desire on the part of the Arabs to go on living under the wing of the former imperial power. Certainly there were many instances when the British were insensitive to the demands of Arab nationalists, and slow to meet the aspirations of Arabs demanding the right to run their own affairs. At the same time, though, some Arabs feel resentful towards their own leaders. Having achieved independence, they ask, why were the new regimes not able to strike more of a balance – governing their own affairs, while retaining at least some of the worthwhile habits and institutions inherited from Britain?

Sudan is one Arab country which, more than most others, absorbed British practices and institutions. Over recent years, however, the Islamic fundamentalist regime in Khartoum has imposed a new and radically different order. Mr Balfour-Paul spent five years in the Sudan Defence Force in the 1940s, and then joined the Sudan Political Service. 'In Sudan, until the present government came to power,' he said, 'they had a great respect for British democratic practices and education and all that because we were there much longer and administered them more directly than other Arab states. Only a few months ago two Sudanese who were once my subordinates, the same age as me, in a district in the Sudan, drove down here to Devon for lunch. They sat here crying, tears pouring out of their eyes. They said: "If you only knew what it's like to have to hate your own country." These are people who were just as interested in independence as any other educated Sudanese. But what has happened in their country just reduced them to tears because they had inherited a certain admiration for the British way of life. They wanted to run Sudan themselves but in the way we had tried to inculcate.'

One could argue, as Mr Balfour-Paul does, that it is to Britain's credit that it did not try to force Middle Eastern countries to adopt more British habits and culture in the way that the French imposed their style on Algeria, Lebanon and Syria. A few tangible British institutions survive in ways that are still just about recognizable, like the Gezira Sporting Club in Cairo, once an exclusive centre of British expatriate life, now a facility open to all with the means to pay. Some traditions, too, linger on. For example, the Jordanian army, modelled closely on British lines, still has a bagpipe band, and Israel continues to follow the tradition established by the British during the Palestine Mandate days of holding football matches on Saturday afternoons, even though Saturday is the sacred day of the week for Jews. But at the official level the relationship between the British and the countries of the Middle East for most of the century was one of master and servant.

At the personal level, though, the relationship was much more complex. Sometimes it was remote, sometimes close. But, despite all the bitterness that from time to time characterized political ties, the relationship was seldom hostile. The Arabs have a remarkable ability to maintain personal relations with foreigners, even though they may be opposed to the policies of their government. Valerie Sale was born in Egypt and lived there for many years. She says that neither her family nor her friends ever experienced any personal hostility towards them, even during the most extreme moments of anti-British feeling among the Egyptians.

'There was,' she recalls, 'a very nice English master at the Egyptian primary school – Mr Bevan. They had one of these riots starting up

– there were about 500 students – and they started to say: "Down with Churchill." He thought he'd better get out while he could. He was the only Englishman in the place and he slipped out the back of the school and got in his car, but the battery was flat. Two minutes later this crowd of boys poured out screaming and yelling anti-British things and they rushed up to him and said: "Push your car for you, sir?" and they pushed him all the way back to his flat. Every now and then they would stop and say: "Down with Churchill", and then push him on until they got him back.'

Not all riots in the Arab world were so gentlemanly. British banks (including one in which my father was working at the time) and other institutions have frequently been the target of mob violence, and Britons – because of their nationality – have been attacked. The Right Reverend John Brown, Bishop of Cyprus and the Gulf, remembers as a young priest in Jordan finding himself caught up with an angry crowd in the West Bank (in those days administered by Jordan) at the time of the Suez crisis in 1956. 'One night in Jericho, everything was in flames, rioters were out in force on the main road. In those days you had to go through the town of Jericho to get across the Jordan valley, which meant passing through the refugee camp. I had a little old and, fortunately, battered Morris 8, and I had a pretty elderly priest with me. Suddenly the car was totally surrounded by scores and scores of rioters all hammering at the window, which I closed very rapidly. They were shouting obscenities at us. As soon as they saw we were English they went wild. Then you could hear the first stone strike and then another; and when one has struck you get lots – the glass broke and came through into the car. In the end it was quite desperate and so I put my foot down and hoped I wouldn't hit anyone. The crowds parted.'

But such outbursts of emotionally charged anti-British feelings – in some cases, officially orchestrated – passed quickly and did no permanent damage to personal relationships. Valerie Sale, looking back on her days in Egypt, believes that 'the people who worked there got on very well with the Egyptians. But you got the odd ones, the snooty ones, who came out for a short time – they didn't want to know. The people in the army were the worst, they were very cliquey and didn't want to know anything outside their own people in their regiment. By and large the people who lived there for a long time had Egyptian friends and were very fond of them.'

In general, though, in my own experience growing up in the Middle

East and that of many Britons I have spoken to, there was not a strong tradition of personal friendliness being converted into strong friendships. The British, by and large, tended to remain isolated from the local communities, sticking to British traditions, and keeping one eye always on the home country. Looking at my father's diaries for the thirty years he spent in the Middle East, for example, I notice that most entries begin with a description of the weather and end with the details of the progress of Bristol Rovers, the football team he supported, or of Gloucestershire County Cricket Club.

As a rule Britons made little attempt to bridge the formidable gulf of temperament, language and culture between the two races. Aside from the difficulties of learning Arabic, Islam has tended to remain a mystery to the British – even among those who have lived in Arab countries for several years. Of all the traditions and customs associated with Islam it is the sacred fasting month of Ramadan which, in my experience, has caused most mystery and irritation to foreigners in the Middle East. During this month Muslims are required to fast during the hours of daylight. Because the Islamic calendar is out of step with the Western one, Ramadan comes at a different time each year. When Muslims are required to fast in a summer month, their energy is sapped long before nightfall.

Most expatriates have stories to tell about the difficulties of getting things done during Ramadan. C.S. Jarvis, a British governor of the Egyptian province of Sinai between the two world wars, recalled in his book *Desert and Delta* the irritation felt by so many foreigners before and since. 'The Christian employer of domestic staff will be called in the morning anything from half an hour to two hours late, will find the water in the bathroom stone-cold, his coffee at breakfast undrinkable, and his eggs uncooked. On setting out after this delightful meal a blear-eyed and corpse-like chauffeur, who has been up all night, will fail to start the car for the simple reason that there is no petrol in the tank and on arrival at the office, which during Ramadan does not open till 10 a.m., the Mahommedan members of the staff will be found to be in a lethargic and stupid state and quite incapable of finding any file or giving a coherent answer on any subject. At night after a badly cooked dinner served by half-witted servants he will be kept awake by the ceaseless chatter of boabs (doorkeepers) at his gateway and by passing parties of revellers moving from one heavy midnight meal to another, and if this does not have the required effect of depriving everyone of slumber artillery salvos are fired at midnight and 3 a.m. to summon the faithful to prayer.'

The sense that the British were often unenlightened onlookers among the Arabs may have been particularly noticeable during Ramadan. But in countless cases Britons were too wrapped up in their own lives to bother much about the Arabs or their customs. Ronald Ballantine, a retired pilot, was based in Cairo during the Second World War. 'We had a lot of fun,' he remembers. 'I suppose we lived in a narrow circle from the point of view of being in a foreign country. We didn't know many Egyptians. I think my wife knew one or two but I certainly didn't.'

While the extent of contact between the British and the Arabs varied considerably, when the two groups did encounter each other in the Middle East the Britons involved were invariably impressed, if not overwhelmed, by the warmth of Arab hospitality. This was true at all times and among all walks of life.

Glencairn Balfour-Paul says he could give scores of examples of the generosity and hospitality he received from Arabs during his working days in the Middle East. He remembers one incident in particular from the Second World War. 'When I was an adjutant in southern Libya in 1942 my commandant took me with him to look out the territory, and we went into this gigantic desert. Eventually we came to a tiny little oasis, with small salt pools, a little hill and two grass huts. There was one old man, two or three women, two goats and some hens. That was all. He didn't know what we were, Germans, English, French or Italians. We had cups of tea with him and exchanged pleasantries and then we drove on. And he insisted, as a matter of honour, of giving up one of his two goats and two of his hens – which was about half his cattle. He wouldn't take anything in exchange and we were loaded with goodies anyway. It's a matter of "sharaf", of honour, for an Arab to be hospitable, but it's humiliating for anyone as mean as me. That happened everywhere one went.'

A decade later, in the lower Gulf states before the discovery of oil, Martin Buckmaster was a young diplomat establishing contact with the various sheikhs and tribal leaders. Viscount Buckmaster recalls being 'constantly overwhelmed almost anywhere where one stopped. The sheikh would slaughter an animal for one, and provide one with a great meal. And on one occasion, I remember, when I had to dash back to my headquarters and couldn't stop he said: "Well, you must have a meal with me. If you don't, I will divorce my wife. And it will be your fault."'

Even in the bustle of the big cities the tradition of hospitality was not lost. Anne Tatham lived in the Lebanese capital, Beirut, for ten years beginning in the late 1950s, when the city had the reputation of being the Paris of the Middle East. She says she will never forget the politeness and warmth of the Arabs. 'One of the greatest things we learnt in the Middle East was the importance of courtesy and hospitality as a means of getting things done. It used to horrify me back in England when you'd sit down in someone's house and no one would say: "Would you like a cup of coffee?", but they would plunge straight in to whatever it was we were going to discuss. You go to a Middle Eastern person's house and they say: "You're very welcome", and they sit you down and give you a cup of coffee and some nuts or something. Then there's a little ritual where they ask you how you are and how your children are. When everybody's sat there comfortably they start to talk about what really matters. They would never start to talk without all the courtesies being observed first.'

Witnessing and, perhaps, absorbing Arab customs of hospitality is one thing. Getting further beneath the skin of the Arabic language and culture is quite another. C.S. Jarvis wrote that 'Arabic is a most difficult language, and so hard to master that during the whole of my service in the East I never met an Englishman who spoke it well enough to pass as a native.'

Whether many Britons have spoken Arabic 'as a native' is doubtful. But within the British foreign service more than a handful have become very proficient indeed in the language – including Mr Balfour-Paul and Viscount Buckmaster. There is a tendency in Britain, not least among those who sympathize with Israel, to see these Arabists as inheritors of a tradition of Britons having a love affair with the Arab world – as being part of a line of descendants that has included Sir Richard Burton, Charles Doughty and T.E. Lawrence.

Bertram Thomas was another in the list. In 1932 he published a book called *Arabia Felix* which described his crossing, as a young political officer, of the Empty Quarter of the Arabian desert. His writings, like others of his and earlier generations, encouraged British readers to view the Arab world through a rosy mist of romance. Mr Thomas took with him as mascot when he set off on his difficult journey from Muscat, on the Gulf of Oman, a

copy of 'Arabia' by Walter de la Mare, a poem which ends with
the lines:

> Still eyes look coldly upon me,
> Cold voices whisper and say –
> He is crazed with the spell of far Arabia,
> They have stolen his wits away.

The opening paragraphs of the book are clearly designed to conjure
up a spell of Arabia. 'It was midnight of the 4th–5th October
1930. The little Arab port of Muscat lay asleep . . . I was secretly
embarking on my long-cherished ambition to unveil the unknown
southern Arabian desert. To-morrow, the news of my disappearance
would startle the bazaar and a variety of fates would doubtless be
invented for me by imaginations of Oriental fertility . . .'

The foreword to Thomas's book was written by T.E. Lawrence. It
is as though he intended his words to be an epitaph to mark the end
of the great British tradition of romantic travel in the Arab world –
travel for travel's sake. 'You see, in my day,' he wrote with a hint of
sadness and nostalgia, 'there were real Arabian veterans. Upon each
return from the East I would repair to Doughty, a looming giant,
white with eighty years, headed and bearded like some renaissance
Isaiah. Doughty seemed a past world, in himself . . .' Lawrence
went on to say that what he called 'the Master Arabians' had all
gone. Now, Arabians 'must frame excuses for travelling. One will
fix latitudes, the silly things, another collect plants or insects (not
to eat, but to bring home), a third make war, which is coals to
Newcastle. We fritter our allegiances and loyalties.'

Despite these comments from Lawrence and his accurate obser-
vation that thereafter people coming to the Middle East would do
so for a specific purpose – i.e. to make a living – the idea that some
romantic affinity ties the British to the Arab world has taken a long
time to fade. It is high time that the myth be laid to rest. And there
is nobody better qualified to do so than Sir James Craig, another
distinguished retired diplomat and a brilliant Arabist. Does he think,
first of all, that there is some kind of special affinity between the
British and the Arabs?

'That's what is often said, particularly by the British,' he replied.
'I'm not sure. If you mean, is there some kind of affinity of
temperament or character, the answer is "No". If you mean that

because of history the Arabs and the British have been thrown together in different ways over a long period of time and know each other rather better than we know other peoples, then there is something in that.'

Sir James traces the origins of the relationship to past centuries when travellers to India started to take an interest in the region they were passing through. 'Then we had a fillip to the study of practical Arabic (not academic Arabic, that was always the sphere of the Germans) once again because of India. Our people there were having to speak languages which had the Arabic alphabet, and large elements of Arabic in their vocabulary; or they were learning Persian, again with strong borrowings from Arabic. So, if you like, they were enticed into Arabic – that's what happened to Philby, for example. He began in the Indian civil service, and learned some Indian languages, then Persian, and then Arabic.'

On the question of a supposed romantic attachment of Britain to the Middle East, Sir James has firm views. 'British Arabists today are often accused of having a love affair with the Arabs which, in my view, is nonsensical. In particular it is alleged that they're all in love with the desert. That may have been true of some people in the old days. It has not been true in my working lifetime. I have never been on a camel in my life.'

Sir James says he remembers, when he first went to the Middle East, being astonished to discover that the Bedouin whom he 'had learnt from British writings to regard as a great crowd of Robin Hoods, wonderfully generous gentlemen, men of honour, living this noble life, the "Noble Savage" and so on – that these same Bedouin were regarded by the town Arabs, who were much the majority, as being crooked, unreliable, treacherous beggars'.

In the view of Sir James Craig there is 'a parallel with the way in which, after Sir Walter Scott, the English regarded the Highlands Scotsmen as being enormously romantic adventurers, whereas the lowland Scots regarded them as being a lot of feckless bandits. So I was never hooked on the Bedouin idea. I quite liked camping in the desert. The Bedouin I met there I found interesting but not entrancing, and very few of my colleagues felt differently. I think if we're talking about Lawrence or Glubb or Philby, then that old myth may have had some reality, but that was a generation or two generations before.'

Glencairn Balfour-Paul also confesses that he was 'not one of those who fell for the spell of Arabia. You may remember R.A.B. Hamilton, who was a good Arabist and who wrote many books about southern Arabia deploring those who did fall under that spell. He called them oafish spirits who gather like dung-flies on a camel track and do us much harm. I was never that. I can truly say that I enjoyed the urban sophisticated Arab just as much as, for different reasons than, the nomad in the desert.'

Bishop John Brown is also an Arabist who has spent much of his working life in the Middle East. In his view the British and the Arabs 'have never integrated. We've made many friends, but that's the highest I'd put it. There's always the point – a certain boundary that you know you can't cross – a significant cultural and social barrier. I'm suspicious of cross-cultural integrations just as I am cynical about Lawrence of Arabia. I don't think that kind of attempt at assimilation is ever going to be successful; it's always going to be part of a myth.'

Sir Anthony Parsons is also a distinguished diplomat and Middle East expert now in retirement. He feels that there is some kind of affinity between the British and the Arabs. But like others he insists that it has nothing to do with 'the old-fashioned Lawrence of Arabia, public school, camel-riding absurdities'. Rather, he sees the affinity relating to the fact that 'we laugh at the same kind of jokes. If there is some absurd situation going on at a public occasion you will often find that the English and the Arabs are both laughing and nobody else has seen the joke.'

His remarks reminded his wife, Sheila, of an occasion many years before in Jerusalem when, as British diplomatic representatives, they were hosting a lunch for the Arab press. 'There was this old man,' she remembers, 'who said he hated the Americans and he hated the French. I thought he was going to say something nice about the English, and I smiled. But he went on to say: "My hatred of them is nothing to my hatred of the British." I had been out of the Arab world for a while and said: "I'm so glad nothing has changed." And we laughed and in spite of it all we were good friends.'

The greatest affinity at the level of humour is to be found between the British and the Egyptians. Both races are self-deprecating by nature and are appreciative of the absurdities of life. Mr Balfour-Paul remembers hosting a dinner one night in Jordan and hearing a Jordanian and an Egyptian 'sitting for hours and hours under the stars exchanging the sort of funny stories that the Egyptians love to tell against their own government. The only one I recall now is of an exchange of telegrams between Nasser and Khrushchev in the fifties when Egypt felt threatened from various directions outside. The following exchange of telegrams took place:

> Nasser to Khrushchev: Send tanks, aeroplanes, guns, ammunition.
> Khrushchev to Nasser: Send cash.
> Nasser to Khrushchev: Have no cash.
> Khrushchev to Nasser: Tighten your belts.
> Nasser to Khrushchev: Send belts.

That joke, Glencairn Balfour-Paul says, 'is very characteristic of a lot of Arabs. What you must never forget is that you mustn't tell those sorts of stories about them. But criticism of their own government or own people is entirely proper and good fun.'

Aside from enjoying their own jokes, there will have been many occasions when the Arabs were amused, as well as bewildered or angered, by what appeared to be fairly eccentric behaviour by the expatriates. At times, the actions of the British, as often as not stimulated by alcohol, could be boorish and rude.

Denis Lunn, a contemporary of my father's in the Imperial Bank of Persia (later the British Bank of the Middle East), described in his autobiography *Rags of Time* spending a night in a hotel in Damascus in 1937 en route to Persia. He and his wife 'were headed towards the restaurant when a deep contralto voice hailed us in English nearby. I turned in the direction of the voice. Three middle-aged women, all obviously British, ensconced in plush armchairs with tumblers in their hands, waved a trio of welcomes and summoned us to join them. There was nothing for it. Introductions followed, and a new round of drinks appeared.' Later, the oldest of the three women 'held forth on the state of the desert, the delay, the lack of comfort in the hotel, the awful food and the general unpleasantness of life for those unjustly compensated paragons whose fates took them to the East. She damned and blasted all and sundry with total disregard for the effect of her loud-voiced invective on others in the room.'

Many decades later in the Gulf I and other passengers were embarrassed on one occasion travelling by plane from Bahrain to Kuwait. The latter state is dry, and a British rugby team from the emirate had been visiting Bahrain for a game and for a good many drinks afterwards. What started with good-humoured singing and monkey-play ended sourly as the plane neared Kuwait. The rugby team, fortified still further by drinks brought on to the plane, started to be abusive about Arabs. The affair ended in fist-fights on the bus taking passengers to the airport terminal.

I have to confess to being party myself to another occasion of alcohol abuse in the Middle East – a less serious occasion and one which provided both amusement and material gain to the onlookers. While attending a course at Tunis University I and my British companions celebrated some milestone or other in the programme by buying several bottles of cheap wine and taking the little train out to the beach beyond Carthage. There, under the stars, we swigged the stuff as if it was water while a grinning circle of Tunisian boys built up around us. The details thereafter are vague. But at some point we foreigners were all in the sea, having left our clothes on the sand. When we emerged, the crowd had dispersed, taking with them our watches and money. We paid for that embarrassing experience in many ways.

The Arabs are as aware as anyone of the effect of alcohol. What they must find puzzling are some of the eccentricities of the British. For example, the way the British have been prepared to put up with considerable discomfort in the pursuit of some mysterious goal or other. The early British archaeologists were a source of curiosity and amusement. In 1926, Sir Flinders Petrie was working at a site in the desert near Gaza. The lack of clean water posed a problem. In her biography of Sir Flinders, *A Life in Archaeology*, Margaret S. Drower described how 'the local wells produced brackish undrinkable water, so a camel had to be sent to Gaza several times a week for a fresh supply ... The camp was completed by an elderly doctor named Parker, who proved a great acquisition: though frail in appearance he was indefatigable on the dig, would get up at four in the morning and thought nothing of walking eighteen miles to Gaza and back in a day ...' Even amid hardships one invariably finds touches of quirky British humour. In 1890, when the Gaza area was under the control of the Ottoman Turks, Sir Flinders was starting another dig. The rule was that he had to be supervised by a certain Ibrahim Effendi, a very reluctant appointee of Ottoman officials in Jerusalem. Once again, 'water was a problem: they got their only potable supply from a deep well at Bureyr six miles away, stagnant and very green and salt: "though I boiled it well, yet the colour and taste of it is almost too much for me. When boiled it is three courses in one, soup, fish and greens." The Effendi was now proving more amenable, even affable. Conversation was sometimes difficult, but Petrie found he could keep him interested by reading out to him from *Whitaker's Almanack* the salaries of government officials in England.'

The Arabs on the Petrie digs must surely have been as baffled by Parker's energy as they must have been bemused by readings from *Whitaker's Almanack*. But it is difficult to imagine what they made of the sight on New Year's Eve 1927 when a party from the dig in the desert 'walked to Gaza for a party, "with their ties and collars and toothbrushes and the ukulele"'.

Thinking up ways of providing entertainment has traditionally occupied much of the time of the British in the Middle East. Valerie Sale remembers as a child in Egypt hilarious treasure hunts around the countryside. Then 'at Christmas every year we had a donkey paper chase for everybody. There used to be about thirty or forty people charging about on donkeys. The Egyptians thought we were crazy, but they loved it.'

A striking feature which emerges from the anecdotes of Britons who lived and worked in the Middle East in decades gone by is one of fun, even if at times it was rather forced. Sir James Craig, remembering his time as a teacher at the Middle East Centre for Arabic Studies (MECAS) at a village in Lebanon in the fifties, says that a pillar of their entertainment was 'the ubiquitous Scottish dancing once a week. The first director there and his wife were extremely enthusiastic and used to put great moral pressure on the students to attend the dancing.' The urge that gripped the British when they lived in the Middle East in past decades (as it does still today) to start performing Scottish dances (and Morris dancing) is inexplicable. It is an obsession that pursued Sir James Craig wherever he went. When I asked him about entertainment in Dubai in the late sixties and early seventies, he replied gloomily: 'There was Scottish dancing. There always is.'

The sense of fun was seldom absent, even when the conditions were primitive or difficult; or when there was danger. Time and again, humour comes to the rescue. Sir Anthony and Lady Parsons laughed as they recalled what could have been a dangerous incident in Bahrain in 1967 at the time of the Arab-Israeli war when anti-Western feelings were running high throughout the Middle East. 'I remember,' Sheila Parsons said, 'when the crowd were getting very excited outside and

Tony got very pompous and started saying we'd got to defend the [British Political] Agency. The British army wanted to come, but Tony said: "Never. If a shot is fired it'll never be forgotten." And I remember you came upstairs and started barking out orders to me like a soldier, saying: "I want all the doors and all the windows locked; and we'll hold them on the stairs" – like General Gordon. I did all this and I may say that our Agency then had a huge balcony overlooking the sea with masses of locks. I locked all these. Then it all died down and Tony came up and said he wanted to listen to the radio – to the resignation of Nasser. But I'd lost the master key – we couldn't unlock any of the doors.'

The Parsons kept cool in a crisis – a constant theme in the anecdotes from the British in the Middle East. Keeping up appearances, especially among British officials, was another priority, even under unusual or difficult conditions. C.S. Jarvis, in *Desert and Delta*, described the dangers, as he saw them, of a British administrator living a lonely life in a remote outpost going native – becoming 'stamped with the Bedouin hall-mark'. C.S. Jarvis continued: 'It may be argued that the wearing of a black tie at night is a queer and petty method of fighting against this Bedouin bewitchment, but it is a gesture, a definite stand in fact, against the very natural desire to let all unnecessary details and routine go by the board. There is something so entirely British about the proceeding that unconsciously one regains every evening something of the Occident that has been lost or Orientalized during the day. Moreover, hygiene demands after twelve hours of burning sun and considerable heat in a dusty country that some sort of toilet is made in the evening even if only for the sake of comfort and personal cleanliness. This being the case, there is no reason why one should not put on the correct dress for the occasion and make one's solitary dinner something of a function.'

A similar attitude, but for different reasons, is described by Sir Gawain Bell. As a young officer, he was in charge of a remote Camel Gendarmerie on the edge of the Negev desert at Beersheba in southern Palestine (then under British control) just before the outbreak of the Second World War. 'After the war had started and we weren't doing too well, it seemed to me that the appearance that one gave to the people generally was important. If they saw Bell looking very gloomy, they'd say: "Oh dear, the British are losing the war." But if they saw him looking cheery, they'd say: "He knows something, something that we don't." So, at night I always wore a dinner jacket for dinner. I was alone, but I had a cook who served me dinner with full ceremony. I tried to make a point too that when I went to the office in the morning I appeared to be perfectly relaxed, to show that there was no problem.'

It wasn't just the British officials who felt they had a duty to keep up appearances. My mother, Muriel Butt, a new bride in the summer of 1938, underwent a gruelling journey across the desert on her way to Iran, where my father was being posted. It was her first experience of the Middle East. Even as she arrived at the Iraq–Iran border it was clear that what was on her mind was the desire to maintain European standards in this strange new region. 'At the customs post,' she recalls, 'there was a tea house where we were handed some cooked chicken wrapped in Persian bread. We were handed this without a plate or anything. We chatted to an American missionary lady, and later when we met she said she remembered the expression on my face as I was handed the chicken. She said I clearly didn't know what to do with it. She also noticed that I was wearing stockings and a white jacket. Everyone else travelled in clothes that didn't show the dirt.'

My mother came to the Middle East to be with my father, Archie Butt. He, in turn, had begun a career for a British bank in the region some years before, not lured by any 'spell of far Arabia', but because at a time of severe economic recession in Britain, the firm offered the chance of a job for a young graduate from Cambridge with a first-class degree in mathematics.

For my parents, setting up home in Iran (or Persia, as it was more commonly called by the British in those days) was a considerable adventure. But British involvement – political, military and commercial – was already well established there and in several areas of the Middle East.

2

THE ROUTE TO INDIA

On one side of Tahrir Square, the stark, dusty and noisy square in the centre of Alexandria, lies a corner of England. The Anglican church of St Mark's, Manchiyeh, is a formidable monument to the days when Britain was the dominant power in Egypt. It is a solid, flat-roofed, pseudo-Byzantine structure that does not look out of place in a Middle Eastern setting, despite the carved frieze high on the outside wall which starts 'The Lord is Gracious His Mercy is Everlasting . . .' E.M. Forster, in his *Alexandria – a History and Guide*, dismissed St Mark's as 'a tolerable building'.

St Mark's is, without question, anachronistic in contemporary Alexandria. Britain's day in Egypt ended in the early 1950s. The British community in Alexandria these days has dwindled almost to insignificance. But the church still contains surprising echoes of past eras. At the end of sung Communion on a Sunday in 1994, the then Archdeacon, Father Howard Levett, read the notices to the little pockets of congregation in the vast church and asked if anyone wanted to add anything. 'We need volunteers,' a well-manicured British voice from the organ loft announced, 'for a cricket match against Cairo. Next Tuesday afternoon at the Greek Club . . .'

Outside St Mark's lies a solid reminder of Britain's former dominance of Egypt. A marble scroll at the doorway reads: 'Sacred to the memory of NCOs and men of the 2nd Batt Duke Of Cornwall's Lt. Infantry who died in Egypt during the campaign of 1882 and subsequent occupation by British forces.' It was in 1882 that Britain established a solid foothold in the Middle East. The occupation of Egypt lasted for more than half a century, and the country became the foundation stone upon which Britain's policy for the whole region was built.

The occupation of Egypt marked the beginning of Britain's role as the most influential colonial power in the Arab world. (I use the word 'colonial' loosely, because, with the exception of Aden, Arab countries did not become British colonies in the strict sense.) The British were not strangers to the Middle East. Arabs, when asked, will point without hesitation to the Crusades of the eleventh and twelfth centuries as the first instance of British and other Western powers meddling in the eastern Mediterranean area. Certainly the experiences of the Crusades coloured the attitudes of the peoples from the two regions towards each other and established prejudices which have never been eradicated. For Europeans, the Crusades represented an attempt by the civilized world to secure the holy sites of Christianity in the face of threats from barbaric Muslim hordes. In the Middle East the episode – not regarded in any sense as a 'crusade' with its modern connotation, nor called by that name – was seen as a crude invasion and occupation by ill-mannered and intemperate barbarians from the west. The fact that the Crusaders were eventually driven out of the region by the Muslim armies has been taken ever since by the Arabs as an allegory for subsequent Western encroachments into the Middle East.

But the seeds of Europe's modern concern with the Middle East were sown with the emergence of Turkish power in the region. The Ottoman empire, with its centre in Constantinople, dominated the Middle East for five centuries up to the First World War. At its height, the empire stretched over a vast area, from Algeria and Tunisia in the west, through Egypt, down the western edge of the Arabian peninsula to include the sacred Islamic sites in Mecca, up the eastern Mediterranean coast and around as far as the Gulf in what is now Iraq and Kuwait. From Turkey westwards the empire took in Albania, and areas of Moldavia to the north.

The Ottoman Sultan in Constantinople was acknowledged by his Muslim subjects throughout the empire as the Caliph of Islam ('caliph' deriving from the Arabic word for 'successor' – the successor to the Prophet Muhammad as leader of the Islamic community). While in some outlying areas Ottoman subjects paid little more than lip-service to Constantinople and local rulers became powerful in their own right, the empire nevertheless represented a formidable power on Europe's doorstep.

The British, like the French, the Dutch and the Portuguese, were keen to use their seafaring and trading prowess to make deals with the Turks and to keep Turkish expansionist aspirations in check. In September 1581 the Levant Company was established in London to do precisely this. The company's charter spoke of how Britain's 'welbeloved Subjects Edward Osborne Alderman of our Citie of London, and Richard Staper of our sayde City Marchant, have by great adventure and industrie, with their great costes and charges, by the space of sundry late yeeres, travailed, and caused travaile to bee taken, as well by secret and good means, as by dangerous ways and passages both by lande and Sea, to finde out and set open a trade of Marchandize and trafique into the Lands, Islands, dominions, and territories of the great Turke . . .' (The text of the Levant Company charter and extracts from other historical records quoted in this chapter are taken from *The Middle East and North Africa in World Politics – A Documentary Record*, Yale University Press, 1975.)

The Levant Company became more than a trading institution. It provided over the next two centuries British diplomatic and consular staff, and generally looked after Britain's interests, gradually succeeding in winning concessions from the Ottoman authorities.

The Ottoman empire, while seeking trading links with its western neighbours, was constrained against expanding its military and political influence in this direction by a constant threat on its eastern flank. The Ottomans and the overwhelming majority of their subjects (most of whom were Arabs) were Sunni Muslims, part of the mainstream branch of Islam. The Muslims of Persia on their eastern borders were Shiites (as the majority of Muslims in Iran are still). The Shiites split away from the mainstream of the Islamic community in a bitter and violent dispute over succession in the decades after the death of the Prophet Muhammad in the seventh century. So hostility between the Ottoman and Persian empires in the seventeenth and eighteenth centuries had an ingredient of religious as well as political rivalry.

At the same time as the Levant Company was making contact with the Ottomans, the British and the Dutch were trying to wrest control of the spice trade routes around the Gulf and the Arabian Sea from the Portuguese. The Persians also were keen to see what appeared to be a Portuguese attempt to establish an empire in the region thwarted. So they welcomed the efforts of the British and Dutch adventurers. British traders in the form of the Muscovy Company had already made an attempt to set up an overland trading route from the Caspian Sea area across Russia to bring Persian silk to Britain. While this arrangement did not last long, Britain's credentials in Persia had been recognized. This process was advanced when a small group of British mercenaries, led by Sir Anthony Sherley, helped to organize the army of Shah Abbas I, a formidable military and political leader.

Shah Abbas's army drove the Portuguese out of southern Persia in 1602. With the help of ships of the British East India Company the Persians forced the Portuguese out of their last positions – on Hormuz island, which, in honour of the Shah, became known as Bandar Abbas.

Through the British East India Company, Britain won considerable privileges, or capitulations, in Persia. The concessions granted by the Shah, when tabulated and signed, stated that 'in the behalf of the supreme Majesty of King James there might continually reside at the court of Shah Ababs an ambassador'. Persian port officials, the Shah decreed, could not exact from British ships 'one farthing more than the accustomed duties which my own subjects pay'. The British were permitted to import whatever they wanted and trade freely, with 'nobody molesting them, or offering them any force or violence'. And in a paragraph designed to guarantee the safety of the British community the Shah agreed that they could keep 'whatsoever sort of arms and weapons in their houses: and if in their travels any person shall steal anything from them, and they in their defence thereof kill him, the governors of that jurisdiction shall not molest them for it . . .'

More than a century later the British East India Company was entrenching itself further in Persia with the establishment of a strong presence at Bushire in the south of the country. A royal decree granted the company the right to 'have as much ground, and in any part of Bushire they choose to build a factory on, or at any other port in the Gulf. They may have as many cannon mounted on it as they choose, but to be no larger than six pound bore: and they may build factory houses in any part of the kingdom they choose.' Bushire became the headquarters of the British East India Company and, in later years and until well into the twentieth century, the centre from which British political and administrative control of the Gulf radiated.

Britain, meanwhile, had consolidated its economic and political relationship with the Ottoman empire, a number of concessions being listed in the Treaty of Capitulations of 1675. Some related specifically to trade. For example, the treaty stipulated that 'duties shall not be demanded or taken of the English or the merchants sailing under the flag of that nation, on any piastres or sequins they may import into our sacred Dominions, or on those they may transport to any other

place'. One item, though, related to the lifestyle of British officials
– a subject close to the heart of expatriates in the Middle East ever
since. It stated that 'no obstruction or hindrance shall be given to the
Ambassadors, Consuls and other Englishmen, who may be desirous
of making wine in their houses, for the consumption of themselves
and families . . .'

Despite the commercial contacts with the world beyond the borders
of the empire, the Ottomans did not encourage change or innovation,
nor even inquisitiveness among their scholars and scientists. To put
the matter bluntly, while Europe was experiencing an explosion of
ideas through the Renaissance, the Reformation and the Counter-
Reformation, the Islamic world remained isolated and introverted.
In terms of technology – military as well as civilian – the Ottomans
began to slip further and further behind. So, in 1798, when Europe
re-entered the Middle East as a military power for the first time since
the Crusades, the Ottomans were in no position to resist.

The intervention came from France, and more particularly from the
young Napoleon Bonaparte. He reckoned he could see a weakness in
Britain's overseas power which he could exploit, and at the same time
win a gigantic prize for his country. Napoleon's idea was to capture
the Ottoman province of Egypt, the strategic crossroads on the route
to India. From Suez, he believed, he could send another French force
to defeat the British in India.

Like other invaders of Egypt before and since, Napoleon landed
at Alexandria. His army then marched along the banks of the
Nile to Cairo. Egypt had been weakened for decades by squabbles
between the Ottoman officials nominally running the country and
the Mamluks (formerly slaves and mercenaries from Turkey and Asia
who had gradually taken power for themselves). The Mamluks were
defeated at the Battle of the Pyramids, and Napoleon's army took
control. On 2 July 1798 Napoleon issued a proclamation to the
Egyptian people. 'For too long,' it read, 'this assortment of slaves
bought in Georgia and the Caucasus has tyrannized the most beautiful
part of the world; but God, on Whom all depends, has ordained that
their empire is finished.' The proclamation warned that any villages
taking up arms against the army would be burnt down, and ended
with the words: 'Each man shall thank God for the destruction of the
Mamluks and shall shout Glory to the Sultan! Glory to the French
Army, friend! May the Mamluks be cursed and the peoples of Egypt
be blessed.'

Neither Napoleon's appeal for loyalty to the Ottoman Sultan nor his attempt to convince the Egyptian people of the altruistic intent of the French occupation was taken at face value either in Constantinople or London. To the Sultan it was immediately clear that unless action was taken, a chunk would be lopped off the Ottoman empire, while Britain realized for the first time that its vital route to India was vulnerable.

This convergence of interests led to military co-operation. Admiral Lord Nelson destroyed Napoleon's fleet in Abuquir Bay in August 1798. A year later, in the face of an Ottoman-led army approaching Egypt down the eastern Mediterranean coast, Napoleon abandoned his troops and returned to France. His bedraggled army hung on for another two years under British and Ottoman pressure, dispirited and in increasingly bad health, before finally being defeated and driven out of Egypt in August 1801.

The three-year French occupation of Egypt opened up an important corner of the Middle East to some of the innovations of Europe for the first time. Napoleon had brought with him scientists, artists and engineers. The printing press and other products of Western technology were introduced into the Arab world.

The long-term impact of Napoleon's foray into Egypt is significant in the context of the eventual collapse of the Ottoman empire and the gradual renaissance of the Middle East. The immediate British priority, though, was to ensure that the route to India would never be threatened again. To guarantee that, Britain realized that it would have to involve itself much more on the ground in the Middle East – which is what began to happen. The French occupation of Egypt – brief though it was – represents a major turning point in the history of the British in the Middle East.

Even while Napoleon was still in Egypt, the British began to shore up their interests along the route to India. On 12 October 1798, two months after the arrival of the French in Cairo, the British East India Company (as agent of the British government) signed a peace treaty with Muscat, the port at the farthest point east in the region where the Arab world stretches over towards the Indian subcontinent. The wording signed by the Imam of Muscat leaves the purpose of the agreement beyond doubt. It says that neither the French nor the Dutch will ever be given 'a place to fix or seat themselves in, nor shall they get ground to stand upon within this state'.

The fate of nations and their leaders is what fills the history books, rather than the fate of humble individuals. But in the British treaty with Muscat there is an intriguing reference to one unfortunate man whose fate was fixed in the accord with Britain without his knowing. Article 4 of the Imam's document states that 'as there is a person of the French nation, who has been for these several years in my service, and who hath now gone in command of one of my vessels to the Mauritius, I shall, immediately on his return, dismiss him from my service and expel him'.

Having secured Muscat, the strategic point needed to guard the sea lanes to India, Britain had to make sure that the land routes through Persia were also safe. In 1814, with the Foreign Office in control of British interests, a Treaty of Defence Alliance was signed with Tehran. The Persian authorities agreed 'not to allow any European army to enter the Persian territory, not to proceed towards India, nor to any ports of that country'.

From 1820 onwards, Britain consolidated further its influence over the territories of the Gulf by signing defence treaties with other rulers. The British secured the support of the sheikhdoms in the fight against piracy and slavery, warning that anyone committing the former offence 'shall be held to have forfeited both life and goods'. The offensive against piracy had considerable success, while that against slavery did not. Cases of slavery in the Gulf were still being uncovered in the middle of the twentieth century, as a later chapter will show.

The agreements signed with the Gulf sheikhdoms gave the latter military protection and bound up their interests with Britain. But Britain still had no intention of committing forces to the Middle East. The region represented little more than the route to India; the priority of foreign policy and diplomacy was to maintain by whatever means necessary favourable relations with the two major powers in the region, the Ottomans and the Persians, to keep the route open and secure. Britain's emergence as an occupying and ruling power – beginning in Egypt – was more an accident of circumstances than a result of long-term design.

The French adventure in Egypt at the end of the eighteenth century had sharpened rivalry between Paris and London. Britain could no longer ignore developments in Egypt, for fear that France might exploit them. After the withdrawal of the French, an Albanian officer who had been drafted into the Ottoman army to fight the occupiers took advantage of the collapse of Mamluk authority and the weakening hold of Constantinople on Egypt to seize power. His name was Muhammad Ali, and he is called the founder of modern Egypt for having reorganized the army along European lines and turned the province into an independent state in everything but name.

The Ottoman authorities, concerned about Muhammad Ali's secessionist ambitions, were happy to gain British support by agreeing to a new commercial agreement which benefited greatly the imperialist-minded Palmerston government. The agreement waived Ottoman trading monopolies and gave Britain the right to trade throughout the empire, paying duty of only three per cent. Muhammad Ali decided that this would be damaging to Egypt, so refused to accept the new terms. In 1839 he flexed his muscles further by occupying Syria. But the move was short-lived. Britain was unhappy at seeing Egyptian power expanding so rapidly; and because the British had won such favourable economic concessions from Constantinople they were willing to help the Ottomans force the Egyptian army out of Syria. Britain convened a conference in London in 1840 for the Pacification of the Levant, attended by French, Austrian, Prussian and Russian representatives. The five powers ordered Muhammad Ali to remove his army from Syria, but at the same time they granted his family hereditary viceroyship of Egypt. Muhammad Ali rejected the military ultimatum, but eventually gave in under British military pressure.

Muhammad Ali was succeeded by his grandson Abbas, who granted the British the right to build the first railway in the country (and one of the first outside Europe) between Cairo and Alexandria. The job was supervised between 1851 and 1856 by Robert Stephenson, son of George, the inventor of the steam engine. The Railway Museum in Cairo contains the engine carriage built for Abbas's successor, Said. The engine has an ornately designed brass funnel, while the décor inside the carriage is heavy Victorian, with inlaid mahogany and a barrel ceiling. The name Muhammad Said Pasha is lacquered in maroon and gold on the outside, while a small brass plaque reads: 'No. 1295 Robert Stephenson. Newcastle-upon-Tyne'.

But while Britain had a hand in establishing rail transport in Egypt, it was distressed to see Abbas give the French the contract to build the Suez Canal – a much bigger and infinitely more prestigious project. The canal was finished in 1869, but the cost was crippling. Said's successor, Ismail, who had taken on the title of Khedive, had launched his country on an ambitious programme of modernization and spending. Egypt was on the verge of bankruptcy and Britain, seeing an opportunity of exerting its influence in the country once more, bought shares in the Suez Canal Company. From that time on, until nationalization by President Nasser in 1956, the canal remained under Anglo-French ownership.

Having gained joint control of the waterway through Egypt, Britain did not seek further footholds in the country. A statement of British policy in Egypt late in 1879 stated that the aim was 'the maintenance of neutrality of that country, that is to say, the maintenance of such a state of things that no great Power shall be more powerful there than England'.

But events outside Britain's control were moving fast. The Khedive Ismail was replaced in 1879 by Tewfik, who struggled to contain the growing nationalist demands of his people, who were suffering high taxation because of the profligate spending of the ruling family over the decades. More importantly the Khedive faced nationalist unrest within the Egyptian army. The nationalists were seeking political independence from Ottoman governors and economic inde-pendence from Britain and France.

A key figure in the movement was an army officer, Colonel Ahmed Arabi. The Khedive tried to play a double game, meeting some of Arabi's demands and even bringing him into cabinet, while secretly trying to find a way of ousting him. Amid this political turmoil, with the cry for independence getting louder and louder, Britain still hoped that the Ottoman Sultan would find a way of re-establishing the authority of the Khedive and calming passions – though in fact the Sultan was backing both Tewfik and Arabi and waiting to see who came out on top. In London, meanwhile, it was felt that at worst the Ottoman authorities might have to take brief military action under Anglo-French supervision to restore order in Egypt.

But neither the Sultan nor Tewfik could influence the nationalists. In May 1882, with the Egyptian army enjoying enormous popular support and appearing to threaten the rule of the Khedive, Britain and France strengthened their naval presence off Alexandria. The show of force had the opposite of the desired effect – it fanned the anger of the nationalists, leading in June to serious rioting in Alexandria in which several hundred people were killed or injured, including about fifty Europeans. With Arabi and his supporters taking control of Alexandria, thousands of Westerners fled the city. Britain was uncertain about what to do, still hoping for some kind of joint international action to restore order. On 10 July 1882 the British issued an ultimatum to Arabi: if he did not remove gun batteries and dismantle the fortifications that he was building around Alexandria, the city would be bombarded.

The ultimatum was rejected, and Alexandria came under British bombardment for ten hours, suffering fires and major damage. The Egyptian army left the city, and on 13 July a British marine force landed there and re-established order. France by this stage had indicated that it was not inclined to get involved in any military operation and the Italians had declined a request from Britain. With Arabi continuing to issue defiant statements and winning popular support, the Gladstone government vacillated over whether or not to take further action. Finally Gladstone won cabinet approval for military intervention in Egypt, which the government justified on the grounds of the perceived threat to the Suez Canal caused by the turmoil in the country. British warships closed the canal at Port Said, and an expeditionary force, commanded by Sir Garnet Wolseley, landed on Egyptian soil at Alexandria. The poorly armed and trained Arabi forces were defeated at the battle of Tel el-Kebir, on the edge of the Nile Delta north-east of Cairo, on 13 September 1882. Fifty-two British troops were killed, and twenty-two went missing. Many thousands of Egyptians were killed. 'I do not believe,' Sir Garnet Wolseley wrote later, 'that in any previous period of our military history has the British Infantry distinguished itself more than upon this occasion.'

With the arrival of the British army in Cairo and the surrender of Arabi (who spent the next eighteen years in exile in Ceylon), calm returned to the country. Like occupying powers before and since, Britain found that it was easier to capture territory than to give it up. Even though Egypt was strategically important − essential, in fact − as a link in the chain to India, the British government would have preferred not to be burdened with administering such a large country. In January 1883 the government issued a circular outlining its policy in Egypt. It declared that Britain had succeeded in restoring peace and order, 'and although for the present a British force remains in Egypt for the preservation of public tranquillity, Her Majesty's Government are desirous of withdrawing it as soon as the state of the country, and the organization of proper means for the maintenance of the Khedive's authority, will admit of it'. Britain, in other words, would have preferred to see a return to the previous status quo in which Egypt remained a province of the Ottoman empire under close British military scrutiny.

But Khedive Tewfik was not in a position to regain authority, having lost the respect of his people by his handling of the Arabi affair. Also, while Arabi had been soundly defeated, the seeds of nationalism had taken firm root in Egyptian soil. Therefore, to guarantee the security of Egypt, the British could not risk pulling out. The Union Jack was hoisted over the Citadel in Cairo and barracks were built for British troops. Britain became the effective power in the land, with the Khedive, who had British decorations conferred on him during a military review in Cairo, little more than a figurehead ruler.

After centuries in which Britain had been a trader in the Middle East and had policed the routes to India, in 1882 the Lion arrived in the Sand.

3

THE ROAD TO INDEPENDENCE

'When I have finished dressing I send for a cab to go to the club, as I have given up breakfasting in. Suleiman "fancies" himself as a cook, but he is wrong ... The driver, who has his head muffled against the cold, without waiting for orders, starts his horses off at a slow amble in the wrong direction. When my voice has penetrated the shawl, he slowly hauls them round, beating them for not knowing the way, and we proceed towards the club.'

Thus a typical day under way for a bachelor civil servant in the British-run administration in Egypt, as described by Lord Edward Cecil, who served there for eighteen years. The description appears in his book *The Leisure of an Egyptian Official*, published in 1921, which provides a light-hearted (but arrogant and racist, too) view of the society which he served.

By the early 1920s British control over Egypt was well established. Having arrived in 1882, the British authorities had come to the reluctant conclusion as the months passed that to pull out would risk a power vacuum which might be filled with elements hostile to British interests. The route to India still needed to be kept secure. The threat to political calm in Egypt was perceived as coming from the nationalist movement. This had received a blow when the Arabi revolt was crushed; but the determination of the Egyptians to continue the struggle for independence and self-rule was not weakened.

In theory, Egypt was still an Ottoman province governed by the Khedive. But in practice, power lay in the hands of the British Agent and Consul General, Evelyn Baring. He later became Lord Cromer with the title of High Commissioner, and in his eighteen-year term of office he put a distinctive mark on the style of British rule which is detectable in the tone of Lord Edward Cecil's memoirs.

Above all, while taking a patronizing and condescending interest in the well-being of Egyptian peasants, Lord Cromer saw to it that urban dwellers were not encouraged to pursue their education much beyond primary level. Places of higher education, he argued, became seed-beds of nationalism. Lord Cromer held strong views on the dangers of nationalism. He believed that Egyptians would never be capable of governing themselves. In the end, he conceded, some kind of autonomy might be possible. But the process 'may take years – possibly generations . . . but if the Egyptians of the rising generation will have the wisdom and foresight to work cordially and patiently, in co-operation with European sympathizers, to attain it, it may possibly in time be found capable of realization'.

Given such a strong belief that the Egyptians were incapable of doing anything properly for themselves, it was hardly surprising that the British felt they had to occupy the key jobs in Egypt. As a result, the ministries and government departments became top-heavy with foreigners. C.S. Jarvis, in his memoirs, wrote that in the period just before and just after the First World War, 'all the important positions in the country and practically all the executive posts were in the hands of the British to the total exclusion of Egyptians . . . In the very early days of the British occupation of Egypt it was the intention to administer the country as a temporary measure with the minimum of British advisers in the various Ministries, leaving the executive control of the government work to the existing Egyptian officials. This was a most excellent idea in theory, but in practice did not work because the normal Briton with his very rigid standards of efficiency and moral integrity is very rarely sufficiently plastic to reconcile himself to the laxer methods of the East, and is quite unable to carry on his department when he knows that it is permeated by peculation, nepotism, and all the other adjuncts of Oriental officialdom.'

As some employees of His Majesty's Government in Cairo were struggling with the various 'adjuncts of Oriental officialdom', others were looking beyond the shores and borders of Egypt. One problem lay in Sudan, which was nominally under the authority of the Khedive in Cairo. There emerged in Sudan an early proponent of pan-Arab Islamic fundamentalism. He was Muhammad Ahmed, who proclaimed himself, with considerable popular support, the Mahdi, an almost divine Muslim leader sent to bring justice to the world. The Mahdi called both for foreigners to be expelled and for Islamic states to unite. He thus represented a threat to Egypt; and his presence on the country's southern flank strengthened the argument that Britain should remain. General Gordon was chosen as the commander of a British force sent to defeat the Mahdi. The five-month siege of Gordon in Khartoum in 1884 and his ultimate murder – speared to death on the steps of Government House – were followed closely and passionately in Britain. To the horror of the British public the Mahdi (the 'mad Mahdi' as he was often called) was victorious.

The problem remained that if Sudan was in turmoil, Egypt's security was under threat. Eventually an Anglo-Egyptian force led by the commander of the Egyptian army, Sir Herbert Kitchener, defeated the Khalifa, the Mahdi's successor, and his supporters in 1898. From then until 1956 an Anglo-Egyptian condominium controlled Sudan, although practical power in Khartoum lay in the hands of the governor-general, who was nominated by the British before being formally appointed by the Khedive – and in later years by the king – of Egypt.

Aside from the problems of Sudan, British colonial officials in Cairo had other developments further afield to ponder over. In particular they were concerned about what might become of the ailing Ottoman empire once it fell. With the outbreak of the First World War, the need to take action was obvious. The Turks sided with Germany against Britain and its allies. They were thus in a position to threaten British interests in the Middle East in two areas – in Egypt, which controlled the Suez Canal and Red Sea routes to India, and in Iraq, which guarded the northern entrance to the Gulf, another way to India. This latter area was also becoming important in its own right as a potential source of oil wealth.

After much debate and pondering in Cairo and London, Britain sought the support of the Arab Governor of Mecca (the Sharif), Hussein. Sharif Hussein wanted to see the Turks driven out of Hejaz, the western part of the Arabian peninsula, so that he could establish his own power. He was well aware of the growing strength of his Arab rivals, the fanatically pious Wahhabi Muslims from the eastern areas of the Arabian peninsula led by Ibn Saud. With the encouragement of T.E. Lawrence (events dramatized in the film *Lawrence of Arabia*) and other British officials based in Cairo, Sharif Hussein agreed to declare an Arab Revolt against Turkish domination. In return he was given by Britain what history has shown to be a vague and unsatisfactory promise of independence for the Arabs in the lands liberated from Turkish control.

In June 1916 Sharif Hussein declared the Arab Revolt to be under way. The Ottoman garrison in Mecca was overrun, and the Sharif was accorded the title of King of Hejaz. Some Arab units fought with the Allies, who, in December 1916, having resisted a Turkish assault on the Suez Canal, began the battle to drive the enemy northwards out of Palestine and Syria. When General Murray, the commander of the Allied army, failed at great cost in British lives and morale to dislodge the Turks from Gaza, he was replaced by General Allenby. Allenby defeated the Turks in battles both at Gaza and Beersheba, and on 9 December 1917 arrived triumphantly in Jerusalem. From there his army later went on to liberate Damascus and the whole of Syria from Turkish control.

Many thousands of Britons got their only experience of the Middle East in the course of serving with the army during the First World War. For most of them, especially ordinary soldiers, the impression was not very favourable, coloured by memories of hardship and atrocities.

When I asked Jimmy Page, now aged ninety-nine and living in the Star and Garter Home for ex-servicemen in Richmond, about his first impressions of Cairo, he practically spat back the reply. 'Foul. Huh. More poverty than you'd care to contemplate.'

Jimmy Page later moved out of Cairo and fought under Allenby in the battles both for Gaza and Beersheba. But at the time, like his comrades, he had no clear idea of the bigger picture of the war, and his memories are a collection of images. 'When we moved into Palestine with Allenby we almost lost touch with civilization. We had to be fairly brutal. Not individually, but there was a need to be fairly brutal. There were little villages, I can't name them now. I remember Ramallah, not far from Jerusalem. There were all sorts of little villages scattered around – it wasn't convenient to leave them with their guns. I remember being put in charge of two wagons, with six horses on each wagon, to clear out a village. Not only were they harbouring snipers, they were in our line. And one of the wagons was taken up by blind people. There was a lot of glaucoma over there at that time. We had one wagon loaded up with about thirty old people; the other one had their belongings. What happened to those people, God knows. I took them back behind the line and I went the other way. God knows what happened. One woman bore a child on the side of the road.' Mr Page paused as the image from 1917 reformed in his mind.

I asked him about his memories of the scenery in the Holy Land.

'The labourers had gone in terracing the hills,' he said. 'They'd built stone walls which held the drift of soil downwards. All with rough stone and rock. There were terraces there all planted with fig trees or grapes or something. But to whom it belonged, God only knows.'

Was it beautiful?

'I think I would have preferred the Commercial Road,' he said and laughed.

More than anything else, Mr Page remembers the hardships of the First World War in the Middle East. He slept 'on the deck for four years and seven months. All the time on the ground, the only place to sleep. We had a rubberized thing to put down on the floor – even in the desert it strikes up very cold from underneath. Even the *Daily Mirror* underneath would have been very useful.'

When I asked about the food they were given during the campaign, Mr Page again spat out the words. 'Practically nothing,' he said. 'Have you ever heard of Fray and Bentos bully beef? Can you imagine this in a temperature of over ninety degrees when you could have poured it out? Can you imagine what it was like to have more flies than you can possibly imagine? There was no DDT in those days and the flies were there in their trillions. And we were lousy with lice. The Turk wasn't pleasant. He was well backed up by the German. The Turks were indeed good soldiers. And moreover they held the trump hand, they were at the top looking down.'

As for the course of the war, Jimmy Page remembers that there was 'rumour, only rumour. And much of the things we heard of course had about the same semblance of truth as Goebbels.' And news from home amounted to 'at most . . . an occasional letter from my mother. And my poor mother, who was probably waiting for letters from me, didn't get them. I had no facilities for writing, just a bloody stupid post card which says "I am well", "I am not well", "I'm in hospital", "I am not in hospital". I could only fill that in with a bit of black lead. If it ever reached her I don't know. I believe my mother went through hell.'

Jimmy Page's war ended on the road to Damascus. 'I was put in charge of some teams of horses and drivers,' he remembers, 'and we had to clean up the Damascus road of all the impedimenta that the Turks had run away and left. That was why we couldn't go on to Damascus, on the only road open. We had a park of Turkish guns that were captured and it was largely the work of me and half a dozen of my drivers who went out and collected them.'

During his time in the Middle East Jimmy Page and his comrades had 'very little contact with Arabs. We met them when they came along with a few eggs, or oranges or figs. If we had money we bought them. But money was very scarce.' His knowledge of Arabic was limited to 'swear words. I could say "good day" or "goodbye". I could say "Good day, bint", "Good day, miss". What we needed for chasing skirts.'

In Cairo, on free evenings 'it was only the brothel that wasn't out of bounds – one could go to the brothel. There were restaurants if you had money, but you needed very little money in the brothel.' Evenings in the field or desert were for sleeping and nothing else. 'We had nothing else to do,' Jimmy Page says. 'They kept us going as long as they could. The horses still had to be watered and fed, and their eyes and noses sponged out because of the dust. We were either grooming horses, cleaning harnesses or digging gun pits. We had no leisure.'

While Mr Page and his fellow-soldiers slogged their way through each long day, the military progress in the Palestine campaign was being monitored by British officials in Cairo. At the same time, officials of the British-controlled government in India were busy making sure that the alternative route to the jewel in the British imperial crown – through Iraq (Mesopotamia as it was called then) and Persia – did not fall into enemy hands. Oil was another consideration – large quantities were found in Persia in 1908, and the British government bought a controlling interest in the Anglo-Persian Oil Company in 1914. It seemed certain that Mesopotamia would also have sizeable oil reserves.

Before the outbreak of hostilities, the British in the Gulf region were getting prepared. In October 1914 news that the Turks had entered the war on the side of Germany reached a British warship in the Shatt al-Arab waterway, Iraq's link with the Gulf. The message in English from the local Ottoman authorities read: 'Please leave the Shatt before 24 hours.' But the ultimatum was ignored, and a British force quickly occupied the port city of Basra, which lies at the head of the waterway. A few days later an expeditionary force was on its way from India.

The Mesopotamia campaign, like that in Palestine, afforded to thousands of Britons a brief glimpse of the Middle East. Edmund Candler was an official eyewitness, and later wrote his memoirs entitled *The Long Road to Baghdad*. Just as Jimmy Page had little time or energy to appreciate the beauty and significance of the Holy Land, so soldiers in Iraq were not always impressed by the historical significance of the landscape in the land that boasts of being the cradle of civilization. 'We had entered the oldest country in the world,' Candler wrote, describing the journey up the River Tigris from Basra. 'Qurna, where we anchored in the morning, is the reputed site of the Garden of Eden . . . Upstream the biblical tradition holds. The second night we moored by Ezra's Tomb, a domed shrine silhouetted among the palms in the clear starlight. One could not help moralising upon the new lap we were pursuing in the continuity of history when one heard a lowlander of Perth point out the scribe's resting place to his mate as "yon corner-hoos".'

Once again, though, it was the suffering that stuck most vividly in Candler's mind as the Turks were gradually pushed back in a long series of gruelling encounters. At the battle of Sheikh Saad in January 1916, for example, 'we lost 4,262 of General Aylmer's column in this frontal attack upon the advanced trenches of the enemy, a force equal to half the garrison we were relieving. A hundred and thirty-three British officers fell in the action. But it is not the long roll of honour that lends bitterness to the thought of that unhappy day; it is the tragic memory of the wounded. Never since the Crimea can there have been such a collection of maimed and untended humanity in a British camp as were gathered on the Tigris bank on the night of January 7th . . . While our casualties in the battle were over 4,000, there was barely provision for 250 beds.'

Eventually Baghdad fell, but not before an ignominious British withdrawal from the city of Kut after a long and costly siege. There was also intense summer heat to suffer. Candler described one of the side effects of sunshine. The dancing mirage, he wrote, 'plays one a hundred tricks. My sapper friend put up a direction post for prismatic compass survey, a little mound with a flag on it. When he started back to camp he took down the flag. He had left the mount a mile behind when, looking back, he saw what he thought was an Arab pursuing him. He lay down and covered the figure with his rifle and called to his orderly to do the same. They lay in wait while the Arab still came on at the same rapid stride, his cloak flying in the wind. Whole minutes passed, yet though he never ceased to move he came no nearer. They approached and found it was the little mound, no more than a foot high.'

Baghdad offered some compensation after the gruelling weeks of battle. Cheering crowds came out on to streets to greet the Anglo-Indian force. 'Among them were girls and matrons of fair complexion and unveiled, whose forwardness was almost embarrassing to men who had seen nothing in the shape of woman for years beyond black bundles filling their pitchers on the Tigris bank.'

For the British back in Cairo, there was plenty of female company and plenty of entertainment. But official entertaining was circumscribed out of respect for those fighting the war. The British High Commissioner, Sir Reginald Wingate, decreed that no alcohol would be allowed in his house until peace was proclaimed. 'Dinner at the Residency in those days,' C.S. Jarvis wrote in his memoirs, 'was, therefore, rather a gloomy business, and the butler who came round with the drinks did nothing to enliven matters, for the tone of his voice, when asking the question "Lemonade or barley water, sir?" suggested the death sentence at the Old Bailey.'

Sir Reginald's dinner guests worked out that the only way of surviving the meal was to drink enough in advance to sustain them through the six courses. But Candler wrote that 'the result was not entirely happy, for until one has tried one does not realize how difficult it is to get sufficient alcohol on board to make one a cheery dinner companion when one is diluting the stock the whole time with barley water or lemonade. It takes a considerable amount of practice to discover the exact quantity one must consume at 7.50 p.m. to carry one through till 10 p.m. without becoming too cheery and forthcoming with the soup. The marked feature at the Residency dinners until 1918 was the extraordinary cheerfulness that started with the hors d'oeuvre and lasted to the entree, and the rather funereal gloom that fell on the party when they reached the dessert stage.'

For officials and the public in London the immediate preoccupation in the war years was probably more with events closer to home than those in the Middle East campaign. But in certain offices in Whitehall attention was being focused on how the territories captured from the Turks should be administered after the war. A promise, remember, had been made to Sharif Hussein of Mecca on behalf of the Arabs. But the picture was now more complicated. Britain and France had already agreed to Russia's demand for sovereignty over Constantinople and the Dardanelles. France also had ambitions, claiming Lebanon and Syria as regions of special interest to it. In the end, Britain came to the conclusion that on this instance it would be better to accommodate its old rival rather than antagonize it. So during a series of meetings in London at the end of 1915 and early 1916, Britain and France drew up a secret agreement (the Sykes-Picot agreement, a name that to this day in Arab ears evokes a sense of British betrayal) dividing up the territory at the eastern end of the Mediterranean and in Iraq between them.

Changes were made later to the agreement, which was publicized for the first time, to Britain's embarrassment, by the Bolsheviks after the Russian Revolution in 1917. But, to the indignation of the Arabs, the Sykes-Picot accord formed the basis on which the twentieth-century map of the Middle East was drawn. In the years after the First World War borders were drawn by Britain and France for the newly created states of Lebanon, Syria, Transjordan (later to become Jordan) and Iraq. France had mandatory control over the first two; Britain over the second two.

Britain also faced the problem of what to do with the Hashemite family of King Hussein of Hejaz, the former Sharif of Mecca. Hussein's ambition of becoming king of all the Arabs came to nothing. He was driven out of Hejaz in 1926 by the Wahhabis. Their leader, Ibn Saud, became king of a united Saudi Arabia in 1932.

Hussein was an old and bitter man, and the British apparently felt no pangs of conscience about cutting him off from the spoils. But they felt an obligation to his two sons Feisal and Abdullah, who had fought in the liberation of Arab lands. The solution they came up with was to make Feisal the king of Iraq, while Abdullah was installed as Emir of Transjordan.

Britain's Mandate in Iraq ended in 1932, when the kingdom became nominally independent. In practice, though, the British retained a strong influence in the country, as much as anything to protect their oil interests.

In Transjordan, Emir Abdullah (the grandfather of the current Hashemite ruler, King Hussein) was proclaimed King of Jordan after the Second World War when the Mandate ended. But once again the British retained strong military and political influence, in addition to providing vital financial aid, for another decade.

Under the various post-First World War settlements, Palestine (including Jerusalem) was handed to Britain in 1920 under a League of Nations mandate. Palestine became the biggest problem for the British in the Middle East because of a promise made to the Jews in November 1917. It was a form of words which became known thereafter as the Balfour Declaration. The Foreign Secretary, Lord Balfour, reacting to a campaign by Zionist supporters, wrote a letter to a leading member of the Jewish community committing Britain's support for 'the establishment in Palestine of a national home for the Jewish people'. The homeland was to be set up, the letter continued, without doing anything that might 'prejudice the civil and religious rights of existing non-Jewish communities in Palestine'.

As the decades passed, the contradictions inherent in the Balfour Declaration came back to haunt and taunt the British administrators. Britain was faced with two competing moral claims for the land of Palestine; and Britain had promised to pursue the rights of one claimant without damaging the interests of the other. British officials, troops and members of the Palestine police force found themselves in an impossible position. Sir Ronald Storrs, the first Governor of Jerusalem, wrote in his memoirs, *Orientations*, that 'two hours of Arab grievances drive me into the Synagogue, while after an intensive course of Zionist propaganda I am prepared to embrace Islam'. Before long the British were caught not just in the crossfire of moral and political debate, but in the dangerous crossfire of street violence.

Various commissions were established in London and dispatched to Palestine, and White Papers were published aimed at establishing a middle way to satisfy both the Jews and the Arabs. But finding a compromise between two such strong moral claims proved impossible, particularly with the mass slaughter of Jews by the Nazis in Europe gnawing at the conscience of the West, combined with the major problem of what should become of the tens of thousands of Jewish refugees. Long before the British pulled out of Palestine the Mandate authorities had managed to antagonize both sides in the dispute and were becoming the targets of the violence perpetrated both by the Arabs and the Jews.

At the beginning of 1947, Britain admitted defeat and handed the issue over to the United Nations. The state of Israel was established in May 1948. Israel was immediately attacked by its Arab neighbours, and in the war which followed was able to acquire around twenty-five per cent more territory than it had been granted under a UN partition plan put forward the previous year.

By 1948, Arab countries were fast winning independence. But in practice, Britain's grip on the region remained strong. Sir Anthony

Parsons, a retired British diplomat, recalls that in the post-Second World War years British influence 'did seem really eternal. Having been in the Middle East on and off from the early 1940s, after the defeat of the German and Italian forces in the Western desert, as a British officer you could literally travel with no identification documents, no stopping at frontiers, the whole way from Morocco just about to Afghanistan. Even when I got to Baghdad in the early fifties, we were very much the paramount power. As a very junior diplomat I was automatically on hobnobbing terms with the chief of the general staff and senior officers of the Iraqi armed forces and so on. I had easy access to all their garrisons. So our position did seem pretty well unchallengeable. But while I was there of course it was quite clear that the picture was changing – the revolution in Egypt had a profound effect.'

The revolution in Egypt erupted seventy years after the moment when the Lion had first arrived in the Sand. Egypt at the halfway point of the twentieth century remained under strong British influence. The uncertainty of its status within the Ottoman empire had ended in 1914 when the Turks joined the war against the Allies, and Egypt became a British protectorate. The imposition of protectorate status did not mean that Britain's troubles in Egypt were over – on the contrary. After the First World War, for example, British administrators and troops faced what amounted to a revolution when popular Egyptian expectation that independence would be granted was not met. In 1922 British rule was terminated, and Egypt became a nominally independent state under strong British tutelage. Britain retained responsibility for the security of the communications of the British Empire, and for the defence of Egypt and Sudan. This was not a formula likely to please Egyptian nationalists, and it did not do so.

While the number of British civil servants was cut drastically as part of the independence agreement of 1922, the presence of Britons in Egypt was still considerable, and official attitudes towards the Egyptians had changed little from those during Lord Cromer's days. C.S. Jarvis wrote about the appointment in 1925 of Lord Lloyd as British High Commissioner. The new appointee was 'horrified on arrival in Egypt to find how the post of High Commissioner had fallen from its high estate. He at once insisted on the reintroduction of all the special rights and privileges that had been accorded to High Commissioners in the past. Whenever he travelled he demanded a special train; he arrived at and departed from Cairo station by the royal gates; and at all functions and ceremonies special arrangements had to be made to ensure his arrival just before the King and his departure immediately afterwards ... Lord Lloyd clearly realized that for Great Britain's representative to be herded among the ministers of minor powers at state functions was to advertise to all and sundry that England no longer insisted on a special position in the country.'

That special position was maintained, even though more concessions were made to the nationalists in a treaty signed in 1936. At the outbreak of the Second World War, the Egyptians' demands for total independence were put on hold while their country became a garrison for Allied troops (much as it had done in the previous war) and a battleground (in the western desert) against the Italians and the Germans. After the war, the nationalist pressure on the British resumed.

The Arab-Israeli war of 1948, and the catastrophic performance of the Arabs, produced a mood of anger and depression throughout the region. In Egypt, the country's military failure was seen to be the product of years of inept and corrupt rule – symbolized by the weak monarchy, which appeared to be a puppet of the British will. The Egyptians never forgot an incident in 1942 when the British High Commissioner, Sir Miles Lampson, ordered tanks to surround King Farouk's palace before going in to insist on a change of government – an incident described in a later chapter.

In July 1952 a group of disillusioned young army officers who had seen the inadequacies of the army at first hand in 1948 and decided that their country's years of humiliation should end seized power. One of the officers, Gemal Abdul-Nasser, later became president of the republic. A new era of pan-Arab nationalism had begun, and the sun was setting on Britain's day in the Middle East.

In 1954 an agreement was reached with Britain for the withdrawal of the last of its forces from Egyptian soil, while civilian maintenance of the Suez Canal continued. During the 1950s a strong anti-Western – and particularly anti-British – mood developed in most areas of the Arab world. Britain perceived the pan-Arab movement as a danger because it might provide a channel for Soviet and East bloc infiltration into the Middle East. The British tried to counter this with the formation of the Baghdad Pact, an anti-communist alliance linking Pakistan, Iraq, Iran and Turkey. President Nasser, using the powerful transmitters of the Voice of the Arabs radio station in Cairo to beam his message to the masses around the region, denounced the accord in the strongest terms possible. Britain tried to persuade Jordan to join the Baghdad Pact, but popular opposition forced King Hussein to refuse. And in the atmosphere of hostility towards Britain he had no choice but to dismiss the British commander of the Arab Legion (a highly efficient Arab fighting force led by British officers), Glubb Pasha.

Nasser had another reason for feeling disenchanted with the West. He became increasingly impatient at it's dilatory attitude towards funding that Egypt had requested for the Aswan High Dam project on the River Nile. The delays prompted him to start turning to East bloc countries for aid and military assistance. This in turn prompted Western powers to show their disapproval by withdrawing their offer of aid for the dam project. Nasser responded in July 1956 by nationalizing the Anglo-French Suez Canal Company. The British government were incensed, and the Prime Minister, Sir Anthony Eden, converted a personal loathing of Nasser (comparing him to Hitler) into a single-minded obsession to cut him down to size. This led to secret contacts with France and Israel, and a deal was struck. Israel, in response to cross-border attacks, invaded Egypt and advanced on the Canal. Britain and France, as guarantor powers, issued an ultimatum to both sides to withdraw. Egypt rejected the ultimatum, giving Britain the opportunity it had been seeking to send in its own troops with the aim of bringing down Nasser.

But Britain's days of dictating events in the region were over. International opinion, not least that of the United States, was against the Suez operation, and Britain was forced to withdraw ignominiously, while Nasser capitalized on what was perceived throughout the Arab world as a brilliantly successful strike against Western imperialism. Even within Britain, opinion was sharply divided. Britain's secret collusion with France and Israel only emerged later, adding even more disgrace to what was one of the country's most inglorious moments in the region.

In the aftermath of Suez, and with Arab hatred both of Israel and the West growing, it was going to be hard for pro-Western regimes to survive. Sir Anthony Parsons served in Iraq during the fifties, and he noticed the change that had begun with the 1952 coup led by army officers in Egypt. Officers in the Iraqi armed forces, he says, 'were all clearly dying to do the same. Not so much because they hated us, rather because they had to prove their independence. That current was running through the country. At the same time it became apparent that the Palestine problem was increasingly permeating the political structure of Iraq and also the military structure. It was noticeable that if you called on an Iraqi officers' mess there were no placards, or plaques or memorials to people who had been killed in some action in the Second World War. They were all to do with the '48 war in Palestine. There were generally three boards – lightly wounded, heavily wounded, and killed. If you were killed you appeared on all three. This was their preoccupation. It was pretty clear to me that by the time I left Baghdad in '54 that there were two very strong currents running: one of them was rejection of the Anglo-American notion that the enemy was the Soviet Union. As far as the Iraqi army was concerned there was only one external enemy and that was Israel, and to try and pretend to them that they were under threat from the Soviet Union was just a pure waste of time. Secondly, there was a desire to emulate what the Egyptian officers, Nasser and company, had done. It came as no surprise to me four years later when the regime was overthrown.'

The military coup in Iraq, in July 1958, was bloody. Young King Feisal, the grandson of the man originally put on the throne by Britain, was assassinated in his palace. Also murdered were other members of the royal family and the pro-British prime minister, Nuri Said, who had been a formidable political player in the country for many years. His mutilated body was dragged in triumph through the streets of Baghdad. With the collapse of the monarchy in Iraq the Baghdad Pact disintegrated and other pro-Western states in the Middle East suddenly looked vulnerable. President Chamoun of Lebanon asked for and was provided with the help of United States marines, who came ashore briefly in Beirut.

Alan Munro began a diplomatic career in the Middle East in Beirut shortly after the coup in Iraq. In terms of the effect on British policy towards the Arab world, he describes the overthrow of the monarchy and the Suez débâcle in 1956 as 'seismic shocks'. In the decade since 1948, when – as Sir Anthony Parsons recalled earlier in this chapter – British influence was paramount, much had changed. But the British were still reluctant to accept that their days of influence were drawing to a close. Sir Alan recalls that in 1958 'as a young man embarking on a career in the Middle East, one was carried forward still by the idea of a British political presence, buttressed by a military presence in the Gulf, Jordan and North Africa, which still looked fairly secure and necessary to the stability of the region and for the benefit of its people. The Middle East still represented an area of considerable political and economic importance for Britain. Prior to the Second World War, and during it, we had built up strong connections and a position of underpinning for a number of regimes. It takes time for such a culture to change.'

One of the countries still underpinned by Britain was Jordan. When the monarchy in Iraq was overthrown, British troops were flown to Jordan. Like Iraq, the Hashemite Kingdom of Jordan was a product of British colonial policy in the wake of the First World War. Against the background of popular pan-Arab sentiments King Hussein had distanced himself as much as he could from Britain. But in the eyes of many Arabs, Jordan, with its British-style monarchy, was anachronistic in the new climate of anti-Western feelings. But the King survived and survives still. Despite coup attempts and attacks on his life he has shown more political adroitness and won more personal respect than any other leader in the Arab world.

Two dramatic events in later years shook the Jordanian monarchy more than any other. The first was the Arab-Israeli war in June 1967. This was a disaster for the Arabs. President Nasser was the key player. Bombastic speeches, broadcast by the Voice of the Arabs into homes all over the region, spoke of how Israel would be crushed. The Arab people wanted to believe this and did not take much convincing that the Egyptian leader would act according to his word. Matters came to a head when President Nasser asked the United Nations to withdraw troops from Sinai and closed the Straits of Tiran (the entrance to the Gulf of Aqaba and the approach to the Israeli port of Eilat) to Israeli shipping. 'The Jews threaten war,' Nasser declared. 'We tell them you are welcome, we are ready for war, but under no circumstances will we abandon any of our rights. The water is ours.'

The Arab people waited eagerly for the moment of victory. But the war, when it came, was over in just six days. The Egyptian air force was destroyed on the ground, and its army soundly defeated. Jordan and Syria also suffered costly defeats.

Most humiliating of all for the Arabs was the loss of territory. When the fighting ended, Israel had captured the Sinai peninsula from Egypt and occupied the Gaza Strip, a small, desolate coastal area south of Israel densely packed with Palestinian refugees. The

Israelis had also occupied the West Bank of the River Jordan and the Syrian Golan Heights. The biggest Arab loss of all was the eastern half of Jerusalem, the site of the Aqsa mosque and the Dome of the Rock, sacred sites for Muslims. The mosque complex is built on the ruins of the original ancient Jewish temple, the western wall (or Wailing Wall) of which remains, making this part of Jerusalem the biggest prize of all for Israel.

Nasser was the architect of pan-Arab nationalism, and the fiasco of the six-day war against Israel meant the discrediting of that policy and soon afterwards the death of the man himself. Nasser talked himself into a war when his country and the Arabs as a whole were unprepared for one.

The second dramatic event to shake the Jordanian monarchy was a direct consequence of the 1967 war. The fighting and the territorial gains made by Israel caused a big increase in the number of Palestinian refugees, many of whom ended up in Jordan. Also, the failure of the Arab regimes to defeat Israel and restore Palestinian rights prompted the Palestinians to start taking matters into their own hands. The Palestine Liberation Organization (PLO), led by Yasser Arafat, emerged as both a political and a guerrilla force in the Middle East. The PLO began to use Jordan as a base for raids against Israel. These actions prompted harsh cross-border military retaliation leading to Jordanian civilian casualties. Inside Jordan the PLO began to operate almost like a state within a state, angering those Jordanians who were not of Palestinian origin and threatening the monarchy. The hijacking of Western airliners and their much-publicized blowing up of a Jordanian airfield were among the actions which made King Hussein decide that enough was enough. He ordered his army on to the offensive against the PLO. In the bloody civil war which followed in September 1970 ('Black September', as the Palestinians called it) the PLO was eventually defeated and driven out of Jordan.

The Palestinians rebased themselves in Lebanon, where the PLO once again established a state within a state. The presence of the Palestinians upset the delicate political balance in Lebanon, leading eventually to the long years of civil war in that country which broke out in the middle of the 1970s. But by that point Britain had bowed out of the region altogether.

Britain's last zone of direct influence in the Middle East was in the Gulf. While wars and other dramatic events were being played out in Egypt, Israel and the states round about, the atmosphere in the eastern region of the Middle East was much calmer. The most significant development there was the discovery and exploitation of oil, in which Britain played an important part.

Even before the start of the twentieth century Persia (Iran) had been strategically important for Britain because of its location on the route to India. Keeping the country neutral had been the subject of lengthy diplomacy involving the British and the Russians. In 1907 Britain and Russia signed an agreement under which Persia was divided into two spheres of influence, with the British taking the south and the Russians the north. The south-western corner of the country was declared neutral. Six years earlier the Shah had granted William Knox D'Arcy, an Englishman with experience of successful and lucrative mining in Australia, a sixty-year concession to prospect for and exploit oil and gas. After a barren start (during which the Burmah Oil Company of Britain linked up with the D'Arcy project), oil was eventually discovered at Masjid-i-Suleiman in the south-west of the country in 1908, and the Anglo-Persian Oil Company was formed.

With the rapid expansion of the Royal Navy in the years that followed and the conversion from coal to oil-powered engines, members of the British government (and in particular Winston Churchill) saw the value of the Persian oilfields as a source of fuel for ships. In June 1914, on the eve of the First World War, the British government bought a controlling interest in the business – which later became first the Anglo-Iranian Oil Company and later British Petroleum (BP). Iran, therefore, was the first Middle East oil producer.

Iraq followed, but not before wrangling over the sovereignty of the Mosul region, where oil reserves were reckoned to lie, was resolved. In the various post-First World War debates over the shape of the Middle East, Turkey (the defeated Ottoman imperial power) claimed control of Mosul. Calouste Gulbenkian, a wealthy Armenian merchant, had been interested in the possibility of oil exploration in the former empire since the 1890s, and the discovery of oil in Iran increased the interest in Iraq. In 1912 Mr Gulbenkian and the Anglo-Saxon Oil Company (Shell) became shareholders in the Turkish Petroleum Company (TPC) which planned exploration and exploitation of oil in an area in the east of the Ottoman empire around Baghdad and northwards. The First World War broke out before exploration and surveying could get under way. After the war the pressure to explore for oil in Iraq resumed. In the end, in 1925 the TPC was reconstituted: Mr Gulbenkian kept a five per cent share, and the remaining ninety-five per cent was split four ways between BP, Shell, Compagnie Française des Pétroles and an American group of companies. In 1928 the name of the company was changed to the Iraq Petroleum Company (IPC).

At around the same time a 'Red Line' was drawn through the Middle East. This meant, to put a complicated arrangement in simple terms, that the IPC group of companies had a right to exploit oil in a region which included Lebanon, Jordan, Syria, Iraq, and the Gulf states of Qatar, Abu Dhabi and Oman.

By the late 1920s Britain had made sure that the Mosul area was firmly within the borders of British-controlled Iraq. Exploration and drilling began in the Kirkuk area, and oil was discovered in October 1927. As one historical record relates, 'subsequent drilling on the Kirkuk structure rapidly established it as an oilfield of the very first importance'.

The problem then was to find a way of getting oil from northern Iraq to the Mediterranean for shipment to Europe. The answer was provided by what in the late 1920s and early 1930s was an astonishing engineering feat. A twelve-inch pipeline was laid from Kirkuk to the Mediterranean coast at Haifa – a distance of about 550 miles, much of the way through desert and other difficult terrain. Pumping stations were set up at intervals to help the passage of oil to the sea.

Bahrain became an oil exporter in 1934, and in the decades which followed the search spread with increasing American investment into Saudi Arabia, where exports began in 1938, and the other Gulf states. Britain's interest in the search for oil brought many of its nationals to the region, playing pioneer roles, often under appallingly difficult conditions, as subsequent chapters will show.

The discovery of oil in the eastern quarter of the Middle East also began to transform Britain's political interest in the region. With the development of air travel, the sea and land routes to India gradually became less important, and establishing the security of the oilfields emerged as the new priority.

Britain's relationship with most of the Gulf sheikhdoms was well established before the discovery of oil because of the various defence and friendship pacts signed in the nineteenth century. Relations with Iran had also been close. But from 1920 onwards, Reza Shah trimmed the privileges that Britain and other countries had enjoyed.

Iran came back into Britain's focus during the Second World War when Germany invaded the Soviet Union. The fear of the Allies was that the Germans might move on down and across the border into Iran. This could enable the Germans to capture the Iranian oilfields. While Reza Shah insisted that his country was neutral, pro-German sentiments in the country were considerable and Nazi undercover agents were doing their best to encourage anti-Allied feelings. In 1941, with the German threat growing, Reza Shah cited his country's neutrality and refused to allow arms to be transported to the Soviet Union. As a result, in August of that year, British troops from Iraq invaded Iran from the south (with United States troops following later), while Soviet troops came in from the north. The following month Reza Shah abdicated and was succeeded by his son, Muhammad Reza Pahlavi. In 1943 Iran abandoned its neutrality and declared war on Germany. In 1946 British and American troops withdrew.

Iran came under British scrutiny yet again at the beginning of the next decade. Nationalist feelings were directed against the Anglo-Iranian Oil Company, which was regarded as making excessive profits at the expense of the country at a time when Iran urgently needed funds for development plans. The leading nationalist politician was Muhammad Mossadeq, who became prime minister in 1951. To the fury of the British government he nationalized the oil industry, including the Anglo-Iranian Oil Company. Britain appealed unsuccessfully to the International Court of Justice, but was successful in encouraging international companies to boycott Iranian oil. In August 1953 the Shah tried to challenge Mossadeq and dismissed him from office, appointing a loyalist as prime minister. But in so doing the Shah was forced to flee the country. However, a plot was hatched by the CIA, with British help, to remove Mossadeq, and six days later the Shah returned. Management of the oil industry was then rearranged, with a consortium of American, Dutch and British firms making up the National Iranian Oil Company.

The Mossadeq affair spelt the end of Britain's prominent role in

Iran. But British dominance in the lower Gulf states lasted another two decades. In 1967 Britain withdrew under severe nationalist pressure and amid scenes of violence from Aden, which had been a Crown Colony for nearly 140 years. At that point, though, there seemed to be no prospect of Britain closing down its military bases in Bahrain and the other Gulf states. Indeed, the rulers of these sheikhdoms were insistent that they did not want to lose British military protection.

The British Labour government of the day, amid rumours of a Gulf withdrawal, sent a minister to the region in 1968 to reassure the rulers that Britain had no intention of going. But no sooner had he done that than he was sent back to the Gulf to say that Britain was indeed intending to withdraw all its forces by the end of 1971. The Gulf states were stunned. When the moment came Bahrain, Qatar and Oman became independent nations, while the Trucial States banded together to form the United Arab Emirates – consisting of Abu Dhabi, Dubai, Sharjah, Ras al-Khaimah, Ajman, Fujairah and Umm al-Qaiwain.

Over the previous decades Britain had frequently abandoned its various positions of privilege and influence in the Middle East under Arab nationalist pressure. It was ironic and sad that the announcement of its final withdrawal from the Gulf should have taken place against the wishes of the local rulers and in a manner which appeared to them to be less than honourable. Glencairn Balfour-Paul was serving as a British diplomat in Bahrain at the time, and says he was surprised at the manner in which Britain's decision to leave the Gulf was conveyed to the rulers. 'We knew that Britain's moment in the Middle East was ending,' he says, 'but we didn't think it would end quite so quickly or in the unexpected way it did, with the two ministerial visits. I was appalled by the fact that we appeared to have misled the rulers only two months before into thinking that we would continue to defend them and support them as long as our mutual interests made this necessary. But one saw that it had to come and I think that the government's decision, though it was conveyed in a rather careless manner, was probably the right one.'

As the British forces left their bases in the Gulf, the era of the Lion in the Sand, which had begun with the arrival of an expeditionary force in Alexandria in 1882, came to an end. The events of this era provided the backdrop for the lives of the individuals who set up temporary homes in the Middle East to make a living or to support husbands and families. It is with their stories and adventures that the following pages are filled.

Part 2

PERSIA, IRAQ AND THE GULF

4

GETTING THERE IN ONE PIECE

My father and I stood on the flattened sand apron at Doha airport in Qatar. It was sometime in the late 1950s. There were words exchanged – my father expressed consternation. The flight was overbooked by one, and we were the last to arrive for the flight to Bahrain. 'Don't worry,' I heard the English pilot say, 'the little boy can sit on the box at the back.' So when the de Havilland Heron took off for the short flight across the sea, I sat on the airline dispatch box on the floor at the back. Nobody seemed to mind.

At around the same time my father was flying down to one of the smallest emirates in the lower Gulf. The pilot was having trouble spotting the oil drums which marked the location of the runway in the desert, so he asked my father to come alongside and help him find the landing-strip.

Those were days of casual and relaxed attitudes to flying in the Gulf, uninhibited by tight rules and regulations. Even though air travel by this time was well established in most corners of the world, in the Gulf it still remained something of an adventure – or so it seemed to me then. What I did not know until I was much older was how tame my parents' adventures were at that time, compared with the rigours of travel which they and other Britons had experienced in the Middle East in the previous decades.

Many of the early journeyers to Iraq and Persia (which from 1935 was known as Iran) in the days before regular and reliable air travel, found themselves taking a unique desert ferry service known as the Nairn transport. It was started as a taxi service across the desert from Damascus to Baghdad, and was pioneered by two brothers from New Zealand, Norman and Gerald Nairn. They had stayed on in the Middle East after serving with the Allied armed forces in battles with the Turks during the First World War. John M. Munro, in his book *The Nairn Way – Desert Bus to Baghdad*, describes how in April 1923 the Nairns made their first experimental trip. They took with them a Bedouin guide, and were helped further in their navigation by the 'air furrow', a line that had been ploughed straight across the desert from Amman to Ramadi. It had been designed to assist Royal Air Force pilots, who were at that time operating a fortnightly air service between Cairo and Baghdad. The group completed the 550-mile journey overland safely in three days.

But further experiments were required to establish the best route, given the difficult and varied nature of the terrain. In the words of John M. Munro, 'unlike the deserts of central Arabia, where billows of soft, shifting sand make travel on foot or even in jeeps with a four-wheel drive a painful, if not hazardous experience, the Syrian Desert is a vast, undulating plain, its surface strewn with gravel, and pock-marked with clumps of dusty, grey-green vegetation'.

Another problem was to ensure the safety of the passenger service from attack by the Bedouin. The Nairns negotiated a guarantee of safe passage from a local Syrian sheikh. He not only had influence over tribes in the desert, but was a keen smuggler and therefore had an interest in seeing the opening up of the desert to faster means of transport than the camel to enable his men to dodge customs officials.

By the end of 1923 convoys of Nairn cars were starting to carry mail, and then passengers, from Damascus to Baghdad. As George Green discovered when he travelled the route in 1928.

Mr Green, now in his eighties, accepted a job at the age of nineteen which would take him to Persia. He was to work for a company in Isfahan analysing the morphine content of opium. Like so many others who travelled in these early days, Mr Green found simply getting to the Middle East something of an adventure. Sitting in his home in Sussex he recalled the planning stage of his journey to the unknown. 'I went to Thomas Cook's in Ludgate Circus. I said I wanted to go to Isfahan. They didn't know where that was, so the man got a map out and I put my finger on the map to show him. He said he could get me to Baghdad, but no further.' Mr Green managed to pick up a copy of *Marlborough Self-Taught Persian* (the much-thumbed red-covered book is still in his possession) and in November 1928 set off to the East.

The first part of his journey was by train and boat from London to Marseilles. The next lap was by ship from southern France to the Lebanese capital, Beirut. The trip from Beirut over the Lebanese mountains to Damascus was by car. From there to Baghdad the terrain is desert. Mr Green had a seat booked in a special Nairn taxi. The vehicle was 'a large American car. Cans of petrol and luggage were strapped to the running boards. One passenger sat in the front, and three in the back with their feet on mail bags. There was no road, and the driver navigated using a compass and the stars.' This leg of the journey took thirty-six hours. In later years a variety of buses operated a faster service.

Having reached Baghdad, the planned stage of Mr Green's journey was over. He bought a train ticket and travelled by rail across the Persian border to Kermanshah. From there to his final destination, Mr Green hitchhiked, getting a lift in a lorry part of the way and making himself understood as best he could with the help of his *Marlborough Self-Taught Persian*. In this way he was forced to learn and speak Farsi (the Persian language). As Mr Green today describes the process: 'You shave in cold water until you learn the word for hot.' In later years Mr Green was given the nickname Sabsi – the Farsi word for green – in recognition of his skill in speaking the language.

Mr Green's journey ended when he arrived one evening in Isfahan. 'One of the things I remember,' he said, 'was waiting outside the house where I was to stay. Out of the darkness appeared a clown, a Columbine and a fireman. They were having a fancy-dress party.' Mr Green had arrived among the British in the Middle East.

In later years, the Damascus–Baghdad stage of the journey out to Iraq and Iran (which Britons, for many years after 1935, still referred to as Persia) still involved travel by Nairn transport, although the service gradually became faster and more sophisticated. Sir Roderick Sarell, who joined the British Consular Service in 1936, travelled by Nairn transport on the way out to his first posting in Iran. Passing through Damascus he had dinner with Gerald Nairn. 'He told me about how they had begun the service and about the desert. It was fine in dry weather, but after rain it was a different matter. Nairn said that he had been marooned for three days by mud on one occasion and in fact had had to have supplies flown out from Damascus. Having pioneered the route he then evolved his very original bus for those days. It had a long fuselage of an aircraft type where we sat four abreast in aircraft seats. It was pivoted on the front with a single pivot which was mounted on a lorry tyre to provide suspension. A six-wheel tractor pulled the fuselage. It was a very early form of articulated lorry, and was an efficient and comfortable conveyance. It left Damascus in those days at seven in the morning and took twenty-four hours to reach Baghdad. Quite soon afterwards this was accelerated to eighteen hours. The desert is flat and free of vegetation. But there is a certain amount of undulation which provided for the famous notice in the Nairn buses which said: "When the bus stops, Ladies will disperse to the left, and Gentlemen to the right".'

How often did it stop?

'Sufficiently often, I don't recall exactly how often. But we were all young, so it didn't have to stop too often.'

Answering the call of nature presented a problem for my mother – a young and sensitive English bride out from London, in the Middle East for the first time – even before she boarded the Nairn bus in her journey to Persia in 1938. When she and my father arrived by ship in Beirut they found themselves in the port, about to share a taxi to Damascus. 'I suddenly said that I couldn't go to Damascus without visiting a loo,' my mother remembers. 'They asked a policeman, who asked someone else. Eventually a procession formed along the quayside – me in a white suit and a hat – with some small boys joining in. Something was happening, and they were saying: "Where are you taking the lady?" I was escorted into a house and a madame met me. I was escorted upstairs to the loo, and the driver sat on the stairs waiting for me to come out. Then we all marched back to the car. It ended up being quite a procession.'

The taxi set off 'at breakneck speed over the mountains, round hairpin bends, to Damascus. We were booked on the air-conditioned Nairn to go across the desert. But when we got there we were told that the air-conditioned coach had been taken over by the Persian court. The Shah had become engaged to an Egyptian princess, and they had been taking presents to her. So we were crossing the desert in an open-window coach in July. There were a lot of schoolgirls coming from boarding school in Beirut to their homes in Baghdad – they were singing "Rose Marie".'

My mother was constantly distracted by mirages in the desert. 'I kept asking them to tell the driver to stop under the trees by the lake – but the others couldn't see anything. Then we stopped in the desert and they said: "Men that side, women this side." I said: "No thank you." I couldn't do that.'

Relief came finally when the bus stopped at Rutbah wells, a *Beau Geste*-style desert fortress which served as a resthouse. Here the

C.S. Jarvis, a British administrator in Sinai between the wars, discussing fishing with Egyptian peasants.

Peake Pasha, commander of the Arab Legion of Transjordan before Glubb Pasha.

A rest-stop in the Syrian–Iraqi desert for a pioneering crossing by the Nairn transport service.

A 1930s brochure shows the revolutionary design of a bus built by the Nairns for the Damascus–Baghdad desert crossing.

British and Dominion troops in the Middle East during the Second World War teaching the art of darts to desert Arabs.

Sir Gawain Bell organized camel and horse races in the Negev desert to promote friendship between Allied troops and the Bedouin.

Sir Anthony Parsons, one of many distinguished British Arabist diplomats, in conversation with Sheikh Isa, ruler of Bahrain.

Well-hole no. 1 at Baba Gurgur in northern Iraq in October 1927, operated by the British-run Iraq Petroleum Company (IPC).

travelling British – as so often in the Middle East – found a link with home. 'A Bristolian was in charge of the resthouse,' my mother recalls. 'We sat there in the desert talking to him about Bristol Rovers. We then continued our journey at about ten o'clock at night, and the man we'd been speaking to gave me a huge grey blanket. I said it was the last thing I wanted, having been roasted all day. But I did need it. The night was bitterly cold.'

The Nairn experience was only part of the adventure of travelling to Iraq and Iran in the pre-Second World War days. Before the traveller left Britain he or she had to assemble enough clothing and equipment to last for a posting of several years in a part of the world where few items other than the most basic could be bought.

Sir Roderick Sarell remembers getting together all the household goods he would require, plus two years' supply of groceries. 'Luckily my mother had had experience in Tunis after the First World War, where my father was posted as consul, in ordering such supplies from the Army & Navy Stores – so she was able to guide me in the things I should provide for, such as tea and marmalade. The supplies available in Persia were perfectly adequate for day-to-day living. A gaping lack, which is a comment on my innocence, was any supplies of drink. But on arrival in Persia I was entitled to three months' duty-free import. So this gap, particularly supplies of whisky and gin, was readily restored by orders from Bombay. But in our ordinary kit we had all the crockery, all the glass, all the cutlery that we needed. A 1939 Army & Navy catalogue lists a canteen for twelve, A1 plate, at thirty-six pounds. The same in solid silver, forty-five pounds. But this must be read against the background of a salary of three hundred pounds a year, with an outfit allowance of one hundred and twenty pounds.'

My mother, setting off from London a couple of years later, also remembers taking 'as much as we could, as we were going for five years. We took sheets, blankets, china and glassware. Furniture polish. Mrs Beeton's recipe book, which had good household advice. I didn't know that I'd eventually be making my own furniture polish and that sort of thing. I also took material – we had a great pile of luggage.'

Sir Roderick Sarell told me about setting off with his huge mound of luggage on the Orient Express, which ran from London to Venice. The fare, by sleeper, cost eight pounds ten shillings. 'We had a first-class dinner with excellent wine on board. We woke up at that magical moment when you go through the Swiss Alps, seeing them from your sleeper window, and travelled across the Po valley, lunching as we passed the lakes, fetching up in Venice at about four o'clock in the afternoon. I should mention in passing that I was an experienced traveller because my father had been a consul. One thing I learned was that you do not part with your heavy luggage, so I had insisted on taking every last piece of kit with me on the train. I was a bit shaken; it cost, I think, fourteen pounds for my share of the load – it was well worth it, but it required checking at the major stops such as Paris and again at Venice. There I was met by Thomas Cook. I realized in Venice that I had reached the edge of the Middle East because largesse, I saw, was being distributed to facilitate the movement of the luggage. I was not involved in that, and away it went on board a delightful Lloyd Triestino's ship called the *Marco Polo* which alas was sunk in Tobruk during the war. As of right I travelled first class. The voyage, Venice to Haifa, was very pleasant. We stopped at Bari, and our next call was Alexandria where, through my sister, I knew the daughter of the consul general. He received us most hospitably. We had a very pleasant day before getting on board for a rather uncomfortable passage to Haifa.'

The overland route took the young Roderick Sarell to Damascus and Baghdad, and then across the border through a bitterly cold Persian winter towards Tehran. 'The journey became increasingly difficult,' Sir Roderick said, 'because of the snow and ice. And instead of our heavy luggage being transported by lorry, it was strapped on and around two large taxis. In particular, there was a large case of crockery strapped to the back of one car. Going down the mountain passes it caused the taxi to slither from side to side in a discouraging manner.'

A stop was made at the Grand Hôtel de France in the city of Ghazvin for lunch. 'It had the superficial trappings of European facilities. But the facility immediately outside the dining room had one startling defect. It had the modern water flush with a high-level tank. Unfortunately the connection to the pan had come away. And the unwary traveller, on pulling the flush, flushed his feet and not the pan. I suffered this interesting experience myself.'

After spending Christmas in Tehran, Mr Sarell carried on with his long and meandering journey to his destination, Shiraz. Isfahan was the next stop on the way. In the mid-1990s, looking back on that amazing journey six decades earlier from the comfort of his armchair in his Berkshire home, Sir Roderick said that arriving in Isfahan gave him 'one of the most fascinating and dramatic experiences of my life. The winters were cold and dry, and the atmosphere of astonishing clarity. The road into Isfahan comes into the great Medan e-Shah, one of the great squares of the world. We entered it on a clear, starlit night with the stars, as they do in that type of climate, appearing to hang out of the sky with astonishing brilliance and the entire Medan with its mosques and the gateway to the old palace standing out in astonishing beauty.' Sir Roderick paused for a few seconds as he recaptured the scene, and in the stillness one could hear the clock ticking in the room and the soft cooing of pigeons in the trees outside.

Weeks after setting off from London, the young consular officer reached his destination. 'The saying in Persia is that oases have to be earned. When you've had a long and dusty journey through the desert, which is what most of Persia consists of, hard gravel desert with mountain ranges each side, to suddenly come on a large tract of green vegetation is an unforgettable experience. This was rendered more dramatic in Shiraz by the fact that the road from Isfahan came through a gap in the mountains and dropped abruptly into Shiraz, lying in the valley below. This pass was known as the Tange Allahu Akbar – the pass of 'God is most great', because the weary traveller arriving by caravan, coming suddenly upon this marvellous sight of vegetation, would cry out: "God is indeed most great."'

With so many connections to be made, and so many forms of transport involved, it is not surprising that the travellers in those early days – with their mountains of luggage – never knew how long a journey might take. In the winter months, for example, a traveller might find himself stuck in Damascus waiting for floods in the desert to subside. In 1937 Denis Lunn decided to drive out from England with his wife in the Chevrolet which they had been given as a wedding present to the Persian city of Khorramshahr to take up his latest posting in the Imperial Bank of Persia. But, he wrote in his autobiography, *Rags of Time*, the RAC, 'when confronted with a request for detailed routes, urged strongly against driving through the Balkans and Turkey . . . and this recommendation was one I could neither challenge nor wisely disregard'. So the Lunns put the car on a ship from Trieste to Haifa, drove to Damascus and made contact with the Nairn company. 'In 1937 the Nairn organization offered as a sideline to its trans-desert crossing a sort of pathfinders' service for private cars whose owners lacked experience of the desert.' But the news from the Nairn company was not good. 'On arrival at Damascus that November evening we learnt to our dismay that the desert was in flood, with no crossing possible for at least three days. This was a doubly serious blow. I was due in Khorramshahr the following Tuesday and did not relish facing criticism from my new chief for being late, however unavoidable the delay might be. Also, the last ten days had eaten seriously into my end-of-leave resources.'

Another complication could be regulations relating to border crossings. My mother, in Iraq in 1938, remembers well her first crossing into Iran. 'We had to go down to the bazaar first, early in the morning, to get a permit to enter the country – you could only get it the day you were going. I sat in the bazaar, and I didn't like that because I had to be left in the car while my husband went in. I was surrounded by donkeys and people just starting their day, shouting and yelling. At the police post to enter Persia it turned out we hadn't the right documents and had to return to Baghdad on a rocky road. We then returned to customs at twelve o'clock and they closed at twelve. They opened all our luggage and they stripped the car. They said we couldn't take in the silver. But in the end, because they were closing, they put everything back and just charged us for the cloth. There was an American missionary woman at the post with her three children. She was bringing in cocoa powder in a valise full of shoes and the bag had burst. All the shoes were full of cocoa and I thought: 'Oh dear, do we get like that living out here?'

As well as passing customs, travellers also had to conform with the health regulations of the various Middle Eastern countries they were entering, as Kenneth Bradford, en route to Iran in the late forties, discovered. 'We spent two periods in quarantine because the ship I went out on had called into Alexandria and they had a cholera epidemic there. And although we had been inoculated against cholera, the authorities in both Lebanon and Iraq insisted on putting us into quarantine. So it took over a month to get to Tehran.'

Some travellers in the Middle East in the pre-Second World War days were not encumbered by schedules. Pamela Fletcher, now Pamela Cooper, was taken as a young lady by her godmother on extensive foreign excursions. In 1935 they went on a tour of the Holy Land. 'After the hunting finished,' Mrs Cooper said, 'off we went on these lovely journeys. I must have done about five with her, but the one to the Middle East was an early one to see the wild flowers and to make a Christian pilgrimage. *In the Steps of the Master*, by H.V.

Morton, had just come out, and we took the book with us. We also had his dragoman [interpreter], Michael Khouri, who lived on the walls of Acre. Off we went – from Victoria down on the Orient Express. It was really good then, you know. Each of us had a salon, you didn't have to climb up into a bunk. We got into our wonderful navy blue *salons-lits* wherever we went. The meals were absolutely delicious in the nice dining room. We had a lovely travelling maid, Miss Last. There were four of us with Miss Last. One was rather isolated looking out of the window, but it was magic. It was made for you by the "brown nanny" – the Thomas Cook representative. Mr Cook met us everywhere, and looked after us. Obviously we picked up a lot of queer people – three ladies, and I was the only young one. Whenever we alighted from the train, if someone unsuitable attached himself to us there was Mr Cook's representative to welcome us. And of course in those days people didn't travel. Everywhere we were met by people from the embassy and so on.'

From Istanbul, the party went by train to Haifa. Mrs Cooper remembers that they 'had next door to us a lovely Turkish general who never got out of his pyjamas. He had a very nice ADC who took photos of me in the corridors. We talked and talked. The train was going very slowly through the Taurus mountains and he wanted us to get out and go hawking. We couldn't do that, of course. The general was going off to raise some troops somewhere.'

The journey continued into Syria. 'We arrived at Aleppo, and that was where we left the sort of grandeur of Europe. It was terrific – Palmyra, then Baalbek in Lebanon. We travelled in motor cars from Aleppo onwards – one for our luggage, one for ourselves. The flowers were marvellous.'

From Lebanon, the young Miss Fletcher and her godmother continued southwards to the Holy Land. 'We went to the Christian pilgrimage places, like Galilee, which was wonderful. We stayed at the King David Hotel in Jerusalem. I remember it was very comfortable and luxurious with its Sudanese and Nubian servants.'

After the Holy Land, the party crossed the River Jordan and went to Amman. Miss Fletcher was taken to meet King Abdullah. 'He didn't sleep in his palace, he slept in a tent. It was very informal. You were led up and you said: "Hello" and "How do you do?", and you gave a little bob and had some coffee. He was very much an Arab sheikh in the desert; it wasn't at all formal. The King was small and squat and had a big, strong face.'

Before leaving Jordan the English ladies were invited by Captain F.G. Peake, Peake Pasha, the commander of King Abdullah's army, to visit Petra. With the spectacular rose-red Nabataean city hewn out of the rock as the setting, a Bedouin feast was prepared in honour of the visitors. 'Peake Pasha rode into Petra looking absolutely fantastic on his stallion with his scarlet cloak. He was a rather mild man, but you know there were lots of stories among the Arabs about his temper.' At the feast, the Bedouin sang songs and Peake Pasha made a speech. One of the Bedouin sang a song about Miss Fletcher and how beautiful she was, and Miss Fletcher didn't understand a word of it. I remember Peake Pasha had a very elegant French lady with him who was the first person I ever saw in wonderful khaki jodhpurs. She was very chic, and I think she got a song too. The feast was massive – they killed the sheep and we sat around the fire late into the night. And all the Bedouin came up and ate all the remains of the feast. And there were more songs – about my godmother and her generosity, and so on. They sang in that lovely old quarter-tone chant. And then they got more and more excited and the children came around. They were a rather wild tribe down there. They didn't have much contact with the outside world. We slept in a cave. It was all very exciting.'

I asked Mrs Cooper if the party saw other foreign tourists during their travels.

'Just a few privileged people. Not many British, a few Americans. On the whole they were either specialists or had fallen in love with the Arabs, those kinds. I suppose you could travel easily with quite a lot of money. I think my godmother sprinkled a lot of money around on the way. It was rather like travelling with royalty. Her tipping was so lavish that as we left the Luxor hotel in Egypt I remember a tiny boy rushing out and jumping on the running board of the car. "Please, please, lady, you've not seen me." He had his little dishcloth, he was obviously a scullion or something. She was wonderful, but goodness knows what she gave. It was all very romantic for people like us. One came across rich Americans; but the masses didn't travel. I was in heaven.'

When the Second World War broke out, travelling to the Middle East was neither leisurely nor romantic. Troops and civilians on the move faced the same dangers in that region as in other theatres of war. The outbreak of war also coincided with the beginning of the era of organized and regular air travel. It was the era of the flying-boat – the craft that briefly provided a link between the leisure, luxury and romance of sea travel and the functional efficiency of air transport. But travelling by flying-boat, despite the relatively low speed and range of the craft, was not always a relaxing experience, particularly in the heat of summer. Alaric Jacob, a news correspondent in the Second World War, wrote in *A Traveller's War* about a flight from the Cape to Cairo in 1941 by an Imperial Airways flying-boat. 'Khartoum,' he observed, 'looks like a mere village at the place where the two great Niles meet. We come in at about ten thousand feet, where it's quite cold, but when we step out of the cabin into the motor-launch the heat rises up off the water and strikes a blow that nearly knocks us over. Today is the first of August. It is 110 degrees in the shade. And Heaven knows what in the sun. Covering the hundred yards from the launch to the waiting car, the sun falls upon one's back like the flame of a blow-torch. Never have I felt such heat. I believe if someone were to plaster a raw egg on my shoulder it would fry before I reach that car. A naval officer's wife who is one of the passengers becomes faint from the sudden transition from ice-box to oven and has to be helped into the car. Someone gets a damp handkerchief to put around her head.'

After an overnight stay in Khartoum, the passengers prepared to resume their journey. 'Eviscerated like Toast Melba after a grilling night, we clambered into the flying-boat again at 6.45 a.m. and were stewed inside the hull for half an hour while the engineers fiddled with the engines. The take-off, followed by a rapid soaring to 10,000 feet, was a vast relief. Soon we rejoiced to feel cold again.'

Immediately after the Second World War, civil air transport came into its own. But sea travel was still common; and the Middle East offered for many Britons who had suffered the rigours and deprivations of the war in Europe a pleasant escape. George McGeachie, en route to Abadan in Iran to take up a job with the oil company, sailed to Alexandria on the *Caernarvon Castle*. Because of troubles in Palestine, he was forced to wait a week in Alexandria, followed by ten days in Cairo. There he stayed at the famous Shepheard's Hotel, which, he says, 'was tremendous. You can imagine the effect that had on a twenty-three-year-old like myself after the austerity of wartime Britain, with the blackouts and the shortage of food. Here you had this wide-open world, the incredible array of fruit that one saw in the market, the shops, and the busy toing and froing of merchants. The luxury of the old Shepheard's Hotel with the servants, the food – it was an entirely different world. Later we had a marvellously luxurious two days in the Grand Orient Hotel in Damascus. It was a different world.'

As the war years receded, so the number of Britons seeking jobs in the Middle East grew. Travel, while much slower than today, was more often than not by air, a move that put paid to the Nairn bus and other early forms of transport. Journeys to the Middle East by sea became increasingly rare. But in 1952 the Parsons family travelled by ship to Iraq. Mr Parsons (later Sir Anthony) was starting out his diplomatic career in the Middle East. The story of his journey to the region is a fitting epitaph to the days of leisurely, luxurious and romantic travel in the region.

The Parsons booked a passage for themselves and their two small sons on a cargo boat from London. Travelling for eight weeks with two very small, hyperactive boys, he recalls, was an unforgettable experience. 'It was rough in the Bay of Biscay. The boys had thrown all their toys over the side of the ship – and quite a lot of the ship's equipment, too – before we even reached Gibraltar. The captain's chessmen had also disappeared by that time.'

The ship, it turned out, was not well organized. 'The captain had rather unwisely loaded the cargo in the wrong order so we had to do a lot of going backwards and forwards unloading cargo in one place and then coming back and unloading cargo at an earlier port. He also had masses of cement on the top of the hold. It poured with rain when we were in Oran in North Africa and the cement turned to concrete and that held us up quite a lot. When we got down into the Red Sea and the Arabian Sea – and it was pretty warm and things were really getting pretty bad – the boys got up into the chart room one afternoon when the captain presumably was having a kip and tore up all his maps – which may explain some of the delays in the journey. We were then told fresh water was getting short and would we only have baths when we simply had to. I was sitting on the deck one afternoon and I noticed water pouring out of the corridor and down some steps. The boys had gone into two of the bathrooms and turned on all the taps absolutely full blast. We spent the afternoon mopping up, not daring to tell the captain that almost all the ship's fresh water had gone.'

Once in the Persian Gulf, nature took a hand to subdue the two small boys. 'A plague of locusts so terrified them that they went into their cabins and stayed there for about thirty-six hours. We eventually got to Iraq after stopping at some very interesting places. I remember

Kuwait was simply a little mud-walled city. We disembarked at Basra and I went politely to the captain and said: "You have had a frightful time with my family and I would really like you to tell me how much I owe you for all the damage the boys have done." He simply said: "Look, honestly, just to get your family off this ship is all the reward I could possibly ask for."'

5

PERSIA: A LITTLE DREAM WORLD

'**A**lways wear your topi until the sun is well down in the evening.
'The habit of running from office to office without a topi is dangerous in the extreme.'

So began a memorandum written in 1928 and issued thereafter to employees of the Anglo-Persian Oil Company arriving in Abadan or at the oilfields. Abadan, situated in the hot and arid south-west corner of Iran (or Persia, as it was commonly still called many years after 1935 when the Shah officially changed its name to Iran), contained the biggest oil refinery in the world, making it the centre of the company's operations. According to *The History of the British Petroleum Company* by J.H. Bamberg, 'by 1928 Abadan had become in some respects a boom town and a centre of opportunism both for officials, who regarded service in Khuzistan [province] as more like exile than promotion, and local entrepreneurs who controlled the bazaars and other commercial activity in the area'.

There was clearly something of a frontier spirit among the British employees. In May 1929, when disturbances broke out among Persian workers at the refinery who were making certain demands of the management, the British took their own measures to counteract the troubles. Persian rioters tried 'to penetrate the refinery fences and in the scuffling one or two of the Company's staff in the grounds became involved, including Andrew S. McQueen, a former Scottish boxing champion'.

The boom town of Abadan had been created by the Anglo-Persian (from 1935, the Anglo-Iranian) Oil Company from nothing. George McGeachie, an Anglo-Iranian employee after the Second World War, says that in Persia, as in the Gulf states in later years, oil companies needed to import a lot more than drilling equipment. 'If you go into the Gulf states you can see the very complicated and complex operations that the companies have for the finding, producing, refining and exporting of oil. And in Abadan, as in the Gulf, everything had to be provided by the company. Water, sewerage, housing, electricity – we had our own power stations – married accommodation, which meant furniture and so on – everything was supplied by the company. We ran our own schools in several areas. We built and ran our own church, and we had vicars who came out on contract.'

George 'Sabsi' Green, who had worked in Persia at the age of nineteen, came out to the country again in 1934, when he was in his mid-twenties, as an employee of the Anglo-Persian company. He travelled by the oil tanker *The British Hope*. The crew and passengers 'used to swim in one of the oil tanks which had been cleaned out and filled with sea water. It was pretty smelly.'

Mr Green was immediately allocated bachelor accommodation when he arrived in Abadan. For married couples and families, though, the picture was not so simple. Leonora Goad, who first went to Iran in 1935, remembers that in the early days married accommodation was scarce. 'You had to wait until someone offered you a bungalow, and you came out for the summer. We were known as the "summer brides". Eventually you got your own bungalow.'

The principle of women being allowed into the male world of Abadan caused some ruffling of feathers. One senior official felt, J.H. Bamberg records, 'that rather than relying on domestic servants, wives should involve themselves actively in household duties. He suggested that the Company should therefore provide facilities "to allow them to do a great deal of cooking", noting that the "mere fact of us supplying service imposes on the married man a higher standard of living than he would normally be accustomed to in this country".' Another official, meanwhile, declared that he was 'not very keen on women messing at the Restaurant as they are a damned nuisance outside their normal surroundings and the Restaurant is absolutely full to capacity'.

Contrary to the management suggestions, wives certainly did not take the place of servants; and the inevitable presence of wives and families became totally accepted.

Mrs Goad finally lost her status of 'summer bride', and she and her husband were provided with housing in the Company compound. Settling in was 'not like living in a foreign country. Older hands held a party for you, and you soon became absorbed. It was a self-contained community with a good common spirit. There were rows of bungalows, nearly all of which had gardens. Our first bungalow was very primitive. It had no air-conditioning, only ceiling fans. Later we had air-conditioning. At first there was also no refrigerator, only an ice-box propped on stilts. Ice was delivered every morning – if the staff were there, and alive and awake, they collected it for you.'

The Goads had a cook and a houseboy, and 'maybe someone under him to do the dirty work and put the beds out on the lawn because we slept outside in summer'.

Did Mrs Goad remember any of the servants from that time? 'There was Domingo, an Indian cook. He could make spun-sugar toffee baskets. We also had a cook we called "Minargarene", because he couldn't say "margarine".' Otherwise the Persian servants 'had perfectly ordinary names – Hassan, Ali, Muhammad. They came and went with great regularity, and with many of your personal possessions as well. They were light-fingered. You locked up your stores in which you kept imported food. You put these things under lock and key and doled them out when the cook needed them.'

Local products and produce were brought from the bazaar by the cook, so the Goads had little contact with life outside the oil company compound. 'You didn't really see the shacks and mud-huts and things. When you went to the bazaar you only went to a few shops. If you wanted to buy a carpet or have something made, they came to your bungalow. We were isolated from the poor section of the local population. We were cocooned in our area.'

The expatriate community was also largely isolated from the local population in their day-to-day work. In the thirties there were only a handful of Persians holding positions of responsibility in the Anglo-Persian Company, and mixing was limited. The Persians' accommodation (many had left homes elsewhere in the country to work in this remote province) and recreation facilities were located on the opposite side of the refinery from the one where the Goads and other foreigners lived. Mrs Goad concedes that the British community 'didn't know a great many Persians'. J.H. Bamberg, writing of this period, says that the Company compound 'took on some of the characteristics of a social enclave in Iran. Men and women who in Britain would for the most part have blended inconspicuously into their surroundings became, in Iran, a privileged élite, easily caricatured as the stereotype of the British abroad in the age of empire.'

The attitude of Company officials did nothing to encourage Iranians to seek senior positions and thus mix more with the foreigners. A

Company document of the time defined the type of Iranian who would be likely to secure a senior post and warned of the dangers of the new appointee helping the spread of nationalist feelings. The potential applicant would be 'probably of good social standing and may even have a British University education, but when in the South [of Iran] he is, both by his natural inclination to seek out his own fellow countrymen and by a peculiar disinclination of the average Britisher to meet on a pleasant social basis with foreigners, driven to seek the society of Junior Customs and other Government officials in Abadan under whose influence he becomes imbued with intensely Nationalistic and anti-foreign prejudices which are common to practically all the juniors in Persian Government billets at the present day'.

The whole subject of labour relations was complicated not only by concerns about nationalists, but also by a lack of clear policy on the part of Company management. It is fascinating to see the way in which the issue of who might be best suited to deal with labour relations was debated in terms so peculiar to the class-sensitive British. J.H. Bamberg quotes one senior official of the day as saying that labour relations were 'a specialised affair' requiring 'the instinctive knowledge which comes from close acquaintance with the people'. Personnel officers, the official felt, should have 'a first class public school background' and preferably the District Officer mentality as he had known it in India. However, another senior official expressed doubts about 'Varsity chaps'. He believed that the best personnel officers came from the ranks of 'sons of clergymen, doctors, land agents, etc. whose parents have sent them to good second class public schools, and kept them there until they are 18, and then expect them to make their own way in life'.

While such debates were taking place in Company offices, daily life in the cocooned world of the compound was carrying on. In the evenings, Mrs Goad remembers, 'there was lots of socializing. We had to make our own amusements.' Aside from dinner parties and bridge evenings there was a chance to get involved in amateur dramatics. Mrs Goad smiled at the memory. 'We did reviews and things like *Blithe Spirit*. I played Madame Arcati – that was my great triumph.'

Other evenings were spent listening to gramophone records or dancing to them. 'These were our dancing days. There was the Charleston and the Lambeth Walk. We loved all the Glenn Miller music and the music from the shows. We had musical evenings outside, and my husband would play jazz and classics. "Red Hot Pennies" was a favourite.'

Among the expatriates in Abadan was a big contingent of Scots. So the Caledonian Ball and Burns Night were important dates in the calendar. On these occasions, one can be certain, no attention was paid to the Company's advice to young bachelors (which accompanied the warning about the danger of not wearing topis), that 'if you must drink alcohol, do so after sun down and then only in moderation'.

'Sabsi' Green's memory of these days is that the community in Abadan 'worked hard, played hard and drank hard. My main interest was the cricket section. The wicket was made of crushed shells and straw rolled hard, and coir matting. It favoured the fast bowlers. The outfield was bare desert earth. Everyone thought we were mad to play cricket with the temperature 120 degrees in the shade. We had annual fixtures – we played Baghdad, the Air Force at Basra and each other. We also played against the oilfields and then we'd have a riotous weekend.'

Riotous times were also being enjoyed in the late thirties and forties in Tehran, the capital and business centre of Iran. Located here was the head office of the other great British institution in the country (alongside the oil company) in the first half of the century, the Imperial Bank of Persia (later, of Iran). Up to 1930 it had been the government bank, responsible for the issue of notes. A decade later, even though its official role had been curtailed, it was still a formidable power in the land, with its ornately decorated headquarters building dominating the main square in Tehran and with branches around the southern part of the country.

In 1935, Angus Macqueen, a young bachelor, arrived in Tehran and met up with his former colleague and socializing companion from the London office, Archie Butt, my late father. In contrast to having been penniless employees in days of recession in England they found in Tehran that they had some spare money. 'Your father led me astray far too much in those days,' Mr Macqueen told me, with a twinkle in his eye. 'We used to go to a nightclub where we signed chits, and the owner of it came round to the bank on pay day and collected his dues. Others were involved as well, but Archie and I in particular would meet in the Tehran Club in the evening and there we'd play snooker. We'd leave the club perhaps about ten or ten-thirty, and then go down to the cabarets. Most of the girls were Hungarian and Romanian and were very attractive and amusing. Archie and I held the record of not being home to the mess for thirteen nights running until three-thirty in the morning. We stayed there in the cabaret until three-thirty, and then got our droshky home to the mess. The office started at seven-thirty. But we did have, more often than not, a siesta in the afternoon. Because we'd leave the bank at two o'clock or shortly after, and then not start playing tennis or golf till four-thirty.'

I asked Mr Macqueen if alcohol was freely available in Tehran in those days.

'Very much so, and it wasn't so frightfully expensive because they made their own beer there, and vodka was cheap. They made their own vodka at Pahlevi on the Caspian Sea and the Germans made beer in Tehran. We drank pegs in the club, but I don't think that going to the cabaret we'd venture into whisky because it was too expensive. There were no restrictions on drink in the Tehran clubs or in the cabarets or restaurants.'

Both my father and Mr Macqueen spoke Farsi. But neither in Tehran nor in the provinces was there close social contact between the British and the Iranians because the Shah expressly forbade it. For some Britons, with a real desire to get to know the language and culture of the country, this was a cause of frustration.

Roderick Sarell became interested in Iran through reading books before he arrived in Shiraz as a language graduate in the Consular Service in 1936. He remembers being 'provided with a *munshi*, which is what the clerical Persians were called, an agreeable man who unfortunately knew nothing of grammar. As someone schooled in learning languages in English schools one sought the familiar landmarks of grammar and syntax. One was constantly frustrated with the reply: "Oh, but it sounds pretty."' With the acquisition of a Persian grammar book from England Mr Sarell (as Sir Roderick was in those days) made better progress. But he was frustrated at not being able to practise the language to the full with Iranians. 'I raised this question many years later with the former prime minister who was later murdered, Shahpour Bakhtiar. He explained that the attitude dated back to the intolerable arrogance and excesses of the Russians under the capitulations which made the Shah decide to limit any relationship between Persians and foreigners. He had forbidden Persians to mix with foreigners. This made it almost impossible to have any Persian friends on an easy basis. We did get to know one or two, and of course we had Persian servants with whom we had to converse by necessity. Some of the office staff were Persians, others were Indians. Social intercourse was forbidden. That was very sad.'

Denis Lunn, working for the Imperial Bank of Iran, was also aware of how the British community was forced in on itself because of official restrictions. 'Life in the Persian provinces,' he wrote in *Rags of Time*, 'delightful in so many ways, could also engender deep and sometimes lasting human frictions. These provincial foreign communities were mostly tiny – the British Consulate, occasionally that of another country, the Bank, Oil Company representatives here and there, perhaps a business man in charge of a British trading house and, in all the larger provincial cities, the well-established American Presbyterian Mission or the clerical, medical and educational members of the Church Missionary Society, the C.M.S. Throughout the 1930s relations with cultivated Persian *indigenes* remained limited to the official, fraternisation being strictly forbidden by authority. H.I.M. Reza Shah distrusted any meeting of minds between his subjects and the foreigner. So, at his insistence, xenophobia ruled.'

Despite the attitude which Iranians were required to adopt towards foreigners, Sir Roderick Sarell says he never encountered hostility. 'The Persians were uniformly friendly and hospitable – quite charming. Even in remote country areas. It was rather quaint in Bakhtiari, we travelled up a long valley and camped in a building at the top. An old boy came to see us and said: "Of course it's very sad, the young men are no good nowadays. A few years ago you would never have got up that valley alive."' He meant it. It was a sad reminiscence.' The local tribes had been disarmed by this time, Sir Roderick said, and so there were good supplies of game in the hills for the expatriates who were allowed guns. 'Shiraz is in a valley and there are ranges of hills rising up several thousand feet each side of it. We would get up there at dawn and go in pursuit of the moufflon and the ibex of which there were quite an adequate supply. My shooting expeditions were the most humane imaginable because I never hit anything. But they gave us wonderful exercise.'

Back in the office the work of British diplomats in Iran continued to centre on keeping secure their country's interests in that corner of the world. The British had originally established the pockets of their community in Persia and come to an arrangement with Russia in order to secure a route to India and stop any threat to the oilfields from across the northern border. In the 1930s there was still a considerable taste of India in the country, especially in the cities of Shiraz and Bushire. But the Indian influence was waning. In the Consular Service in Shiraz, Sir Roderick Sarell says, 'I missed having my personal Lancer guard by eight years. The missionaries could remember being escorted the half mile or so from the mission hospital to the Consulate by outriders of the Lancer guard.'

In Bushire Angus Macqueen recalls that there was 'very much the atmosphere of India. In the office we had a small boy who had what was called the punka in the roof. He sat on the floor with the rope attached to his toes and he moved his foot, which moved the punka up there. That brought air over the manager's desk.'

What helped to push attention away from India and even more towards the west was the outbreak of the Second World War in September 1939. The British community in Iran was uncertain what to do. The vast majority stayed where they were, keeping the oil company, the bank and other British institutions going.

In fact, my mother, living in Mashad, where my father had been posted, had a particularly pressing reason to stay: early in September 1939 she was about to give birth to her first baby. 'The American mission were delighted to find that someone was going to have a baby there – a European, that is – they had plenty of Persian babies. I attended the hospital and made my first mistake in Persian. The lady doctor was late, and when she came in she said; "My face is black," and I said: "Oh no, you look very nice." What she meant was "black with shame", a Persian expression.'

When my mother started labour she 'went by horse-drawn carriage the two miles to the hospital. When we got to the narrow shopping street with shops either side of the road the surface was cobblestones; it was enough to bring any baby on. We arrived at two in the morning and the lights went out. I was left on a landing in the dark expecting my first baby. Archie went to find a doctor. I was in a terrible state of nerves. Dr Cochrane came. I was left in a room with no bell, so they brought a huge bowl and ladle and I was to bang on the bowl with the ladle if I wanted anything. I lay there for ever making no progress – I didn't know what was to happen anyway. Occasionally a nurse would look in and I tried to say in my bad Persian: "What's happening? Where's the doctor?" They'd sent Archie home, telling him it would be hours and I felt very much alone. Then from the mosque opposite came the call of dawn from the muezzin – it was beautiful and yet it was eerie. I felt as if I was transported back to centuries before.'

Finally the moment came for my mother to be taken to the labour room. 'They bound me up like a mummy in sheets and then two men came in with a big carpet on poles hanging from their shoulders. They laid the carpet down and the nurses lifted me on to it. Then the men hoisted the poles on to their shoulders – crossed over the poles so I was completely encased in this large carpet – and I was taken to the labour room. No man was allowed to see me. It seemed a long journey in the carpet. It swayed as we went, and I couldn't see a thing. I had no idea where I was going. I was frightened to death and I didn't know anything about having a baby – that was the worst part. At twelve o'clock that day John was born. Mashad then was a long way off the beaten track.'

My mother's second son, Nigel, was born in 1942, in wartime Tehran. She went into labour in the middle of the night when there was a curfew in force. 'Every crossroad had policemen on it and a couple of soldiers with fixed bayonets. We weren't supposed to be out in the curfew. They'd open the car doors and the bayonets would come in either side. The soldiers asked what we were doing. It was obvious, I was trying to have a baby. We got to the nursing home, and the baby was born just after the doctor arrived – he was delayed because he had had to come through the curfew as well. The baby was put on a chair in the middle of the room while the medical staff dealt with my haemorrhage. When they finally got back to the baby he was completely covered with sandfly bites.'

In the three years between the births of her two sons, my mother and other Britons in Iran lived through days of great anxiety as they listened with increasing concern to news reports of the Axis advances both in Europe and North Africa. The British Legation headed by Sir Reader Bullard had plenty to worry about in April 1941 as Freya Stark relates in one of her books. Miss Stark, who was acting as an adviser to the British government on propaganda in the Middle East, stayed at the Legation for a few days. She wrote in *Dust in the Lion's Paw*: 'In the morning I woke to a scent of wallflowers in the Legation garden, where two happy bachelor ducks and a library of good books solaced Sir Reader Bullard's harassed leisure. The shadow of the Greek retreat hung over us, and anxiety for Egypt, and absence of Iraq news [where a pro-German government had come to power].'

When the Soviet Union entered the war in July 1941, with the Germans advancing through their country, the crisis in Iran deepened. Reza Shah, citing his country's neutrality, refused to allow the Allies to ship supplies across Iran to the Russians. This prompted the invasion of the country in August 1941 by British troops from the south and Russian troops from the north. But initially they did not plan to enter Tehran. When the invasion began, there were fears of unrest and opposition among the Iranian population. Plans to shelter British civilians in the Legation premises were put into effect. 'The trouble came in the early hours one morning,' my mother said. 'We'd had a message from Anthony Eden saying: "We hope you'll behave in the correct manner of people under siege, we can't do anything to help you." I suppose it meant "Die like Britons". We were told to get in the cars and get to the Legation as quickly as we could. And we were told we might meet trouble on the way. As it happened, we didn't meet any trouble.'

It had been decided that my mother, with her two-year-old son, John, should be 'dropped at the top gate of the up-country embassy. I was loaded with bags plus a toddler, and it was four o'clock in the morning. Every veranda had an armed watchman who came out to see who we were. The only way I could keep John on his feet was to walk very slowly (I couldn't carry him) and say nursery rhymes – like "Hickory, Dickory, Dock" – and he held on to my dress. It was so lonely except for all the watchmen at each house. There were people on Consul Bailey's veranda where I was staying and they looked astonished to see us arrive like that.'

One day, while sheltering in the Legation compound, 'all the women were asked to sew a huge white cross by joining bits of sheeting cloth together. It was put right across the grass in the centre of the compound and in between the houses for the Allied planes coming in to see where we were.' But, after a week, there had been no need for Allied air attacks on Tehran – the British army had been able to enter the country without opposition, and the families were allowed to return home.

But Reza Shah was still asserting the neutrality of Iran, and refusing to round up or deport Germans who were stirring up anti-British feelings among the Iranians. With tension rising in Tehran, one of the British war reporters to arrive in the capital was Richard Dimbleby. In his book *The Frontiers are Green* he described how he made his way around urgently trying to glean information. 'Tehran,' he wrote, 'is full of these one-horse vehicles that we called "droshkys". They take the place of taxis found in other capitals. If you are not in a hurry there are worse ways to travel than in one of these loosely sprung carriages, rumbling along the paved and cobbled roads behind their mangy horses. But I was in a great hurry to reach the British Legation and the conveyance seemed desperately slow. Each time I told the driver to hurry, he flicked his ancient mare with the whip, and we sprinted for perhaps five yards before relapsing into the original jog-trot. In due course we turned in through the Legation archway and stopped in the gravel drive outside the main building. The headquarters of the British Mission to Iran stand in pleasant grounds bounded by a high wall, inside which the staff had worked and British residents of Tehran had sheltered while we were fighting the Persian army. Now the Legation was back to normal, at least outwardly. There were great banks of flowers outside and plenty of inviting shade in the stone passages and verandas of the building.'

Within Tehran, meanwhile, opposition to the vacillating attitude of the Shah was growing. One morning in September 1941 my mother was trying to get the news from London on the radio when she heard the voice of Richard Dimbleby, trying to link up by short wave with the BBC in London. 'He was calling out saying he had important news, he was yelling, but couldn't get an answer. It was close-down time. "I've important news," he said, "that I want you at the Home Service to receive." It was the news that the Shah had abdicated. Traffic began pelting through the streets, people were running in all directions to get home. All the shops shut down.'

Eventually Richard Dimbleby got his broadcast through to London; but in his account of the day in his memoirs he omits mention of those frustrating moments at the Tehran radio station trying to reach London. 'At lunchtime,' he wrote, 'while I was reporting to London by short wave . . .' – and continued his narrative.

The abdication of the Shah heralded the arrival of British and Russian troops in the capital and the rounding up of Germans. Richard Dimbleby saw a 'long line of Persian army lorries being loaded with the baggage of the German women and children who were leaving by road for Turkey'.

Angus Macqueen remembers that the secretary of the Tehran Club was a German. 'It was known that he was the number one agent. But he was a very pleasant person – played tennis and bridge. He was taken prisoner by us, he and other Germans. But he had a rather pleasant life. He wasn't put in prison in Persia or sent anywhere in the Middle East; he was sent to Australia. And when the war was over he returned to Tehran and took up the duties he had before, representing a big German firm. We all met up again.'

With news of the horrors of the war in Europe reaching Iran, one might think that Britons there would have felt an obligation to get back and help their compatriots. Denis Lunn has written of the debate that took place within his own mind during the early years of wartime. He even went to the British Legation in Tehran to discuss with Sir Reader Bullard the possibility of returning to Europe 'to shoot Germans'. But Sir Reader made it clear that it was the duty and responsibility of Britons to remain at their posts to maintain British interests and to counter the German threat to Iran and its oilfields. In November 1941 an Order in Council was promulgated and signed by the Foreign Secretary, Anthony Eden, under which British males were restrained formally and legally from leaving their posts in Iran, 'thus,' in Mr Lunn's words, 'giving teeth to the earlier unofficial instruction'. The Order stated that 'the Anglo-Iranian Oil Company and the Imperial Bank of Iran are undertakings the carrying on of which is essential for the prosecution of the war'.

As well as keeping British institutions going, some Britons in Iran during the war also played an active part in countering German attempts at winning over the Iranians to the Axis cause. In their branches around Iran, staff in the Imperial Bank were in a good position for intelligence gathering. 'In my own case in Shiraz in 1943,' Angus Macqueen said, 'the Germans had dropped one or two of their friends into the Kashkai tribe which had its main numbers in the surrounding area. While I was in Shiraz, notes – currency notes, treasury notes – were brought in by some of the Kashkais to the office. There were only two of us there. I took the notes down to the Consul where there were government intelligence people apart from the ordinary diplomats. The notes were sent back home and within thirty-six hours the Consul was informed that these notes were all fraudulent and had been printed by the Germans, presumably in Germany, for circulation around the Middle East. So in that case we did serve a useful purpose. We were definitely playing a role in the war.'

When the war ended, life for Britons in Iran – in the oil industry and elsewhere – returned to normal. At Abadan, superficially nothing much had changed. George McGeachie arrived there in late 1945. 'It was a very comfortable life. In many ways you were isolated from the traumas of the outside world. The Company took care of you. The

Company did everything. There was a club, a restaurant, two lovely swimming pools, a sailing club, a golf club, and in many ways it was a little dream world.'

At the centre of social life in Abadan was the Gymkhana Club. Mr McGeachie remembers that 'it had all the facilities: reading rooms, a billiard room, the central Restaurant – with a capital "R" – was located there. And whereas one could go into the other restaurants in Abadan with a pair of shorts and an open-necked shirt, in the Gymkhana Club you dressed properly: white trousers, white shirt and of course in summer one always wore a topi. This was *de rigueur*. There were touches of empire still left there in the late forties. It was a superb club, and the atmosphere was tremendous.'

In those days, too, the British oil company community still tended to live apart from the indigenous community. Even in later years, Mr McGeachie says, 'you had quite a number of expatriates who came out for three or four years, on short-term assignments, with little or no intention of making a career out there, and so their horizons were to an extent limited. But after 1945 the gates opened up and more and more Iranians who'd been educated overseas – in Europe and America – joined the company. You had greater mixing of the communities. For example in Iran, when I went back after my leave in 1948, most of my friends were Iranians, and I kept in touch even after the evacuation in 1951.'

The roots of the nationalization crisis which led to the evacuation of foreign employees of the Anglo-Iranian Oil Company lay in grievances that had been building up for several years. The Iranians felt that the British company was unfairly exploiting their country's natural resources by failing to channel a sufficient amount of oil revenue into the national coffers. But there was another side to the grievance. Iranians felt that they deserved greater representation within the management of the company.

The management, as we have seen, had had reservations in the 1930s about bringing Iranian graduates into the company for fear that they would introduce nationalist sentiments. But some young men who had studied abroad were recruited then. 'Sabsi' Green showed me a presentation plate engraved with the names of the members of the cricket club in Abadan from that time, and I was surprised to notice two Iranians among them – the Iranians, like the Arabs, having generally shown no inclination whatsoever to adopt Britain's national summer sport in the way that they took to football.

Mr Green explained that the two men were products of an education in England.

A major disincentive to employ Iranians lay in the country's strong links with India in the early part of the century and the access to the large pool of Indian unskilled and semi-skilled labour. For example, the Anglo-Persian Oil Company began training Iranians as secretaries in 1914. But with scores of qualified Indian secretaries and clerks available, the temptation to employ the latter was great. In 1933, when the Company's concession was renegotiated, a promise was made that more Iranians would be recruited and trained. Mr Green recalls, though, that there was a reluctance to get rid of Indian staff – cooks as much as office workers – and start teaching Persians to do the same jobs. A Company document in 1935 conceded that the introduction of a large Iranian workforce would be a slow process, and spoke of 'a vast gap between the most finished product of our training establishments and a man really competent to take over from our British and Indian workmen'.

Regardless of the Company's reservations, though, the Iranians themselves were not satisfied and their grievance grew. Mr Green acknowledges that the Iranians 'thought they could take responsibility sooner than we thought they could'. At the same time, though, he 'never thought the Company would be forced to leave Persia'.

But many months of complex negotiations on royalties and other terms of the concession failed to produce agreement between the Company and the Iranian government. In 1951, with the Mossadeq government in power, the threat that the oil industry would be nationalized was carried out. Despite protests from Britain and attempts at international mediation, the crisis could not be resolved. George McGeachie says that nationalization 'meant a very rapid rundown. We had close on three thousand expatriate staff in Abadan and the five or six Fields areas where crude oil was produced and then pumped down to Abadan. The three thousand was very rapidly run down to just under three hundred – the hard core – and for about three months it was just them in Abadan. The Fields areas were completely closed down. No crude oil was produced. The refinery gradually ran down and stopped operating. And there we were, the last little group of expatriates. It was a difficult situation. Life wasn't easy. There was a curfew, and we were very closely watched.'

Negotiations to secure the safe withdrawal of the last group of expatriates continued. 'Suddenly, we got notice that we were leaving on the *Mauritius*, a Royal Naval battle cruiser which had been anchored off Abadan for several weeks with three or four destroyers. We were finally evacuated, I think it was on 4 October, round about midday. We were all marshalled down at the Gymkhana Club and then went out by launch to the *Mauritius*.

'When we were on board the naval band started to play and we sailed off to Basra. And that was the end of that particular chapter of Abadan.'

6

IRAQ: FRIENDS AND FOES

The setting was the British Embassy in Baghdad in 1941. Sir Kinahan and Lady Cornwallis were awaiting the arrival for lunch of a prominent Arab visitor to the country. The Ambassador and his wife did not know that the Arab guest they were expecting had been assassinated as he stepped out of his hotel en route to the embassy. After half an hour of waiting, the Oriental Secretary and Counsellor at the embassy, Vyvyan Holt, was informed of the murder. He told the Ambassador and his wife that the guest was not coming. 'It appears that after twenty years' experience of Iraq politics, when Holt heard the news over the telephone, he merely said: "I suppose we needn't wait lunch any longer."' Diplomats in Iraq were too well accustomed to the volatility and brutality of Iraqi politics; there was no sense of shock or consternation.

This brief anecdote, related by Freya Stark in *Dust in the Lion's Paw*, reveals something of the character of Iraq and its relationship with Britain. Politics in Iraq from the First World War through to the brutal overthrow of the monarchy in 1958 and beyond has been bedevilled by violence. And for much of the century – certainly up to 1958 – the British Ambassadors in Baghdad tried to influence and control events in the oil-rich country to Britain's advantage. It was not an easy job. The Iraqi people, a mix of Shiite and Sunni Muslims, Kurds, and Nestorian Christians, never took kindly to the attempts of outside powers to dominate them. At the same time they were quicker than most other Arabs to educate themselves and to develop modern technology, making Iraq one of the most powerful nations in the Middle East in the second half of the century.

While Iraq became independent in name in 1932, Britain remained the power behind the monarchy which it had installed at the end of the First World War. King Feisal I and his successor, King Ghazi,

81

tried hard (the former much harder and more successfully than the latter, who was a fun-loving playboy) to keep the country together amid the competing claims on power from leading clans, from Shiite religious leaders and from army officers. When King Ghazi was killed in a sports-car crash in 1939, power passed to a regent because the successor, Feisal, was a child. Clustered around the monarchy was a group of what might be called Iraqi aristocrats who supported the West. And the thrust of British policy in Iraq up to 1958 was to bolster their position in the country. It was never an easy policy to pursue against the background of entrenched nationalist and anti-colonial feelings among the people. The monarchy, a British creation, was never a popular institution, and special care had to be taken to protect members of the royal family. ('Miss Borland [the British nurse of young King Feisal II] cooks and tastes all the King's food,' Freya Stark noted in 1941.) In the end, British support was not enough to save the monarchy or protect the pro-Western clique around it.

In the post-independence years in the 1930s, despite the power struggles and frequent changes of government, high-society life in Baghdad was continuing. It was a case there, as much as it was in Britain, of who you knew often being more important than who you were. Sir Roderick Sarell remembers arriving in Baghdad in the thirties en route to Iran. 'I was lucky enough to have had as a neighbour in Sussex a great man, Dr Sinderson Pasha, known to the world as Sindbad, who had been physician to King Feisal in Baghdad, and he and his dear wife had me to stay. He was at the customs to meet me at seven in the morning. And I discovered later he'd been called out to a patient at four in the morning. My first impression of Baghdad was the realization that I had crossed the frontier into the zone of Indian influence, the land of tiffin for lunch, of curries and so on. Iraq had been occupied by the Anglo-Indian army in 1918 and was under the influence of the government of India. In the Sinderson household I was known as the Chota Sahib. Although I was not tall, the word *chota*, or small, merely meant that I was not the master of the house. The master of the house was the Burra Sahib, and that was Sindbad. Correctly, because he was a large man. The head of any firm was the Burra Sahib. Through the hospitality of the Sindersons I got a fascinating insight into life in Baghdad. I was delayed there for four days because the passes into Persia were closed by snow, and I was taken in the wake of the Sindersons to the Baghdad club, the Alwiya, where the British disported themselves. The Sindersons knew everyone of consequence, and they took me to dinner and a reception at the Regent of Iraq, where I played a very agreeable game of rummy with the princess, who was Egyptian. I described in my letter home that I had made my first acquaintance at bowing and scraping and saying "Mais oui, Excellence".'

The British presence in Baghdad at this time was buttressed by the Royal Air Force, who had a base at Hinaidi, a few miles from the city. The branch in Baghdad of the British-run Imperial Bank of Persia provided banking services to the RAF. As a junior on the staff Angus Macqueen had the job once or twice a week of seeing to the airmen's financial needs. It was not, he says, an arduous job. 'There was very little work attached. The RAF started work at about six in the morning because of the heat in Baghdad and finished about eleven. My job was to pay them out their ten pounds or twenty pounds they wanted to draw for spending in the clubs and nightclubs of Baghdad; and also to receive the mess accounts and the receipts from their own messes. But I had two assistants with me, Iraqis, and I didn't arrive until about half past ten in the morning, when they were just completing their duties for the day. So I'm afraid the British bank officer joined the officers in their mess at eleven o'clock, and we spent a very pleasant two hours there while the two clerks looked after the accounts. It gave one an opportunity of meeting the RAF people, and they also appreciated my being with them because they had very little opportunity of meeting people outside. We played bridge regularly with them and went back to the messes. And we introduced them to other people in Baghdad – to some of the female residents. This carried on until after the war years when the Iraqis took over Hinaidi and the RAF moved to Habbaniya.'

The British community in Iraq in those day, Mr Macqueen says, was 'frightfully big because we were still running quite a number of the government departments. That stopped during the war.' The British, he recalls too, led a hectic social life centred on the club in Baghdad. 'I fell ill – it was called heat exhaustion. The heat was terrific. One did play tennis, no doubt when the temperature was such that one would have been better staying indoors. I think, though, it was burning the candle at both ends that brought about the illness to some extent. But the heart was affected and they decided that another summer might not be frightfully good for my health, so I was transferred to Tehran.'

With the outbreak of the Second World War the atmosphere changed radically in Baghdad. Rumours had spread through Iraq that King Ghazi, who died in a car crash, had in fact been murdered by the British because of his nationalist views. The rumours encouraged the mood of popular revolt against British interference in Iraq. In March 1941 a group of Iraqi nationalists – civilians and military – who were hostile to Britain seized power. The leader of the nationalists, Rashid Ali al-Gailani, became prime minister. The group had enjoyed German support while they were plotting their putsch, and when they came to power it was immediately clear that their sympathy was indeed for the Axis rather than the Allied powers. With Germany looking increasingly likely at that stage to win the war the nationalists saw a chance of co-operating with the Axis side to remove British influence from Iraq.

After the change of government the Regent and leading pro-British politicians fled to the country. Freya Stark, who was attached to the British Embassy as an adviser during this time, said the Regent got away by 'lying under cushions in the U.S.A. Minister's car with the Minister sitting in it. No one looked, though the bridges were guarded. Rashid Ali's men searched the palace from floor to ceiling and would no doubt have murdered him.'

Miss Stark then described in detail the weeks that followed, as the British came under increasing pressure. She was greatly impressed by the coolness of the British Ambassador, Sir Kinahan Cornwallis. 'I used to enjoy the way his pale blue eyes became small, with the pupils like pin-points, when he considered an idea or a person, listening with an air of leisure long ago acquired. He once told me he did all his paper work when the day was over and kept his office hours for visitors and coffee; but never missed a Friday's shooting in the years of his service.'

As the crisis in Baghdad developed Freya Stark felt more and more that Britain had not done enough to promote its cause among the Iraqi people, depending too heavily on the influence of a small minority. 'I had expected no Iraqis at my tea party,' a diary entry of April 1941 reads, 'but twenty-nine turned up, all very friendly. How right it was not to cancel! It would be a great mistake not to encourage those who are prepared to show themselves on our side.'

In a similar vein a few days later Miss Stark put in writing her belief that 'our Military Mission should see to it that *every young*

Iraqi officer has some sort of social relation with the English here,' adding that the current crisis could have been avoided if the policy had been adopted earlier.

The crisis deepened with RAF Habbaniya becoming encircled and attacked by the Iraqi army, and the British Embassy in Baghdad under siege, cut off from the outside world. 'The Chancery is a bonfire,' Miss Stark wrote in May 1941, 'mountains of archives being burnt in the court, prodded by staff with rakes; black cinders like crows winged with little flames fly into the sunlight . . . Petrol tins of sand everywhere for bombs; cars parked on lawn; men sprawling asleep round the blue-tiled fountain in the hall to be cool; nurses. Lucknow feeling, very disagreeable. Pathetic looks of dog-like trust of Indians; gloomy looks of Iraqis; imperturbable, hot, but not uncheerful looks of British.'

A picture of life in Habbaniya during the siege was given to Richard Dimbleby by a British military airman who had flown from the base to a desert strip. In *The Frontiers are Green* Mr Dimbleby said the airman spoke of 'the extraordinary coolness and courage of the civilians', while the air operations were 'a hell of a party'. The airman said that 'everyone with the slightest qualification was asking to fly the odd assortment of machines at Habbaniya on their raids against the Iraqis. They had even cleaned up two ancient cannon kept at the station and were counter-shelling the Iraqi batteries overlooking the aerodrome.'

Food during the siege was strictly rationed, but otherwise the British at the base seemed remarkably calm. 'On the whole, it's not too bad,' the airman said in a typically understated British way. 'They've got the cinema going and there are concerts. The women have formed nursing parties and there are fire squads and pickets. But the best thing is to see one of the kites coming in after a raid. The Iraqis follow her all the way and open up on the landing ground the moment she touches down. The pilot whistles across the field and straight into the hangar at a hell of a speed. Then they slam the doors behind him. It's all against the rules, but it works.'

By standing firm at Habbaniya, the British eventually won the day. Axis military support for the Rashid Ali government never arrived, and the sieges of the RAF base and the embassy were ended after a small Anglo-Indian force backed by air power, and joined by troops from the Arab Legion in Transjordan commanded by Glubb Pasha, arrived in Iraq. The Rashid Ali revolt collapsed. The Regent returned, as did Nuri Said, the man with pro-Western sympathies who was to dominate Iraqi politics up to the overthrow of the monarchy. (Alaric Jacob, a correspondent during the Second World War, described in his book *A Traveller's War* a meeting with Nuri Said in Baghdad. The Iraqi prime minister applauded the victories of the Red Army, 'pacing up and down the carpet (Axminster, *not* Persian) in his office which resembled that of a country lawyer in Exeter or Salisbury, except that the sun beat down on mud walls outside'.)

Mr Jacob also witnessed Britain's propaganda efforts in Iraq, which were directed both by Freya Stark and Stewart Perowne. 'Our propaganda which had failed so dismally in other parts of the world,' he wrote, 'was here highly efficient: the Germans could not compete with the British Orientalists who, in this war as in the last, were serving us well from Cairo to Aden and from Beirut to Tehran. The enemy had got off to a flying start. The very intelligent German Legation staff in Baghdad before the war had fomented Rashid Ali's revolt. At first the Axis radio far surpassed our own. Its Arabic crooners and raconteurs of smutty stories had a *succès de scandale* against which the staid, homely programmes of the BBC battled in vain. But the Axis over-reached itself.' To get Britain's message over in outlying regions of Iraq Mr Perowne 'sent cinema vans. From Baghdad, Mosul and Kirkuk, the vans went on tour preceded by posters announcing "The People's Cinema is Coming Tomorrow". At dusk the silver screen was unfurled in the market place and news pictures with an Arabic commentator shown to audiences of five or eight thousand at a time. In the early days the villagers were often mystified to view some obscure member of our Royal Family declaring this or that open, or well and truly laid, but the quality of the films improved until, just before I reached Baghdad, one of them enjoyed a quite embarrassing success. When some Nazi prisoners were shown on the screen, a village headman rushed up and stabbed them with his dagger. It took a little while to repair the screen.'

While all the crises were occurring during the war, Britons employed by the Iraq Petroleum Company (IPC) stuck at their posts. Some of the employees were attached to pumping stations along the 550-mile pipeline that ran from northern Iraq, across the desert to Haifa on the coast of the Mediterranean. Richard Dimbleby was impressed by the way the stations offered touches of rural tranquillity in a bleak and inhospitable setting. 'The company has done its best, with remarkable success,' he wrote, 'to surround each pumping station with an oasis for the enjoyment of its engineers. H.4, H.3, H.2 and H.1, as the pumping stations on the Haifa line are known, are fresh green gardens in the yellow wilderness. Each station has an outer wall and stockade to protect it against marauding bandits. Inside the wall there are trees, flowering shrubs and lawns. The station buildings are of brick and stone, cool and shady. Inside there are comfortable living quarters with fans and refrigerators, and the tinkling of ice is a lovely sound to the traveller from Baghdad who arrives at H.3 on a hot evening.'

Iraq had barely recovered from the upheaval of the Second World War before it was rocked by a major development in the Middle East: the establishment of the state of Israel in 1948. This caused as great a traumatic shock in Iraq as in any Arab state. One effect was the directing of popular anger against the Iraqi Jews, leading to the evacuation of the entire community. Norman Jenkins, who worked for the Rafidain Oil Company, a subsidiary of British Petroleum (BP), remembers in 1952 going with his wife to say farewell to Iraqi Jewish friends. 'One of the scenes that we recall vividly to this day is seeing them off at Baghdad airport where the women were stripped of their jewellery and the men had all their right shoes taken off, so that they went to Israel with one shoe – and that was utter humiliation. One morning the same year I took my children to the convent in Baghdad where they were being educated. And outside were two Jews hanging on scaffolds. They'd been hanged in the morning and were cut down in the evening. I can remember the horror on the children's faces, seeing these two Jewish agents – they were Mossad [Israeli intelligence] agents, obviously, who'd been caught by the Iraqis. Those were the first signs of unrest in Iraq. After the exodus of the Jewish population it more or less settled down.'

Because of Britain's role in the creation of Israel Mr Jenkins recalls that these were tense days for the British community. 'Life wasn't very pleasant. We had to be very circumspect, obviously. But I had an affinity for the Arabs. You know the average man in the street, the average Bedouin, if you like, is a great family man, he's a decent, home-loving person, he loves children, he's very hospitable. He looks after his old people in a way that many of us don't in the West. But Arabs have a streak of cruelty, and as recent events in Kuwait testify [a reference to the 1990 Iraqi invasion of Kuwait], they can be a very terrifying people. There is a lot of truth in the old biblical saying of an eye for an eye and a tooth for a tooth. But there was no hostility directed at us. We all worked together, we got on extremely well. Any hostility was merely centred on the capital. Outside Baghdad, wherever I travelled in Kurdistan or down among the Marsh Arabs in Basra or wherever it was, I found nothing but hospitality and a genuine feeling for the British.'

The 1950s was the era when Arabs, encouraged by President Nasser of Egypt, dreamed of a day when the region would be united under the banner of secular nationalism. It was an era of strong anti-Western sentiments, fanned by stirring broadcasts from the Voice of the Arabs radio station in Cairo. But ignoring pressure from Nasser and from the man in the street, the Iraqi government joined the pro-Western Baghdad Pact.

Nominally, then, Iraq was firmly in the Western camp. And despite the signs of stirring among nationalist politicians and among the population at large, relations between Iraqi and British officials remained good. And for British diplomats like Anthony and Sheila Parsons, life was remarkably easy – and often great fun. Sir Anthony recalls that they 'could travel anywhere with the excuse of flogging a lot of worn-out ex-war material to the Iraqi army. We were able to visit every unit, all over Kurdistan; and we went down to Basra. It was the time we decided to visit the Iraqi navy, which nobody had ever done before. It comprised two gunboats at Amara and we decided to drive – just the two of us.'

The Parsons set off in their un-air-conditioned Humber Hawk on a nine-hour journey through the desert. 'I suddenly noticed that my rather talkative wife had fallen silent. I looked at her and saw that she'd passed out. So I drove the car as near as I could to the Tigris. In those days you used to get cigarettes in tins, so I filled the tins with water and doused her and it had a magical effect. When we reached the navy base we got the most superb welcome, a kind of guard of honour was drawn up. We were absolutely filthy, we were just two great pillars of dust, and we were taken on board the gunboat and shown to our cabin, which was exquisitely clean and white-painted. And there to our infinite relief was a refrigerator. We thought: Iced water, it'll just save our lives. We had an hour to change before an official lunch, and I flung open the fridge and inside there was nothing but one roll of lavatory paper.'

The same evening the Iraqi navy took the Parsons on a river trip.

'It was very romantic in the marshes with the noises of birds. The radio was on and there was Arabic music playing. My wife said to the commander of the gunboat: "What is the singer saying?" He said: "The singer he is saying – 'I am on fire.'" And we suddenly realized he wasn't alone in this because there was the most appalling smell of burning. What had happened was that the inlet on the boat had sucked in a mass of Tigris mud and blocked the whole cooling system and the gunboat was actually catching fire. We had a much longer dinner than we'd expected.'

The days of fun and frivolity ended on 14 July 1958 when two colonels in the Iraqi army led a successful coup. In the process they eliminated the Hashemite monarchy that had been installed by Britain at the end of the First World War. King Feisal II and his entourage were murdered in the royal palace. The hunt then began for Nuri Said, the powerful prime minister who had espoused Britain's cause for so long. Nuri Said was a friend of Freya Stark for thirty-nine years. She called him the 'Grand Old Man of Iraq' and the 'only great man of the Middle East in all those years'. In her autobiography she described how the coup leaders in 1958 hunted him down. 'Nuri tried his telephone on this black morning, and found it cut; immediately suspicious, he made his way to a friend's house on the river bank below and found that telephone cut. They put two and two together and went upstream to Mu'addham to friends who for some reason were unable to shelter the Pasha for long.' He then donned a woman's black coat as a disguise. But with the radio blaring out orders to search out Nuri Said, he could find no place to hide and was eventually spotted and shot dead. But that was not the end of the story. His body was buried in a cemetery quietly after dusk while a curfew was in force, only to be dug up by a mob the next day. His body, and those of others associated with the British-supported Hashemite regime, were then dismembered and dragged by shrieking crowds through the streets of the city, in Miss Stark's words, 'with all the savagery for which Iraq in her long history has ever been notorious'.

Norman Jenkins was a witness of these events. He remembers going to his office in Baghdad as usual the day after the coup. 'There was very little news, and life seemed to be going on as normal. At about midday there were large crowds gathering outside the office. We were ushered up on to a flat roof which overlooked the main street of Baghdad. And there, to my horror, I saw that a man was being dragged through the streets of Baghdad tied to the back of a motorbike. We saw the remains of a bloody body with its hands tied. There was a youth riding the motorbike, shouting slogans. This turned out to be Nuri Said. That really was dreadful. Pretty horrific.'

For all the horrors, Mr Jenkins speaks warmly of his time in Iraq and of his relationship with the Iraqis whom he met. 'I still cherish in my little cabinet at home a medal which was given to me by the Iraq army. I taught them how to play water polo, and on many occasions I refereed them. And it was with great pride and pleasure that the King presented me with the medal.'

The bloody events of July 1958 decisively removed British and Western influence over the running of Iraq; but they did not herald political stability. The monarchy, for all its unacceptable associations with the colonial era, had been a focus for national unity. The new regime of Abdul Karim Kassem, like others in subsequent years, faced the task of balancing the interests and demands of the various clans and ethnic groups. The authorities savagely suppressed dissent against the regime. It was the beginning of a long era in Iraq of fear of the secret police. Foreigners were considered to be potential agents or agitators sent by outside powers, so Iraqis became afraid of being seen talking to them. Harry Odell, an employee of the Iraq Petroleum Company in Kirkuk during this period, recalled that 'when Abdul Karim Kassem overthrew the Nuri Said government, all contact with locals, except at work, stopped. Iraqis ceased appearing at the club or the pool. It was a pity. It was all very sudden, and the Iraqis became very nervous, looking over their shoulders a bit. To begin with, practically all of them continued coming to work. As time went on, some people disappeared off to prison for reasons we didn't know. I had some Iraqis in my department who started getting worried because they may have said some unwise things in the past or have been very pro-British. "Suppose we suddenly disappear," they said, "would you do your best to see that my wife and family are OK?" Of course no one knew what we could do. When one or two did disappear we contacted the families. But they were even more reluctant to get involved with Britishers – they wanted us to stay away for their own safety. At this time, too, army patrols appeared all over the place. Your car was stopped and searched – for guns perhaps, although I don't think they knew what they were looking for. The army just wanted to make a point.'

But even in the aftermath of the bloody coup and with anti-Western feeling running high, the British carried on working there – and even took new jobs. Jean Lewis, keen to see the country where her father had fought in the First World War, was not put off, and accepted a posting with IPC. Miss Lewis joined the band of independent-spirited single women, many of whom I encountered in the 'fifties and 'sixties, who went to the Middle East to do something different, and with more of a sense of adventure than could be found at home.

Miss Lewis, full of enthusiasm, arrived in Iraq 'together with my sewing machine' eager to start the new chapter in her life. But post-coup Iraq took some adjusting to. She learnt quickly, for example, of the dangers that Iraqis faced when they came under the suspicion of the authorities. Soon after her arrival in Baghdad she 'signed up for Arabic lessons. I was five lessons behind in the course, so needed to be taught by an assistant to bring me up to the standard. I had agreed to meet him at a Baghdad hotel at 3.45. When I arrived there was no one there, and the assistant didn't turn up. I heard later that he'd been picked up by Security and questioned. And when he'd said what he was doing, he was jailed for consorting with foreigners. The saddest aspect of my time in Baghdad was that mixing and socializing with Iraqis were not easy. They were afraid to come to your house – it didn't matter that you liked them very much.'

Miss Lewis's British boss in IPC was 'followed everywhere by two Iraqis in a yellow Volkswagen. He got so fed up with them that he went to them and gave them his programme for the day. He even offered them coffee.' At times of unrest in the capital freedom of movement was restricted further by curfews and by the presence of armed militiamen on the streets. 'They were gangs of thugs – fourteen- or fifteen-year-olds – they all had guns, and they were at every intersection. To get to work we had to cross the river and go through five intersections. At every one you had to get out of the car and show your passes, and so on. One day one of the secretaries realized that she didn't have a pass. So she cut a picture out of a magazine and stuck it on a piece of card. She got away with it. They didn't read English.'

Despite the restrictions, Miss Lewis remembers that she was generally able to move around relatively easily. 'One received intelligence as to whether there were any demonstrations. There was a place where we used to go with the dogs near the River Tigris. There was a marvellous place there to walk the dogs.' To get about town Miss Lewis drove an open Armstrong Siddeley which had belonged to the British Consul before the revolution. 'I fell in love with it. It was like a tank. In fact I was once in confrontation with a tank, and it came off worse. A servant one day said: "Memsahib, car too heavy for you. You get little car."'

While Iraq settled into its new post-revolution phase, the IPC staff carried on working much as before. And when the working day had ended expatriates continued to have a life of fun. 'Social life was impossible – it was just endless. The Alwiya club had a pool, a bar, a dining room and a cinema on the lawn. We relied entirely on human companionship. If you liked classical music you'd invite friends to bring their records, and afterwards you'd have spaghetti Bolognese. There was also amateur dramatics – we put on *Present Laughter*, and I helped with the props.'

Accommodation for the three British secretaries in the oil company was provided in a house with zinnias growing in the garden named the 'Hennery'. According to Miss Lewis, it was more popularly called the 'Sex Mess', although the title was misleading. 'We had a watchman who was there constantly. He spied on you. We had one watchman who was so dreadful, lurking around the bushes. You couldn't get up to hanky-panky in those days, it just wasn't on.'

The house was served by an Assyrian maid. 'Every Christmas she used to buy a live turkey. She asked for brandy to put in its food to make its flesh nice and soft. It turned out, though, that the brandy was not going into the turkey but into her.'

Miss Lewis remembers parties being held on the lawn of the 'Hennery' – the only problem coming from the swarms of mosquitoes that bred in the nearby irrigation ditches. From time to time the authorities would try to get rid of the mosquitoes. 'They used to come up and down with a "bug-cart", which was a drum of kerosene on wheels, spraying the ditches. If we were having a drinks party in the garden there'd be a scream: "My God, the bug-cart!", and everyone's drink would be full of kerosene.'

Miss Lewis's position with IPC was as a secretary. But she gradually found herself involved in the field of 'Iraqiization' – putting Iraqis into posts that foreigners had occupied. When the post-revolution authorities scrutinized her papers they noticed that she was not doing the job stated on her permit. So in 1960 she was forced to leave Iraq.

Scores of Britons living in Iraq in the two decades after the revolution were expelled – for a variety of reasons. Towards the end of 1971, a matter of only twenty-four hours before British troops were to withdraw from the lower Gulf states, the Shah of Iran decided to occupy three tiny islands which had been the subject of disputed ownership. The move angered the Arabs in the Gulf and elsewhere. Glencairn Balfour-Paul was the British Ambassador in Baghdad at the time. 'It was the night after Burns Night, and I'd had to give a speech in the Doric and didn't get to bed until late. I woke up, and by force of habit put my hand out and turned on the radio to hear the seven o'clock news from England. And the first item on the news was that the British Ambassador had been expelled from Baghdad. Well, this was total news to me. So I naturally got up hurriedly, went to the office and started ringing up the Ministry of Foreign Affairs to discover what the hell was going on. They wouldn't answer. I couldn't get anyone to speak to me – for two, or two and a half hours.'

In despair, Mr Balfour-Paul drove round to the Ministry. 'I pushed my way into the Protocol Office and said to the two young men sitting at their desks that I wanted to find out what this news was all about. They didn't do anything about it themselves, but they sat amicably beside me on a big sofa opposite the door of the Protocol Office. And we talked for half an hour or more. Just above the door on the wall there was a clock that had stopped, as everybody knew, in 1958 when the revolution took place and the pro-British monarchy was thrown out. It had stopped at nineteen minutes past eleven. Anyhow, we sat there for this long period. Then suddenly, quite surrealistically, the clock started to move forward. And the two Protocol people on either side of me, and I myself, were spellbound by this astonishing, inexplicable fact.'

After the clock had moved on about one minute, the door beneath it opened and Mr Balfour-Paul was told that the head of the Political Department would see the British Ambassador. 'After the usual coffee and amicable conversation the Head of Politics started the next conversation by saying: "First thing I want to say to you is how grateful I am to you for sending me a few weeks ago a copy of the book by your Counsellor Donald Hawley on the Trucial States. Because without having a quick look at it I simply couldn't have written your expulsion order, which I now hand you." This, of course, was to do with the Shah taking over the islands – which were still just our responsibility by twenty-four hours – and the

Iraqis had taken such offence that they were severing relations with the British over it. But without Donald Hawley's book the poor man would not have been able – owing to his ignorance of the geography of the Gulf – to have written my expulsion order. So, that was how I left Iraq. What I liked most about my interview with the Head of the Politics Department on that day was that as soon as he'd told me this and handed me my expulsion order he burst into laughter and clapped me on the back. And we had a tremendous guffaw about the ludicrousness of the situation.'

A year after Mr Balfour-Paul was expelled from Iraq, relations between the Baghdad government and IPC reached crisis point. The Iraqis, like the Iranians two decades earlier, felt that foreign companies were not paying enough to the host country for oil exploitation. Matters came to a head in 1972 when IPC was nationalized and foreigners had to leave. Jennifer Holly, who was married to an Australian employee, was in Kirkuk at the time. She remembers the news of their expulsion reaching them without warning. 'Two soldiers and a security man knocked on the door, came in and ordered us out of the house into a waiting car. I was too angry to be alarmed. I'd spent the whole of the previous day making a chicken mousse, and now it was going to be wasted.'

Did she speak to the security men?

'No, it was better for my husband to talk.'

About twenty Britons were locked in the hotel. They could hear the sound of shooting, but no one was hurt. The atmosphere in the hotel was 'a little bit tense. None of us was too pleased about what was happening. But we had to accept the inevitable.'

The 'inevitable' fate befell IPC workers in countries other than Iraq. In Palestine in 1948, just before the creation of the state of Israel, the company transferred its staff from the oil refinery in Haifa to the facility in Tripoli in northern Lebanon. One of the British employees there was Harry Odell. As a young man, like others, he settled down into a routine of expatriate life centred on the oil company, coming into contact with few Arabs. Until, that is, he fell in love with Abla, a Palestinian from Haifa whom he had seen first from a bus. Abla's family had moved to Lebanon when the Iraq Petroleum Company shifted its refinery operations. Her brothers were IPC employees. Harry and Abla – to the surprise of their respective communities – decided to get married.

The surprise among family and friends in Lebanon was nothing compared with what was to come when Mr Odell broke the news to his relations in Britain. 'They were astonished. They asked whether she owned camels and would be praying five times a day the way Muslims are supposed to. They didn't know anything about the Middle East. People at that time didn't know anything about people outside Britain. But when they saw her they were agreeably surprised.'

Having an Arab wife at that time, Mr Odell says, 'was not totally unique, but exceptional. Generally people in the IPC community in Lebanon were happy and pleased – they knew Abla's brothers. Many senior people came to our wedding.'

Travelling round the Middle East as an Arab married to a Briton working for a British company was a strange experience for Mrs Odell. 'It was quite unfortunate,' she says, 'that we lived in a British community and didn't mix. That's one of the things I'm sorry about. We mixed with the English and not the people of the country we lived in. Whilst the English were there they didn't know how the local people lived – at the same time it was a very good life, with everything laid on for them.'

At times, Mr Odell found that having an Arab wife was a positive advantage. In 1972, just before the nationalization of IPC in Iraq, its subsidiary operation in Syria was taken over by the Damascus government. Mr Odell was chief engineer supervising the IPC pipeline and pumping stations that ran across the country to the Mediterranean port of Banias. Mr Odell was confined to his house, though not expelled from the country. Mrs Odell, who was in Lebanon, heard about her husband's fate and immediately insisted on being allowed into Syria to be with him. 'I contacted our chief representative in Damascus,' Mr Odell said. His wife, meanwhile, by means of conversations in Arabic with the necessary contacts through the necessary channels, was working on the problem from her end. Soon afterwards, Mrs Odell arrived in a convoy of cars. 'It turned out that President Assad of Syria himself had been consulted and gave permission for Abla to join me. This shows me how nice people are. I really love Arabs.'

For a few weeks the Odells remained under house arrest. Mr Odell was nominally still working, but was never allowed back to his office, and eventually the operation began to slow down. Then, the Odells were expelled from Syria. They headed to London expecting another IPC posting abroad.

By that time, though, the company's operations had been nationalized in Iraq and Syria. 'They told me in London that IPC had lost most of its companies,' Mr Odell recalls, 'so, after twenty-five happy years in the Middle East, there was no longer a job for me.'

7

THE GULF: BRITAIN'S PRIVATE RESERVE

'Sharjah was very, very primitive indeed – medieval. One of the things that struck me most forcibly when I arrived was seeing a human hand suspended from a house in the bazaar. It had been cut off a criminal, a thief presumably, in accordance with one of the traditional Muslim punishments. We were living in a little house on the creek which had no proper facilities at all. It was a little Arab house, three or four rooms, built on the creek, and it was pretty well totally lacking in any modern convenience. Sanitation was very primitive too, a lot of dirt. Water was fetched up in tins. It was very, very primitive.'

Sharjah, as Martin Buckmaster found it when he arrived as a diplomat in the early 1950s. The emirates of the Gulf, which within two or three decades were to become among the richest countries in the world, were still marked by backwardness and poverty. The intense summer heat compounded the difficulties faced by the few foreigners found in the region.

The purpose of the official British presence since the nineteenth century had been to maintain good relations with the ruling sheikhs and make sure that Britain's routes to India were not threatened. In this sparsely populated corner of the Middle East a big show of British strength had not been necessary. Viscount Buckmaster says he was the first British political officer to live in Sharjah during the heat of the summer. 'Earlier on the political officer had been sent down from the Political Residency in Bushire in Iran during the winter. Then during the summer it was a local Arab who used to take charge.'

In Kuwait, at the northern end of the Gulf, the heat was no less intense and the conditions no easier. But being situated on the sea next to Iran and Iraq, Kuwait had developed more than most other cities in the Gulf as a trading port. Kenneth Bradford spent his working career with the Imperial Bank of Iran, which became the British Bank of the Middle East (BBME), taking up a posting in Kuwait in 1949. 'Kuwait in those days,' he says, 'was only at the beginning of the oil boom and was still surrounded by its old city walls, the gates of which were shut at night. It was a very small town, but the area within the walls was relatively large, because the walls were always meant as a protection against Bedouin raiders. Flocks could be brought in within the walls in times of danger. But the bank itself had just moved out of an office in the souk to what was considered to be a very grand edifice although it was only a single-storey structure, not unlike a rather elaborate church hall. But it was the only building at the time which was air-conditioned, which encouraged the staff to attend to their duties because it was so much more pleasant in the bank in the afternoon than in their own houses.'

Mr Bradford remembers that expatriate life in those days 'was very circumscribed. There was just home entertainment within quite a small community. Managers entertained members of the royal family and merchants. But there was very little social contact with Kuwaitis because there were very few who were westernized and appreciated perhaps our way of entertaining ourselves. Their families were very large and they lived among the family. The Ruler used to have his majlis [an open gathering at which citizens are free to consult the ruler about any matter] sitting outside the palace during the day, and this was the meeting place for the merchants, who really had a very important part to play in the running of affairs. When one went to and from the bank there were always groups of people sitting out in the majlis if the weather permitted.'

Maintaining friendly relations with the sheikhs and tribal leaders in the Gulf was a priority for British diplomats in the fifties as much as it had been in previous decades. Of particular concern to the ruling families of the lower Gulf at that time was a territorial dispute between the Trucial States and Oman on one side, and Saudi Arabia on the other, which centred on control of the Buraimi oasis. As part of British efforts to support the Trucial States Viscount Buckmaster went in 1952 with Sheikh Zaid, the brother of the Ruler of Abu Dhabi, Sheikh Shakhbut, on the last major camel caravan in the region. It is an experience that Viscount Buckmaster will never forget.

'We went to the Liwa oasis, which lay about one hundred and fifty miles from Abu Dhabi to the south. The object of it all was to explore the area, and get information about the allegiances of the local inhabitants, the two main tribes. All this was brought about by the Saudis' attempt to annex that area to their territory. The Saudis thought that there probably was oil in the area, but none has actually been discovered. They wanted to annex a very large part of the area around Buraimi and Liwa and they worked very hard to that end by bribing the local inhabitants.'

The caravan of fifty-two camels carrying Bedouin from various tribes set off from Abu Dhabi. 'We had a large group of camels carrying dates and rice and things. Each day we used to start off quite early in the morning with a simple meal of bread and coffee and then have two main meals, one at lunchtime and one in the evening. And on each occasion a sheep or goat was slaughtered and eaten with copious quantities of rice in the traditional way. A sheep or a goat has to be slaughtered with its head pointing towards Mecca. In fact it was done very quickly. I don't think the animals suffered enormously. But the head had to be cut off. Then the skin was stripped off and the joints of meat were boiled in one cauldron, and another cauldron had the rice.'

Did the group all eat together?

'Oh yes, very much so. We would sit around in a circle. Big dishes would be prepared, loaded with rice and meat, and we'd all partake.'

What about water?

'Unlike in Sharjah and Abu Dhabi, where the water was very poor, salty and often dirty, the wells of the desert were fairly pure. Each well had its different taste and some of the Bedouin who'd been in that area for a long time could distinguish between wells by their taste, just as one might be able to pinpoint a certain vintage of champagne or claret or whatever it is.'

Each day the caravan would progress about fifteen or twenty miles. 'The camel drivers had to stop for the routine prayers – five prayers a day, dawn, midday, afternoon, sunset and the night prayer two hours after sunset.'

I wondered what Viscount Buckmaster, as the only foreigner, talked about.

'My Arabic wasn't very good then. We used to talk about the desert mainly, the names of different herbs, flowers, camels, things like that. We were cut off completely from the twentieth century, we had no radios, nothing. We were away for two and a half months.

Two months actually going round the desert interviewing the Bedu in the various settlements and another two or three weeks travelling around the islands which were also in dispute.'

Viscount Buckmaster was given a special camel to ride. 'I had the camel that Wilfred Thesiger had when he was out there. It was supposed to be the best camel in Arabia. It was called Ghazala. I was asked to wear Arab clothes, which I did. I was given an Arabic name, Hamad. So although I couldn't behave like a Bedu, I tried to as much as I could.'

I asked Viscount Buckmaster whether he saw that camel caravan as the end of an era.

'Oh definitely so, yes. There were no big camel caravans after that because quite soon after we'd carried out our tour it became normal to visit the area by Land Rover. With sand tyres you could get to pretty well anywhere that a camel had been to.'

Viscount Buckmaster is rare among British Arabists in the foreign service to talk with enthusiasm about travel on camel-back – most of them wanting to distance themselves from the 'Lawrence of Arabia' stereotype. But Julian Walker, who was also a diplomat in the Gulf in the early and mid-fifties, had another reason for not being too keen on camel transport. Camels, he told me, proved to be impractical when he was travelling around the desert trying to map the territory. 'Camels are not very good if you're trying to write notes. You've got a head rope and you may have a stick. You've got no stirrups – you've got to cling on with your knees. The person you're talking to will be a little distance away from you – you can't get down very easily and so it's not a very good means of transport if you're trying to write names, to discuss things with people. It's partly why the Bedu shout, because they shout from one camel to another. I found a donkey far better than a camel, and of course a camel takes time – so we avoided camels. Normally we went by Land Rover – sometimes on foot, sometimes by donkey, sometimes by launch. As a whole I avoided camels, whatever the prestige.'

Mr Walker's first diplomatic posting in the lower Gulf, like Viscount Buckmaster's, was in Sharjah. Conditions were still very difficult, but Mr Walker, many years later, talks about those extraordinary pioneering days in a detached, matter-of-fact way. His position in Sharjah was assistant Political Agent. 'But,' he recalls, 'my first job was not very political, it was trying to get the generators going – there'd been no electricity for the Agency right through the summer, and all three staff there were under doctors' orders having suffered from the heat. The transport was very run down – we had two Land Rovers, one of which we got going, although it had no brakes even then. It was fairly primitive – we lived in the Fort in Sharjah and had to drive in over the dung heaps each day. The Fort had air-conditioning, but you had small, cell-like rooms. The Political Agency itself was crumbling – the Political Agent had his own Louis Quinze-type furniture. We had old Baluchi guards on the front gates. The visa applicants would queue up at the Agency, and go to the lavatory behind the launch which was on the creek. One would go swimming in the creek oneself across to the sandbar facing one – but it was fairly primitive.'

Only a small number of Britons were forced to endure these difficult conditions. Mr Walker says the total community in the lower Gulf in those days numbered no more than one hundred, with more than seventy of these being RAF personnel at the base in Sharjah. Included among the rest were about ten officers serving with the Trucial Oman Scouts (the locally recruited, British-run defence force), plus employees of the BBME and Gray MacKenzie's (trading company), 'and Desmond Macauley at the hospital. There were, when we were lucky, four women in all – all wives: one in Sharjah, one in Dubai, one on Abu Musa island, and one down in Abu Dhabi when they set up the oil company down there. Mainly the British community for parties at Christmas consisted of about twenty-four.'

The day-to-day work of the British diplomats was very varied. As the years passed and the realization grew that the region was rich in oil, mapping the territory became one of the main tasks. 'Before you got boundaries settled it was very difficult to have oil concessions – you had to know where the oil company was going to drill. There were also problems between the states, between Fujairah and Ras al-Khaimah – incidents of shooting and firing and things of that sort. So the Political Agent started out in April 1954 to go on a journey to deal with one boundary between Ras al-Khaimah and Umm al-Qaiwain, and it was supposed to be a boundary over which there was no dispute. He went out with the two sheikhs and the two parties to follow this boundary. And the Ruler of Umm al-Qaiwain led him in one direction, and they seemed to know everything; and the rulers of Ras al-Khaimah were following, waving their arms and saying they were going into Ras al-Khaimah territory. The Political

Agent had a very frustrating bounce up and down sand dunes, getting hotter and more dusty. It became apparent that the frontier that was supposed to be totally undisputed had lots of problems over it. So he came back to pink gins at the Agency and really felt that he couldn't spend all the time that would be needed to deal with those boundaries.'

So the task was handed to Mr Walker, and the mapping party ('myself, my driver and a houseboy to run the camp') set off. 'Firstly one went out with guides from each of the tribes and got the names of places. There were virtually no maps, so I'd go out and camp in a place like the Wadi Gur, which was on the main route going from the east coast to the west coast, and then start with guides from there, find out from them the names of the places and where each of the guides thought their boundaries were, and then work and try and find neutral tribesmen and find out where they thought the boundaries were. We would look up all the history that we had in our old records – British records – and find out where we thought the boundaries were. Then, if possible, we'd come to a decision and go and discuss it with the various rulers – see what objections they had and see what they wanted looked into a bit more.'

To start drawing the maps, Mr Walker borrowed accounting paper from IPC 'because that was the largest paper we could get. I just made compass traverses and notes, and climbed mountains and tried to have a look down from the mountains to see as much as I could. And I went out into the wadis [dried river-beds] by donkey or camel or walked, to find out all I possible could.'

The job 'had its dangers; the area wasn't very secure, therefore strangers were always regarded as hostile. You were better going with a small party because a small party wouldn't look as though it was an attacking and raiding party. Sometimes when they shot towards one, or shot at one, the best thing to do was leave the car, walk up alone towards them and they'd see you weren't hostile. They might even recognize that you weren't an Arab and therefore probably not going to attack them for tribal reasons, and then gradually welcome you. You would send in warning people before if you could to say you were coming.'

When I pressed the issue, Mr Walker admitted that there had been some difficult moments. 'Once I was held up in Fujairah territory by going with the wrong guides from Khor Fakkan. We'd broken a new road through over a mountain pass and followed the track that had been used in the beginning of the 1900s by the rulers of Sharjah to bombard the village with cannons so you could see where the stones had been cleared away, and they weren't very friendly to start with – the ruler of Fujairah's people held me for a bit.'

In the early days of the mapping operation Mr Walker carried a rifle. 'But sleeping with a rifle is not very comfortable, so then I carried a small pistol, and then, in the north, I learned a bit of self-defence. They were very hot-minded people and I don't think they would have liked the drawing of any weapon, so I learned judo and jujitsu but I didn't use it in fact, because one's whole need was to get the trust of the people you were working with, not to antagonize.'

Often the mappers encountered a hazard of a completely different kind in trying to get their work finished: excessive desert hospitality. 'If you were very honoured you would have the cow's milk on the day that the calf was born. In fact the desert people were so hospitable that one would try not to warn them one was coming, and one would try to be in a hurry because otherwise one would be kept for a meal and one would spend four hours while everything was being got ready. One had the meal and then most of the day was lost as far as work was concerned. When we were out camping at one time we lived with a Bedu family. I had an old gentleman coming in in the morning as I was trying to shave, bringing me dried *gammi*, which is a dried goat's cheese held together by goat's hairs; and one side would be the imprint of his floor mat and the other side would be the imprint of his hand. At meals, the sheep's eye wasn't necessarily a thing of honour down there. To the poet you gave the tongue, and the main guest was given the chance to break open the head to eat the brains. The testicles were regarded as a special feature too, and things like that. This was eaten sitting around a mat, with rice and tinned pineapple and maybe tinned cherries for dessert. It depended how far into the desert you went; deeper in the desert there were none of those things.'

Back in the towns, the diplomats had plenty of other varied tasks. Mr Walker remembers, for example, 'having to set up a lunatic asylum with the Trucial Oman Scouts. A Somali came and caused a bit of trouble. He was imprisoned in primitive conditions and then went mad, so we had to set up a lunatic asylum.' Also his job involved countering the slave trade, which despite the treaty drawn up by Britain and signed by tribal leaders in 1820, was continuing. 'We sent up a patrol to capture the last slave trader. He'd captured one or two women – one from Fujairah and some Baluchi ladies from across in Persia and he was going to transport them to Saudi Arabia. It was a long-running practice. He was captured by the Trucial Oman Scouts, and we then had to bring him to trial. I did part of the committal proceedings myself, and he was imprisoned with the Scouts. So it was fairly flexible as to what you did each day.'

Viscount Buckmaster remembers there being two types of slavery – commercial and domestic. 'The commercial involved buying and selling of slaves which went on in the Buraimi Oasis until, I suppose, fifteen or twenty years ago. Children were involved, I'm afraid. They were extracted from Saudi Arabia and sold in the Buraimi Oasis to some of the surrounding sheikhs. But then of course there was also domestic slavery. Pretty well all the rulers had their own domestic slaves who'd lived with them since childhood and were well treated, well fed and given clothing; marriages were arranged for them and everything. If they wanted to obtain release from slavery – it was an interesting custom that prevailed for a long time – they would have to go to the Political Agency and clasp the flag-pole on which the Union Jack was flying, kneel down and clasp it with their two hands and appeal for what was called manumission, freeing from slavery. We used to give them a manumission certificate saying that they'd been freed from their slavery and that no one could interfere with their liberty in future. I released several slaves in that way.'

I asked Viscount Buckmaster whether, in his experience, this ceremony was an emotional occasion for those freed.

'No, I don't think so. Some of them, I'm afraid, after they'd been manumitted, wished that they hadn't taken that step because it was difficult for them to get employment, whereas with the sheikhs they were well looked after, well clothed and fed and so on. And treated very kindly.'

Cracking down on the slave trade and other duties necessitated constant movement between the sheikhdoms of the Trucial States. 'The Gulf in those days, of course,' Glencairn Balfour-Paul says, 'was still a place with no roads and little transport, and you bumped along the coast on tracks visiting the rulers and so on. About which of course you must have heard the famous story about Rupert Hay when he was Political Resident and used to pay very formal visits to the rulers in full kit, full uniform. He was said to have been bumping along the road between Sharjah and the southern emirates with his ADC beside him. And a fearful bump came, and his pickelhaube helmet, you know the thing you wore on the top, went right through the roof of the car, and he was suspended by his chin strap, slowly throttling. And his ADC jumped out and unscrewed the pickelhaube from the top of the helmet and released his boss from instant death. The roads were rather like that.'

As the volume of traffic grew slowly in the Trucial States, it fell to the British diplomats, like Julian Walker, to work out traffic regulations. 'We tried to help with traffic laws as there had been crashes on the open flats between Sharjah and Dubai. It was completely open; but you had two lorries coming towards each other, with neither knowing whether to go to the right or to the left. So we worked out some traffic laws; but by the time the legal advisers in the Foreign Office had dealt with them it was almost a case of "No Parking" on the left-hand side of the streets on odd days of the week, "Go" when the traffic lights are green. But there were no traffic lights. Just as we had a regulation about misuse of the telephone – there were no telephones. I translated this for all the sheikhs and they said: "Thank you for your efforts but we're going to try ourselves." They ended up with something which virtually said only that every car should have a steering wheel, brakes and a horn – that no taxi should carry more than forty passengers. They finally said, I think, that if you're fairly far to the right of the car coming towards you, then go to the right; if not, go to the left. Later on when there were more cars, the cars coming out of town, which would have been heavily laden, were allowed to keep to the track; and cars going into town got off the track. There were no roads, so cars got stuck quite a lot in the sand.'

The overland journey to Abu Dhabi presented a different kind of problem. Kenneth Bradford, working at that time with the BBME in Dubai, remembers that visiting this emirate 'was a great adventure. You had to have some pre-knowledge of the tides. Because having ploughed through the sand to the sheikhdom you then had to cross a creek to get on to the island of Abu Dhabi. That meant describing a considerable arc through the water. At one point you seemed to be half a mile or more from any land in the middle of the sea. It was quite an adventure because you could only do it at low tide. So if you called on the Ruler you had to time your visit to get in and, if possible, out again before the tide started to rise. The Ruler, Sheikh Shakhbut, lived in a fort which was a very impressive structure. There was a tiny customs house, and *barasti* [matted palm fronds] huts for fishermen. Basically I think it would be correct to say that Abu Dhabi at this time didn't exist.'

While Abu Dhabi later became the wealthiest of the emirates in the lower Gulf, in the fifties neighbouring Dubai was the most prosperous sheikhdom. Dubai's prosperity was constructed on trade – the town was built on a creek which provided an excellent harbour. One of the many commodities that passed through Dubai was gold, and a fascinating pattern of semi-legal trade in this precious metal had been established with India. Glencairn Balfour-Paul learnt, while living in Dubai, that the emirate's prosperity was 'based on the fact that the import of gold into India was banned by the Indian government, and the fact that the Gulf states at that time used the India rupee. The rupee coin was worth twice as much in the Gulf as it was in India, for reasons which have always baffled me. However, that enabled the enterprising Dubai subjects to make money – and I may say every single resident of Dubai except the Political Agent had a stake in the gold trade. They would import gold by air from the Bank of England, perfectly legitimately, in ingots which would be piled up at the Dubai airstrip overnight unprotected – a hundred thousand pounds' worth in a heap. Nobody would touch it because they all had a stake in it. It was then put into these dhows which sailed off to the edge of Indian territorial waters, where, by arrangement with wicked Indian boatmen, they would meet Indian boats and offload the gold. It would then be rowed ashore the three miles in the night, taken inland where the Indian peasants were longing for gold, which they bought with rupee notes. These were then taken to a bank and exchanged for rupee coins which were smuggled back to the waiting Dubai boats. If they escaped the Indian navy, which was trying to stop all this, they brought the currency back to Dubai, where they could turn it into sterling at twice the rate, buy another airplane load of gold and repeat the process. One made about an eighty per cent profit on each turn-round.'

The Indian authorities, in their efforts to stop the smuggling of gold, 'posted a trade agent, which was the nearest thing they could get to a spy, in Dubai to try and identify all the boats of the right kind – because they had to be fast to escape the Indian navy sailing out. I was once asked by a Dubai shipowner if I'd like to go pearl-diving with him. I said that nothing would interest me more, so he took me on to his dhow, slaughtering a sheep as I walked up, all that. Off we sailed, up the coast off Umm al-Qaiwain, where pearling was just still going on. And having sat the whole day in the sun watching the pearlers he said: "That's finished." So I said: "Are we going back to Dubai?" And he said: "No, I'm going to drop you at Umm al-Qaiwain, because I'm going on to India. What do you think is underneath you?" The dhow was full of gold, and I – as a foreign diplomat – had been used by this ingenious man as a cover to escape the attentions of the Indian trade agent.'

Episodes like that helped to divert the attention of the small British community away from the primitiveness of the living conditions. Mr Balfour-Paul, in his capacity as a servant of the Queen, had another source of diversion. 'The Political Agent in Dubai, for some reason, had a private bagpiper on the staff – for a Scot like me, of course, it was a splendid thing. He used to play up and down outside my squalid house every evening and accompany me on tour. He did other things as well, I hasten to say. But the Welshman who succeeded me had him struck off the staff. This is the sort of thing that the Welsh do to the Scots. I remember once I was in the very southern bit of Ras al-Khaimah on the Indian ocean at Khor Fakkan, which is the most beautiful beach in the world. I was taking the deputy Political Resident, Sir Horace Phillips, to see the emirates. We were camping on the beach and the most enormous storm I'd ever seen or anyone had ever seen blew up while we were there in our tents. It was pouring with rain and the rain came down from inland, and the sea came in the other way. We just managed to escape and take refuge in an Egyptian schoolmaster's house. And when we went back in the morning there was simply nothing there at all, the tents had all gone into the sea, there was nothing except smooth sand and my bagpiper marching up and down, playing a lament on the pipes. It was quite a romantic moment.'

The biggest problem throughout the Gulf in those days was the heat. The inhabitants of Dubai, resourceful as ever, had devised over the centuries a wind-tower cooling system. Kenneth Bradford speaks highly of the contraption. 'The system was extremely effective. It depended on these tall towers which were open at the bottom and consisted of diagonal walls within the louvred tower itself. So that when the wind blew it was funnelled down into the room below. They were extremely effective to the extent that if you sat under one of the wind-towers in the bank you really had to put paper-weights and things on to the papers, otherwise they'd be blown all over the place. The snag is that the wind is thermal, caused by the rising temperature in the land, so that it blows during the day and gets increasingly strong, and then drops at night. So when you want to go to sleep, and people used to sleep on the roofs of their houses or in their courtyards, you'd be trying to get to sleep in a sort of wet blanket, totally still.'

Another cooling system, the use of the punka, provided a reminder of the days when the whole Gulf region was tied closely to the British presence in India. 'The punka system depends on a supply of low-paid labour to hang on to the rope at one end and move the punka. This is a long piece of wood from which either a rush or a cloth hangs down and moves slowly as the person with the rope pulls it. As it's an extremely boring job and the punka wallah tends to fall asleep if he's not woken up, it's not actually a wildly successful system. We did have in the bank something that in my knowledge is unique, and that is a kerosene-operated fan. This was a table fan which operated with a little burner underneath which worked a pump and turned the fan. The problem with that was that you really had the choice between being asphyxiated by the smell of paraffin or not having the thing working at all. It was used, and while there must have been a lot manufactured, neither I nor anyone I've ever spoken to has ever seen any other example.'

Mr Bradford, representing a British bank in the Trucial States, had as much contact as the diplomats with the ruling families. 'We were really on quite close terms with Sheikh Rashid, the Ruler of Dubai. And when the rulers went out hunting they would quite often drop a gazelle or bustard or whatever they had shot in at the house for us.'

Because the handful of Britons in the Trucial States were on such close terms with the ruling families they had a chance to observe the formalities of Arab hospitality in that part of the world. Mr Bradford remembers one occasion when Sheikh Rashid of Dubai, in a gesture of reconciliation aimed at easing tension between the neighbouring and rival emirates, played host to Sheikh Shakhbut of Abu Dhabi. The Ruler of Abu Dhabi 'was entertained in a typically Arab fashion in the sense that the Ruler of Dubai moved out of his quarters and handed them over to Sheikh Shakhbut, who installed himself in the palace and did entertaining and meeting of people there. For the entire stay he lived in the Ruler of Dubai's quarters as if they were his own. And he gave the typical Arab entertainments. It was an interesting example of how hospitality in an Arab context is conducted and how people go out of their way to be helpful and hospitable. I wouldn't say this is foreign to us, but certainly is something we wouldn't expect to have offered us if we were at someone's house or people came to us.'

From time to time it was the duty of the British community to entertain the Arab ruling families. 'The most impressive party we ever gave was when we had a visit of directors from London. It was a typical Arab-style party. We had the coffee beforehand in the house, which had been totally cleared of furniture, and we ate on the tennis court outside. All the rulers of the Trucial Coast attended, and all together with the rulers, who ate first, and then their retainers, who came in after we had moved off, we entertained well over a hundred people. In addition to that, when it was known that we were giving a big party, as was the case if any of the wealthy merchants gave a party, this news got around the bazaar very quickly. This was because they usually brought in the cook from the local bakery to do the stuffed sheep. So this news spread, and the Bedu who were coming into town for whatever reason would hear about it; and when they had conducted their business they would wait outside the gate. By the time our party was due to start fifty or sixty of them were waiting to partake of whatever was left. We had three large stuffed sheep, plus a lot of other goat and sheep meat; and as we reckoned we were going to entertain around a hundred people there was chicken on the basis of one for each guest. These animals were all brought in live. Our house at that time was on the outskirts of the town, surrounded by sand, and we were awakened that morning to the noise of a hundred chickens having their throats cut and squirming in the sand in their death throes. Anyway, everything was cooked in the sand in the bank "garden".'

On social occasions of this kind, etiquette had to be strictly observed. 'Everything was placed on the floor and you ate with your right hand. You had to grab a piece of meat and you kneaded it into a ball with rice and popped it into your mouth. By and large when the ruler had finished eating he would get up and go and wash his hands, which was a signal for everyone else to follow.'

An Arab feast of a similar kind was put on in Abu Dhabi in 1959 to celebrate the opening of a branch of the BBME – the first bank to operate there. My father, who was manager of the regional operation based in Bahrain, flew down with my mother for the celebration. Although air travel had arrived in the lower Gulf, conditions were still difficult. 'The airstrip has been levelled,' my mother wrote in a journal at the time, 'and a lot of loose sand removed, but over the rest of Abu Dhabi one sinks in at each step, and in places it is a foot deep. Soft, fine, white and powdery sand which gives off a strong glare. Experienced Abu Dhabians wear boots for the sand or else go barefooted.' The bank was a fifteen-minute drive by Land Rover from the airstrip. 'This may sound like an exaggeration, but the only way to keep going on that deep sand is to drive at speed in a zigzag fashion. Wheel marks are quickly covered by the fine sand which is blown over them, and here and there empty oil drums mark out the best track in a particularly bad patch. This method is used at the airstrip, the pilot landing his plane between two lines of oil drums.'

Dominating the sandy landscape was the Ruler's fort. There was little else. 'We are right in the town now, such as it is, and we are turning sharply into a gateless compound, with several Arab buildings in it, and also donkeys, goats and camels. All scatter at our approach with the exception of the camels, who only look contemptuously at the Land Rover, usurper of their desert routes. Another sharp turn, and then we see a very familiar sign over an Arab type of building: The British Bank of the Middle East. We jump down into the soft sand, and climb a few steps to a veranda where a fearsome looking gentleman, complete with rifle, allows us to pass into the bank. The little bank is very pleasant; it mainly consists of one rather long and narrow room, but having windows on either side it is light and airy.' The veranda of a nearby building 'was piled high with carpets, cushions, chairs etc., which had been brought from Dubai by dhow for the feast, together with a master cook and his helpers numbering eight or ten men; also food which included live goats and chickens. All was being prepared in the open air, but a rough shelter from the sun had been erected with poles and tarpaulin, which was being used as a protection for food rather than men. The head cook greeted us, and the little camp was a hive of activity. Rice was being shaken over on large trays time and again before it was passed as ready for cooking. Open fires had the whole goat carcasses cooking slowly over them, and many other pots and pans of food were in process of preparation. The time taken to prepare and cook a feast of this kind is some twelve hours.'

Inside the house, furniture and carpets were being put in place. 'The chairs were arranged around the sitting room, with a large settee at one end on which the Ruler would sit and receive the other guests, and drink coffee until the feast was ready. Meanwhile the veranda had been covered completely with carpets, and cushions had been set at the top end to form seats of honour for the Ruler and whoever he would signify should sit by him. Down the centre of the carpet was laid a narrow white cloth upon which the dishes of food would be placed.'

Socializing of this kind was an all-male affair, and my mother had to be hidden in an upper room of the house until all the guests had gone.

From the tone of my mother's diary of that visit it is clear that she sensed how Abu Dhabi was on the point of sudden change – from a backward desert sheikhdom to a fabulously wealthy oil state. 'Our bedroom faced due east,' she wrote, 'and so we were awake early with the rising sun, and to find quite a fresh breeze blowing in off the sea . . . I am thankful to have seen Abu Dhabi before it is modernised by oil wealth. Its freshness and simplicity will be a happy memory.'

My parents returned to the civilization of Bahrain, where oil revenue had brought about the move towards modernization many decades earlier. By 1959 I had followed the path of my two brothers and my sister to boarding school in Britain. But the previous two years I had lived with my parents in Bahrain. I remember it as an island dominated by the British and by expatriate life. I attended a school run by the RAF to which I was driven each morning by the bank chauffeur in our Humber Hawk. I remember attending a children's party on a visiting British warship, HMS *Ceylon*, and my parents mingling with a crowd on the lawn of the Political Residency at the Queen's birthday party. Apart from on Christmas Day, when Arab merchants – bank customers – called at the house with presents and sat on chairs on the lawn, most of my parents' guests during the year were Europeans or Americans. There was occasionally a trip to the cinema – the open-air one at the RAF base, or the conventional one at the oil company town of Awali. In the summer there was swimming at the Gymkhana Club or on Zellaq beach.

I remember, too, hearing adult talk about anti-British feeling in parts of the island of Muharraq, which is attached to the main island of Bahrain by causeway. It was said that everyone there had a radio and listened to the outbursts of President Nasser of Egypt. This kind of talk had little impact on my life. I did not know that during the Suez crisis there had been trouble on the island. Julian Walker was a diplomat in Bahrain at the time. 'We were almost blockaded in our compound and sent out helicopters to distribute leaflets to try to get the rioters off the streets. There was the feeling of Arab nationalism, and there were riots against the British as a whole, against British property. The causeway between Muharraq and Manama was blocked, the Gray MacKenzie slipway was set on fire, there were demonstrating crowds in the streets and we had to bring in some soldiers. The Ruler put on a curfew. I remember going out by helicopter to distribute leaflets to say that the Ruler had imposed this curfew; but you could look down and still see Bahraini policemen directing traffic, although Gray MacKenzie's was burning and all that.'

Before long, Mr Walker says, order was restored and life for the British in Bahrain returned to normal. 'In the Residency we lived fairly much around the tennis courts, the squash courts and the swimming pool. I used to cycle round the island – I had no car, so I borrowed the cook's bicycle. There were dinner parties at the Residency with Ella Burrows [wife of the Political Resident] calling the square dancing and things like that. I do remember acting in a play, *Lady Windermere's Fan*, with Lady Burrows playing Lady Windermere and us second secretaries acting as waiters and footmen. And there was Scottish dancing, certainly, quite a lot of that.'

The rounds of expatriate entertaining were interrupted – as they had been during the Suez crisis in 1956 – by reaction to the Arab-Israeli war of 1967. The British Agency building in Bahrain was the focus for crowd anger. Sir Anthony Parsons was inside it at the time. 'As soon as the war broke out a crowd gathered outside, and was there permanently until a couple of days after the fighting ended. Some were Palestinians, most were young Bahrainis, a lot of school teachers – a lot I knew personally. I could wave to them from my office. The big lie, when we were accused of flying British aircraft in the pre-emptive attack on the Egyptian air force, had a stimulating effect on the demonstrators. It was very tense, and nobody was thinking of anything but what was going on at the war front at the time. It was the power of radio and the power of Nasserism in Egypt, of Arab nationalism in education in Bahrain. There was great excitement and it was directed against us because we were the only diplomatic post in the place. But it was never vindictive hostility.'

The extraordinary feature of life in the Gulf, from the early fifties until the withdrawal of British forces at the beginning of the seventies, was the lack of hostility towards Britain. All this at a time when Britain was in retreat in every other part of the Middle East. In fact, the thought of the British withdrawal from the Gulf was not – until the last moment – a subject that arose. 'We didn't think ahead that much as to how long we were going to stay,' Julian Walker says. 'What was strange was that in a way we were being welcomed in at that time when Britain was recoiling from colonialism, although this wasn't colonialism – it might have been called paternalism. We were moving in because of the oil companies, while elsewhere we were in retreat.'

The Suez crisis represented the most humiliating retreat of all. Yet amid the outbursts of popular anti-British feeling throughout the Middle East, one Arab ruler in the Gulf remained totally loyal to Britain. When the crisis erupted with the British and French invasion of Egypt, Sheikh Shakhbut of Abu Dhabi contacted the British Political Agency in Sharjah to express his support. Viscount Buckmaster says the Ruler of Abu Dhabi 'was about the only one of the Bedouin leaders who sided with Britain at the time, and he presented me with a very large sword of gold, about two feet long, which I gave to the Agency. He said: "This will show my loyalty to Great Britain and my hostility to the Egyptians and Nasser who've taken over the Suez canal." I knew he'd always been loyal to us. But he was the only Arab ruler of any importance who reacted in this remarkably pro-British way.'

The basis of the Anglo-Arab friendship in the lower Gulf states rested, there can be no doubt, on deep and genuine friendship that developed between the British representatives there in the fifties and sixties and the ruling families. Many of the Britons, now in retirement, who were there at the time speak warmly of their relationships with the sheikhs of the Trucial States and elsewhere. Sir James Craig, a retired ambassador, calls the Gulf rulers 'some of the nicest men I've ever met in my life, with extreme courtesy and great friendliness'. Glencairn Balfour-Paul describes them as 'great characters, all of them, and one enormously enjoyed visiting them'.

Mr Balfour-Paul's special friend was the late Ruler of Dubai, Sheikh Rashid – 'a man who had five right-angles to his nose. He once asked me how much of what he said to me I understood. I said: "I suppose about thirty per cent," or something. He told me that

Craig could understand about forty per cent. "But it doesn't matter if you don't understand what I say," he said, "it's what I don't say that matters." So that of course was the secret of enjoyment or success in the Gulf, understanding what was not said but implied. Anyhow, they were all amusing people. I suppose one of those I enjoyed most was a man who was known as "Electric whiskers" or something – he was the Ruler of Fujairah, the least developed and southernmost of the states. He was invited when I was there, for reasons I don't now remember, to pay a formal visit to England. He'd never been outside the Gulf before, and a great question arose in his mind about how many guns [in salute] he would get on his arrival. Well, I knew from the book that a Gulf ruler was only entitled to one, which didn't sound very good. I mean, the Political Resident got eleven wherever he went. Anyhow I said to him when he asked how many guns he'd get: "How many would you like?" And he said, to my dismay, one hundred and forty-four. I said: "Why one hundred and forty-four?" And he said: "That's the number of guns the British navy shot at my father's palace in 1907, and they're still in the wall." And he thought it would be fair compensation. He only got one, I'm afraid. Anyway, he was great fun.'

The end of direct British influence in the lower Gulf states came abruptly at the beginning of the 1970s. The manner in which it was carried out – as part of hasty cost-cutting measures introduced by the British Labour government of the day – caused distress to those diplomats and others who had worked hard to win the friendship and trust of the Gulf rulers. The sheikhs themselves were not keen to lose British military protection and political support. But it is the view of Sir James Craig that, by the end of the sixties, pressure on Britain to withdraw – sooner rather than later – was growing. The Gulf in the fifties and sixties, with the spread of radio and television broadcasts from Cairo and other Arab capitals, could no longer be kept isolated from the mood of nationalism. 'I can recall visiting the schools, for example, going round the art classes, and all the young children would have drawn pictures of British paratroops landing at Suez and being defeated by the brave Egyptian soldiers. And there would be the occasional march in the streets with people shouting "Long live Nasser", or "Down with Imperialism". It caused my bosses back in London some anxiety. It seemed to me very natural, very reasonable. I think if I'd been an

Arab I'd have felt the same. There was no reason to get too excited. I thought it was obvious that the days of our special relationship with these emirates were coming to an end, not only for political reasons, but because they were going to become rich and would want to flex their own muscles; and they would also receive a great influx of other foreigners. We could no longer preserve these emirates as a kind of game reserve for us.'

Overshadowing all the other changes in the late sixties was the development boom, as oil production and revenue increased. As much as Britons who knew the region in the more primitive days may marvel at the pace and scale of development, some harbour feelings of regret about the passing of the simplicity of life. Sheikh Shakhbut, the Ruler of Abu Dhabi, was forced out of power, with British help, because of his refusal to spend money on developing his country. Glencairn Balfour-Paul, who had a personal role to play in the ousting of the Abu Dhabi sheikh, understands nevertheless why he was reluctant to open up his country to the modern world. 'I think he saw that it would be the end of life as his people knew it. There were only a few thousand of them, and they lived the sort of life they were happy enough with. And of course once you built stadiums all over the country and developed everything it was not going to be the same. They became, in a sense, the pensioners of the state and never did another stroke. When I went back later to Abu Dhabi to ask Sheikh Zaid for money [for a Middle East department at a university in Britain] he was away at camel racing. I saw the programme, and the first prize was a Pontiac. I felt that this was symbolic. Life was changing very fast.'

The days of Martin Buckmaster's tour round the Trucial States by camel caravan – only a matter of a few years before the dramatic transformation of the lower Gulf – suddenly seemed a world away. Today, in retirement in his flat in Chelsea, Viscount Buckmaster still talks with passionate affection for those early days.

Did he consider that the arrival of Land Rovers, bankers and oilmen in a sense broke the idyllic charm of that part of the Arab world?

'Very much so, yes. Rather as those of you who've read Wilfred Thesiger will realize how disturbed he was in his book *Arabian Sands*, at the advent of various things like cars and aeroplanes and so on. It did destroy the idyllic peace and beauty of the area, certainly, yes. Money came rushing in.'

Part 3

EGYPT

8

BETWEEN THE WARS

One of Hugh Holmes's earliest memories is of a voyage on the P & O liner *Caledonia*. He was four years old. The year was 1920, and the ship's destination was Port Said in Egypt. 'I think it was one of the oldest P & O ships, it was only about eight or nine thousand tons, and we went through the Bay of Biscay and right round through the Mediterranean. I think it took about three or four weeks. The passage was very, very stormy, and I can just remember it. We arrived safely, but one wonders why, because in those days it was fairly primitive. The cabins were very small and the service wasn't all that marvellous.'

From Port Said the Holmes family travelled by train to Maadi, which is now an affluent suburb of Cairo. At the time it was a district 'about seven miles south of Cairo right on the banks of the Nile. It consisted of a dozen or so little houses, all occupied by British or European professionals, and a tin church. We had a good club there with a fine swimming pool and a fine golf course, and everything that a British community normally establishes. The church was a small one, but everyone went there.'

Hugh Holmes's father was a judge in the Native Courts, and used to commute to and from Cairo. Later, based in Alexandria, he rose to the pinnacle of the Egyptian legal profession. Even while in Cairo he presided over some of the most serious and controversial trials – including that of the murderers of Sir Lee Stack, the British High Commissioner in Sudan, who was killed in the Egyptian capital in 1924. 'After the conviction of the murderers, my father was very nearly murdered himself. He was on his way to lunch at the Turf Club in Cairo, a famous club where all the top British officials used to gather together. He was walking with a doctor when the doctor was shot dead, obviously in mistake for my father.'

As a child, Hugh Holmes used to play with Egyptian boys from time to time, but his main friends were Europeans. 'I particularly remember the occasion when I went with a little Russian boy called Boris, who I think was the young son of an *émigré* from the Russian Revolution, up to the swimming pool. We managed to burn down all the buildings round it. We were not popular, and I can remember to this day looking across to the old club house, which was four or five hundred yards away. There were thousands of little black boys, little Egyptian boys, with buckets coming towards us, shouting and screaming. My father was not amused until he and the other members of the club discovered that they could claim compensation, so they had a much better swimming pool ever after.'

Another unusual childhood activity, Mr Holmes remembers, incurred the wrath of his father. 'One thing I used to do – looking back I'm horrified at it – I used to get up every morning at six to operate the level crossing on the train line through Maadi. The line went from Cairo, through Maadi, to Helwan. The trains came through very frequently. The signals would go up and I would open the gates and shut them again – I was about six years old at the time. But the Egyptian man who was supposed to do the job was delighted to take his five piastres wages and go and have a coffee. My father, of course, discovered this and was absolutely appalled.'

The Holmes parents led a busy social life, so the children were left for much of the time in the hands of a nanny. 'I also got on terribly well with the servants – the gardeners and the cook. In no time at all I spoke fluent Arabic. It isn't a difficult language if you learn as young as that. Sadly I can't speak it now – well, I suppose I remember some. There were all sorts of things like "*yalla*" – "go away". Or "*mush kwayis*" – "not nice", "not good".'

Learning Arabic and establishing friendship with servants was the experience of another Briton who was brought up in Egypt between the two world wars: Valerie Sale, the daughter of a cotton company director. The family lived in the countryside by the Nile in Upper Egypt. 'It was an idyllic life really because you had a lot of staff. In those days "servant" wasn't a derogatory word – the servants became very loyal and they always used to say "our house" and "our garden" – they felt they belonged to the family and they all stayed forty or fifty years. It was a wonderful feeling to be brought up in that atmosphere.'

The servants spoke only Arabic, never English. 'Some of the people who came out to Egypt, in a snobby way, said: "I'm not going to learn to speak Arabic, the servants can learn English." One awful woman who came out was determined not to speak Arabic, and the servant did his best with her. She was giving a dinner party and she asked for a steak-and-kidney pie. She couldn't get the word "kidneys", but he said he knew what she meant. At the party there was a wonderful pie full of steak and not a kidney in sight. She was livid. She went to the kitchen and asked where they were and he said: "I've got them", and produced a card of trouser buttons.'

Miss Sale remembers, too, that 'servants were so wonderful at helping one. If you had a party, they never asked, they'd go to the next-door neighbours and just take whatever you needed. You might go out to supper and find all your cutlery there, or whatever, flowers from your garden. But it was all done in a very amicable way.'

A particular incident sticks in her mind. 'A friend in Cairo had a very big pompous dinner party one night – he was a bachelor and he wanted everything just perfect. He had leg of lamb, and the poor servant came in from the kitchen, caught his foot on the carpet and went flat on his face; and the leg of lamb rolled under the table and the sauce went and everything. Being very British, nobody said a word and kept talking about the weather and the crops. This poor man picked himself up, disappeared into the kitchen and came back five minutes later with beautifully cooked roast beef and Yorkshire pudding – the lot. When asked afterwards what had happened he said: "I knew the people upstairs were having a dinner party, and they didn't know the lamb had been on the floor; so I took their beef and they took our lamb." The servants were simply wonderful.'

In particular, Miss Sale remembers the chauffeur. 'I grew up with him, he was like a nanny almost. He was so loyal that when we were chucked out in 1956 and the governor came and took over the house the chauffeur fought like a tiger to keep the car and he made such a fuss that he was jailed for quite a long time. When they let him out he got into the house again and he stole for us the radiogram. When I went back to Cairo – I wasn't allowed back for seven years after Suez – he was waiting at the airport for me and the first thing he said was: "I've got your music, I've got your music." I didn't know what he meant – but he'd gone and pinched this thing and hidden it in the house for when I came back.'

There was also a servant who looked after Miss Sale's father and adored him. 'Towards the end of his time there they had student revolts, and one or two bombs were flung about. He wouldn't leave my father and he insisted on sitting beside him wherever he went: "If you go I go." I heard that after Suez he couldn't stick it any longer and he just walked into the river and was never seen again. The Upper Egyptians were terribly loyal.'

The setting of the Sales' house made it a wonderful spot for a child growing up. 'Right in front of the house was the Nile, which in flood time was a mile wide, with sand hills opposite. It was the most beautiful spot, very green with jacaranda and oleanders all round us and bougainvillaea everywhere. It was irrigated by the Nile water. It never rained – the water was brought up in a thing called a *shadoof* – a pole with a bucket on the end of it. The gardeners used to go out and pull this thing up and down, and there was a ditch which you let water into to flood various parts of the flower beds, and this made it very green.'

Miss Sale remembers spending most of her spare time as a child 'with the animals – I had a donkey and my parents had horses. Occasionally another child came to stay. We were never bored. We were very strictly brought up. If you were taken anywhere by your parents you were thrilled to death and you never asked for things. It was a very happy life, a life free of violence or animosity of any kind.'

Valerie Sale's father held the title of British Consul General of Upper Egypt, so the Union Jack flew from the roof of the family house. 'Being the consulate the most extraordinary people would walk in, always very interesting because they were walking through Africa or something. You never knew who would come in. We hardly ever had a meal alone; whoever came in in the evening was automatically asked to stay on to supper. Sometimes we used to have fancy-dress dances. We had a very big veranda and we used to turn it into a jungle or ship's deck or something, spending a few days tenting it all in. They had wonderful tents in Egypt, so we always had parties in the garden.'

The house had five bedrooms upstairs, and three rooms down-stairs. There was an awning on the roof where the family would sleep during the hot months. 'It got too hot to stay in the summer, so we left around April–May and went to Alexandria on the coast. The cotton business closed down and everyone left.'

As far as education was concerned, Miss Sale 'had an English governess who came and stayed with us. I had a wonderful Greek nanny. With all the house staff you felt like one big family; but one was never looked after by them, it was always the Greek nanny and then the governess. Then I went to a tiny prep school in Alexandria before coming to England, where I stayed for the next four years.'

The journey to England was always by ship. 'You travelled with an enormous amount of luggage. There were plenty of porters, and you had a whale of a time on the boat. It was a week from Alexandria to Venice, and then we'd get on the Orient Express through to Dover or else go to Marseilles. But it was a regular thing that everybody did in the summer; or we spent the summer in Alexandria, which was wonderful because of all the sailing and fishing.'

Alexandria between the wars, by all accounts, offered a relaxed and easy lifestyle to the foreign community. Gabriella Barker, who organized concert parties for the forces, described in her autobiography *Desert Angels* the social scene in the city as 'luxurious, gay and charming'. Cherie Conner came to a similar conclusion. Her father was in the military and was sent to Alexandria in the 1930s to set up a hospital. His family joined him in 1936. 'It was a glorious time for a girl to arrive,' Mrs Conner says. 'There were so many parties, and not much for the men to do. So they just enjoyed the beaches. Along the eleven miles of coast there were many casinos, and there were dancing possibilities every night. The tango and the rumba became my passions. Sometimes we went to parties at one of the yacht clubs around the harbour. But the Royal Navy had the most terrific affairs on board ship. You'd go out in a little motor boat and all the ships would be lit up – a fantastic sight. Once there was a party on an aircraft carrier for three thousand people. It was a very glamorous time.'

For an attractive, single girl, there was also a lot of attention from the men. One boyfriend was in the air force and Mrs Conner says he used to fly his plane over her house. 'There were lots of heartbreaks, lots of glamour – it was a very exciting and romantic time.'

Cherie Conner stayed on in Alexandria after her parents left, living in the house of friends of the family. They had a servant who took upon himself the role of guardian of the family's morals. 'Bassiouni had a great sense of what was right and what was wrong in life, and felt it was his duty to see that the family and the guests went the right way. The most amusing thing was that as a Muslim he didn't approve of wine, so never put it on the table. The father of the family would bang on the table and say: "*Bassiouni, the wine!*" And not until the father shouted would Bassiouni bring the wine. He was their guardian angel.'

In general, contact between the British and the Egyptians extended little beyond formal relationships of one kind or another, especially with servants. 'The trouble was,' Hugh Holmes says, 'that all our institutions – our clubs and meeting places – were our own. The British and the Egyptians seldom asked each other to their houses, unless they were like my father – senior British officials asked other senior Egyptians who usually spoke good English or French.'

The British army, which had a considerable presence in Egypt even before the Second World War, tended to remain as isolated from Egyptian life as any other group of expatriates. 'Most of us were stationed in Cairo,' Mr Holmes says. 'We had a marvellous time there, but we lived entirely independently in a very large cantonment just outside the capital. There was another battalion in the old Citadel, another in Kasr el-Nil barracks. But our life was made up of socializing and recreation when we weren't soldiering – particularly playing polo. There was a marvellous club in Cairo, the Gezira. The Egyptians kept the place organized, but as far as I can remember there were no Egyptian members. The club had three or four polo grounds, and we all played almost every afternoon, and we all had our own ponies. The polo was based on regiments, and all the teams were British. There were one or two civilian teams supported by better- off people who could afford to keep ponies.'

When the polo was over for the day, there was still plenty for the British army officers to look forward to before bed. 'In the evenings there would be cocktail parties and nightclubs. It was quite a life. How we did it I don't know, because our pay in those days was ten shillings a day. None of us will ever forget that period.'

At weekends the British officers would 'go to the Suez Canal and to other parts of Egypt, taking our girlfriends with us. On the whole we had a pretty good time. Before the war, both in India and in Egypt, there was something called the fishing fleet. This consisted of second-year or third-year débutantes in London; and if the "debs" hadn't made the grade they were organized by their parents and aunts and people to go to India and Egypt. They were great girls, most of them – they gave us a lot of fun, and that. But there was a golden rule amongst all of us soldiers: never, never get involved with any of those girls unless you eventually could get a chance to see them on their own ground in England. Some didn't wait for that and they regretted it. Anyway that's where we got our girls from. And of course there were marvellous cabaret girls. Some of the cabarets run in very respectable hotels had a series of, I suppose one would call them, call-girls – Greeks and so on. We became great personal friends of theirs. And I often regret that we've never been able to see them since. One or two of them did actually get married to British officers. But the Continental in Cairo and the Excelsior in Alexandria were absolutely famous. And we had a lot of fun.'

In this atmosphere of fun few of the British in Egypt can have paid much attention to the continuing demand of Egyptian nationalists for the ending of British domination of the country's affairs. The biggest outpouring of nationalist and anti-British feeling had come in 1919. Then, as C.S. Jarvis, a senior administrator in Egypt, remarked in *Desert and Delta*, 'the whole of Egypt blazed up into open revolt against the British'. Perversely, from the Egyptians' point of view, the outbreak of violence was taken by British administrators as evidence that the people were ill-prepared to run their own affairs, rather than as a sign of growing popular determination to throw off the foreign yoke. Lord Cromer, at the turn of the century, had doubted the ability of the Egyptians to govern themselves. In 1938, C.S. Jarvis, recalling the 1919 uprising, was writing: 'These incidents happened only nineteen years ago and there is not the slightest reason why they should not happen again. Who could blame Great Britain, therefore, if she adopted the very reasonable attitude of refusing to believe that there were any immediate signs of Egypt being able to govern herself successfully or, what is more important, of being able to protect the very large number of foreigners who own businesses in the Nile Valley.'

So, in the interwar years, the British – in the form of the High Commissioner and later of the Ambassador in Cairo – remained the power behind the throne. In the 1920s, one High Commissioner in particular, Lord Lloyd, had a reputation of wielding authoritarian power. Mr Holmes tells the story of two of Lord Lloyd's ADCs standing in a doorway, unaware that their boss was in earshot. 'Where's God?' one asked. 'I don't know,' replied the other. Lord Lloyd walked up and said: 'God's here, and you're both sacked.' Lord Lloyd, who arrived in Cairo in 1925 having previously served in India, made it his task to re-establish the standard of dignity and respect which he felt befitted the status of British High Commissioner and which he felt had been allowed to slip by previous incumbents.

At the same time, his wife Blanche was determined to raise standards in the Residency. No doubt with memories of the luxury of official accommodation in India still fresh in her mind she was shocked by what she regarded as the tawdriness of the furnishings. The whole house, she wrote, was 'bleak and desolate to a very marked degree ... the hall is carpeted with vivid mustard-coloured squares and hung with faded nondescript velveteen curtains edged with little woolly balls. The big drawing-room gives a general impression of the Royal waiting-room at St Pancras on a large scale, and is full of various ill-assorted furniture ... sofas and armchairs covered with very ordinary flowered chintz suitable for a Vicarage.' Her husband's room was 'worse still: it has in the middle a common yellow deal office table ...'

Despite what the Lloyds regarded as the appallingly inadequate accommodation, they began the task of entertaining the large body of British civil servants still employed in Egypt. The process of replacing British employees with Egyptians was under way, however, and by the end of the thirties the number of Britons holding top jobs in the Egyptian government and administration had been reduced considerably. In the words of C.S. Jarvis, 'during the years between 1927 and 1936 it was discovered that the country could be run with only a sprinkling of British officials in place of the thousand odd who had previously managed the affairs of the country'. An anonymously written preface, published in 1929, to *The Leisure of an Egyptian Official* by Lord Edward Cecil, says that 'the state of Egyptian society described here has already passed away. The patient and incorruptible English Civil Servants have made way for native Ministers and others ...' The Egyptian people 'were brought out of squalor and oppression to prosperity by [Lord Edward Cecil] and others like him who wholeheartedly gave their lives and the best that was in them to the work of regenerating Egypt'. That they gave of their best may not be open to doubt; but the boast that British civil servants brought prosperity to the Egyptian people is blatantly untrue.

It is human nature to resent having one's job taken from one and given to someone whom one regards as inferior. This may account for the uncharitably patronizing tone of Mr Jarvis, writing in *Desert and Delta*, when he implies that the withdrawal of Britons from positions of responsibility invariably meant a lowering of the standards of integrity within the various departments. He quotes several examples of corrupt practices creeping in, including one concerning the annual school examinations. One summer there was a 'quite phenomenal return of successful candidates', including some of the dullest students. 'All might have been well, and the year 1934 would have gone down to posterity as a vintage year for youthful Egyptian brains, but unfortunately a small minority of students, who had been unable to obtain or who had been unwilling to pay the market price for an advance copy of the examination papers, began to complain and the whole scandal came to light. The only people who suffered on this occasion were the unfortunate British schoolmasters, who had their leave curtailed by one month to enable them to preside at a second series of examinations.'

One of the departments which remained in British hands was that of the Cairo City Police. The Commandant was Sir Thomas Russell, known as Russell Pasha. 'I imagine that every inhabitant of Cairo knows him at least by sight and has something more than a healthy respect for him,' Mr Jarvis wrote in 1938. 'They must entertain for him a feeling approaching affection, for during the all-too-frequent rioting in the capital the commonest sight one sees is Russell riding on a conspicuous white horse with a totally inadequate escort, or driving about town in an open car. He has undoubtedly given the rioters and malcontents of Cairo every conceivable opportunity to assassinate him, and his action has not been dictated by bravado; the point is that if a dangerous Oriental mob allows a most conspicuous six-foot police officer to ride or walk through them unharmed they have unconsciously let the wind out of their sails for the time being, and it is very difficult to work up again that state of blind fury that was driving them to stone and assault the police.'

The paradox of Anglo-Egyptian contact during all this period – as in contact between the British and the Arabs elsewhere at different periods – is that despite the general mood of hostility which frequently descended upon Cairo such personal relationships as existed between the two communities were unaffected. The Arabs have a capacity to make and keep a clear distinction between personal and public attitudes. As much as the servants of the Sale family, quoted earlier in this chapter, remained loyal and devoted, so the Egyptian colleagues of Judge Holmes, the father of Mr Holmes, remained friends with him. 'On the whole, in my experience,' Mr Holmes says, 'there was a lot of affection between the top British officials and their top Egyptian opposite numbers. My father had enormous integrity, and that was why, I believe, he was entirely accepted and almost everything he did was considered absolutely all right. A lot of his Egyptian opposite numbers were very devoted to him. I have three silver candlesticks on my dining-room table today which were presented to him by his Egyptian colleagues, inscribed to their "beloved and great friend"; and I have no reason to believe that that wasn't genuine. My father was pensioned by the Egyptian government, and what always impressed me was that right through the worst relationships when we had the Suez affair and all the British and European properties were sequestrated and we were basically at war with them – despite all this, not one day did he not get his pension from Egypt. They were absolutely honourable in that respect'.

But mutual affection and respect among senior officials was not sufficient in itself to prevent the gradual deterioration in Anglo-Egyptian relations. On the surface, much had changed. In 1922 an agreement between the two countries had been reached, stating that 'the British protectorate over Egypt is terminated, and Egypt is declared to be an independent sovereign state'. However, four sub-clauses retained for Britain a number of rights relating to communications and defence. For Egypt the agreement represented only nominal independence and went in no way far enough to satisfy the demands of the nationalists. In 1936, an Anglo-Egyptian Treaty was signed, formally ending the British military occupation of Egypt. Once again, though, there were strings attached. The agreement stated that British troops would not leave the country, but be withdrawn gradually to the Suez Canal Zone and Sinai. British military aircraft also retained the right to fly through Egyptian airspace. Even more important from Britain's point of view was the right to reoccupy Egypt and have full use of ports and other facilities in the event of war breaking out.

As the Second World War approached, the rioting and the clamour of the Egyptian people for full independence from Britain increased. When war was declared in September 1939 Britain revoked the clause in the 1936 Treaty relating to wartime reoccupation, and the focus in Egypt as elsewhere shifted from domestic to international matters. The intensity of the demand for full sovereignty from Britain did not diminish; but with Egypt rapidly being turned into a garrison for the Allies, the British had no time or inclination to address the question.

9

CAIRO DANCED

'That first night in from the desert I made a quick round of the bars. The terraces were crowded far into the crisp moonlit night; dance bands played, roses bloomed, laughter still ruled. Out there whence I had flown there was the terrifying rumbling and squeaking of tanks manoeuvring at night, the pinging bark of their guns. Here the only percussion came from the gourds and drums of conga orchestras. Cairo danced.'

These words were written by Alaric Jacob, a news correspondent in Egypt, describing the atmosphere in Cairo in June 1942, as the Axis armies advanced on Alexandria.

Egypt, officially neutral despite the enormous British military presence on its soil, had become part of the theatre of the Second World War in June 1940 when Italy threw in its lot with Germany. In September, Italian forces crossed into Egypt from neighbouring Libya, and confronted the Allies. The incursion was brief. By the end of 1940 all Italian forces had been driven out. But in April the following year, with German reinforcement, there was another incursion towards Alexandria, and the city began to be bombed.

The Egyptians had to take seriously the possibility of an Axis victory. Many senior officials (including the Chief of Staff) felt that the best course of action was to abandon the stance of neutrality and support the Axis powers as a way of getting rid of the British. Others, King Farouk among them, believed that Egypt should assert its neutrality more forcefully. The issue contributed to a severe crisis in Anglo-Egyptian relations, and more particularly in relations between King Farouk and the British Ambassador, Sir Miles Lampson (later Lord Killearn). Their relationship had never been comfortable. The King, in the words of Peter Mansfield in *The British in Egypt*, 'lacked the courage and strength of character to choose a position on which to stand his ground against Lampson. Instead he found ways of provoking and irritating the British ambassador on minor matters such as by keeping him waiting for appointments. Lampson took to making satirical remarks on social occasions about the king which were invariably relayed to the palace.'

Internal political developments in January 1942 brought the crisis to a head. The resignation of the Egyptian prime minister presented an opportunity, Sir Miles Lampson concluded, to install a government led by Nahas Pasha which, he believed, would work in the interests of the Allies and deal forcefully with pro-Axis sympathizers in Egypt. As Mr Mansfield has written, 'Rommel was advancing in Cyrenaica and the cry of "Long Live Rommel" was being heard in the streets of Cairo; there was a rumour that a suite had already been booked in his name at Shepheard's Hotel.'

King Farouk refused to bow to British pressure, provoking the anger of Sir Miles, who sent an ultimatum to the palace: appoint Nahas Pasha or abdicate. On 4 February 1942, with the King continuing to stand his ground, Sir Miles ordered the British army to surround the royal palace while he personally confronted the Egyptian monarch. In his diaries he recorded the report of the incident which he sent to the Foreign Office. 'At 9pm I arrived at the Palace accompanied by General Stone and an impressive display of specially picked stalwart military officers armed to the teeth. On the way we passed through lines of military transport looming up through the darkened streets on their way to take up positions around the Palace. I could see by the startled expression of the Court Chamberlains who received me at the entrance that this imposing arrival registered an immediate preliminary effect. Whilst we waited upstairs I could hear the rumble of tanks and armoured cars taking up their positions round the Palace.' Sir Miles handed King Farouk the text of the letter of abdication, 'saying he must sign it at once or I should have something else and more unpleasant with which to confront him'. The King backed down and 'with considerable emotion' agreed to summon Nahas Pasha, the man Britain wanted to be the next prime minister of Egypt. As Sir Miles left the palace, he reported to his Foreign Office chiefs with – surely – excessive glee and an unwarranted degree of arrogant condescension, that the Court Chamberlains filling the corridors resembled 'a crowd of scared hens'. This outrageous act of high-handed diplomacy helped to trigger the upheaval in Egypt ten years later which saw the overthrowing of the monarchy and the removal, finally, of British influence in the country.

But in February 1942, with Nahas Pasha installed as prime minister, British attention turned once again to the deserts of Libya and Egypt, where the Axis forces were enjoying success. One crisis had passed; but a large and potentially much more serious one loomed, with the prospect of a battle to defend Egypt.

These were clearly very unsettling times. News from the war front was bad, and the domestic political scene in Egypt was unsettled. Was Alaric Jacob exaggerating, then, when he spoke of there being a party atmosphere in the capital in the summer of 1942? Was it really possible that 'Cairo danced' while Egypt was gripped both by political tension and the imminent threat of an Allied defeat in the Libyan and Egyptian desert? I asked Cherry Ballantine, who lived in Cairo during the war. 'Yes,' she replied, 'we danced. We danced with the people who were coming back from the desert and who were very keen to do so. I don't think it was insensitive, I think it was a good thing in fact. Lady Wavell [wife of General Wavell, the commander of British forces] started dances at the Gezira Club called the Lonely Officers' Balls – an unfortunate name. They were for officers who hadn't got any friends or relations; and we all used to be rounded up to attend and they were very good fun.'

Even Freya Stark, committed to the cause of British propaganda and the goal of winning the hearts of the Arabs to the Allied cause, was touched by the frivolity of the mood in the Egyptian capital. She wrote with some warmth in *Dust in the Lion's Paw* that 'no one can forget the gaiety and glitter of Cairo as the desert war went on'.

Pamela Hore-Ruthven (now Pamela Cooper) worked with Freya Stark in Cairo and remembers well the atmosphere in Cairo during this period. Mrs Hore-Ruthven arrived with her husband, Pat, at the start of the war. She went home to Ireland to give birth to her first son, whom she left aged three months to return to Cairo. 'I was excited at getting back, but depressed at leaving my child. I flew back on a flying-boat. We stopped at Lisbon. We had to keep coming down – it was too extraordinary, rock-rock-rock, and the little ladder to get you into a boat.'

In Cairo, Pamela Cooper remembers, 'it was tremendous fun. We had a wonderful time every night; it was dancing and parties and so on, dancing on the roof of the Continental and Shepheard's Hotel, and a lot of private parties. I remember the music, tunes like "Begin the Beguine", "Smoke Gets in Your Eyes", "My Heart Belongs to Daddy", "Cheek to Cheek". Then there were all those blades like Peter Sterling – his flat where all the boys from the desert came. Pat was in and out of Cairo. He wasn't a great dancer. The first time I met him he was dancing with a cushion at Cambridge.'

One of the great centres of fashionable socializing was the home of Momo Marriott, wife of Major-General Sir John Marriott. Pamela Cooper remembers Sir John as a military hero. ('He'd conquered a mountain in Eritrea with a pistol, or something. He was a lovely little man.') Momo, on the other hand, was the life and soul of the party. 'She kept a salon where anyone amusing or of any importance used to go for dinner. It was where all the heroes from the desert used to hang out. She kept a sort of open house. Really Cairo in those days was Momo's house and her little general of a husband appeared occasionally from the desert or Eritrea or somewhere. I brought Pat there one day when he came back from the desert. He was absolutely fantastic, like a wild gypsy, dark with curly black hair and a huge nose, looking very lean and thin. I heard Momo say: "Darling, I hope I see you incessantly"; and Pat went all down the drive outside Momo's house in the lovely garden, doing the Irish jig and singing: "Momo is going to see me incessantly, Momo is going to see me incessantly." And this was a sort of song among the desert boys. I think there were awful goings on, but they were great fun.'

Great fun especially, perhaps, for beautiful young women. Alaric Jacob pointed out, for example, that 'something like two or three hundred European women had personally at their beck and call anywhere between 30,000 and 40,000 men ... It would be foolish and impossible to enumerate all the Cairene beauties of the period – a period which has now passed into history, for the gaiety and attraction of Cairo at this time depended absolutely upon the continuance of the war in the desert just as the gaiety of the Brussels ball on the eve of Waterloo depended on the bloody events that were to ensue. For Cairo well knew its own naughtiness – knew that the only justification for such unethical behaviour in the midst of a bloody war was the proximity of the war itself.'

In Cairo, unlike in Alexandria, the war was a very distant phenomenon which seldom touched even the edges of life in the capital. Mr Jacob writes of dining on the roof of the Continental. 'An alert sounded during dinner and searchlights swept the sky but so feeble were their thrusts in the light of a great orange moon that they could not have picked out any raiders had any shown up, and none did.' Mr Jacob then 'danced in the garden at Shepheard's', before taking in 'the cabaret at Madame Badia's with its bevies of Tummy Dancers'.

Another British correspondent, James Lansdale Hodson, was struck by the oriental dancing. In *War in the Sun* he saw 'one of those Eastern women dancers whose method is to move slowly round the arena, smiling, but contorting herself, as though in ecstasy of desire, or pain, or both. My companion remarked: "It's said of her that her navel winks." She was quite pretty and appeared to enjoy herself.' Mr Hodson, like Mr Jacob, did not miss the irony of such a carefree life being lived in Cairo, so near to the battlefront. 'A few hundred miles from here troops are grilling in the desert and being killed. This night on the restaurant roof might be Paris or some other fashionable capital in peace.'

Cairo was colourful by day and night, 'full of gaudy young officers of fancy regiments on leave. They, and some of the Dominion troops, whose hobby was detaching the gharry horses from their shafts and running races around the Metropolitan Hotel at one o'clock in the morning, were responsible for giving the town a "playboy" atmosphere which it did not truly deserve.'

The party atmosphere concealed a capital of jangling nerves. According to Richard Dimbleby, in *The Frontiers are Green*, it was a city 'full of rumour and anxiety'. Most of those Britons left in Cairo had jobs connected directly or indirectly with the war effort. But because of their ease of living, compared with the rigours of the battle in the desert, they were the object of ribaldry and scorn from the desert troops. They were branded with such names as the Gabardine Swine, the Long-Range Groppi Group (named after Groppi's, a fashionable tea house in Cairo), Groppi's Horse, or the Gezira Hussars.

The Gezira Club continued during the war, as it was in pre-war days, to be one of the main centres of expatriate life. It was one of the first things that Mr Jacob noticed on his arrival in the Egyptian capital, as his flying-boat descended towards the Nile. 'Here beneath us,' he noted, 'is Cairo, the largest city in Africa – a race-course, what looks like a country-club with people splashing in a swimming-pool.' As had been the case before the outbreak of war, the Gezira Club was a preserve for the Cairo élite. Cherry Ballantine says the club was the centre for 'a lot of sport, very good tennis, swimming and polo. There were some Egyptian members, but I didn't know any personally. It was almost exclusively British during the war.'

The British passion for sport in Egypt bemused a French war correspondent, Eve Curie. In *Journey Among Warriors* she described a journey from Cairo to the Suez Canal. 'We passed a peculiar golf course with no "greens", no grass: a "sand golf", really. Captain Plevins, whom everybody called "Jupiter", remarked on this occasion that all Englishmen were mad: "only mad people would think of having a golf course in the sand". He repeated, with evident satisfaction: "We are a crazy people," and tried to prove it by driving faster still on the straight, monotonous road.'

The golf course and the Gezira Club were as inaccessible for most of the British troops in Egypt as they were for the Egyptians. The inhabitants of Cairo became observers as their city was taken over by thousands of foreigners, most of whom had almost certainly never before travelled beyond the shores of Britain. The soldiers' experience of the Middle East differed radically from that of most other Britons this century. The majority went through choice; they also had the luxury of time and could immerse themselves slowly in the region – as much or as little as they wanted. By contrast, during the war thousands of British troops were dipped in and out without choice or ceremony. It was a searing experience, fixing images of the Arab world in their minds which were often as sharp as they were, inevitably, superficial.

For the troops, Cairo was a centre for rest and recreation. For them, there was no invitation to Momo's dinner table. William Stannard, of the Royal Northumberland Fusiliers, told me that the British army did not lay on entertainment, so the majority of soldiers went to cabarets and beer bars. 'The main source of amusement was drinking in the cabarets and in the bars. In Cairo there was a street of ill-repute which was called the Birka, and there one could go and indulge for a matter of ten piastres, which was the equivalent of two bob in those days, and that was it. In Alexandria there wasn't such a place, but there was a notorious place called Beera Street – Beer Street; not that there were any brothels there. I don't remember any brothels in Alexandria, so you had to go further afield for your amusement if you wanted it. But quite a lot of chaps were satisfied just to go into the cabarets and bars, drink what they could hold or afford and wend their way back to barracks for a good kip.'

There was also the chance of meeting women at dances. 'There were one or two selected places where you could go. In Cairo we had a place called Spiro's where one or two of us who were very keen on dancing used to eventually make our way. We went there and conducted ourselves correctly for the very simple reason that if we didn't, we wouldn't get any girls to dance with. Every young girl was chaperoned; the chaperon would come across and ask you in pidgin English, or sometimes in very excellent English: "Would you care to dance with my protégée?" So we danced. It was great fun, really.'

Similar reminiscences of nights out in Cairo came from another British soldier of the day, Edward Phelps. 'You'd no sooner go into a club or cabaret than you'd have a beautiful young lady sitting next to you. But I remember it was all very expensive. The Egyptians were friendly, but you weren't allowed to talk to the bints – otherwise you'd get a dagger in your back. They'd tell you to hurry up and get away.'

Alexandria was the other major centre where British troops were sent for rest and recreation. Peter Lewis, who arrived in Egypt in May 1942 with the Durham Light Infantry, says that 'everybody liked Alexandria; the beaches were nice. It was different to Cairo, which was a bit smelly. If you went on a train from Alex to Cairo, you could smell Cairo as you approached; coming the other way you could smell the sea breezes.' In the evenings, the British troops in Alexandria had their favourite bars. 'We went to one on the sea front. We used to use the Cecil Hotel quite a lot. There wasn't really anything else to do. You could go to the cinema – we sometimes went in the afternoon because it was nice and cool. They had a form of air-conditioning. It was so hot outside.'

Mr Lewis and his comrades met Egyptians in Alexandria only occasionally – 'sometimes in the nightclubs – one or two. But the clubs were expensive. They had dancers – belly dancers and all that.'

When the bars and clubs closed the British troops, as they made their way by taxi back to barracks, would sometimes become victims of robberies. Mr Lewis says the soldiers learned to take precautions to prevent this happening. 'On several occasions the taxis drove through the rough parts of Alexandria and the occupants were jumped – the taxi would stop and several Arabs would come rushing out and take away whatever they wanted to take. So eventually we actually had to take our revolvers out and stick them in the bloke's neck and say:

"You're going to Sid Bish – the rest camp – and you're not stopping anywhere." And that was all right. We never knocked anybody about, but having heard of people being jumped it seemed only sensible to issue a threat without harming them in any way.'

Another danger faced by civilians as much as by the military in Alexandria came from German spies. They were trying to undermine the morale of the population, as much as to assess the strength and the strategy of the Allied forces, at a time when the German army was pushing eastwards towards Alexandria. Gabriella Barker ran a concert party for the troops. In her book *Desert Angels* she described how, in June 1942, one morning after the city had been bombed by the Germans, the telephone rang.

'A very English-speaking voice said: "Is that you, Gabriella?"

"Yes," I said. "Who are you?"

"I am Rex. I just want to tell you that the enemy will be in Alexandria very soon. You'd better get out."'

Mrs Barker remembered being confused. She had met many men during the war, and she racked her brain trying to think who Rex might be. While the caller waited, Mrs Barker called her husband to the phone.

'"Cyril, old boy," the voice said, "the game is up."' The caller would not say where he was, only that it was a trunk call. 'My husband knew at once,' Mrs Barker wrote, 'that it was a lie, as in Egypt the trunk calls have a special ring.'

Another fifth columnist was unmasked at around the same time in a tense confrontation with a young British lady, Valerie Sale. 'I was in Upper Egypt once, at home, just before the Battle of El Alamein. Our head *sufragi* came in and said: "There's an American soldier to see your father [the British Consul for the region]." My father was out, so I went and I saw him standing at the bottom of the stairs in khaki with a big revolver. He had his hands on his hips and spoke with a very American voice. He said his company had gone into the Sudan and he'd missed the last convoy and he wanted permission from my father to cross the frontier. Then he said: "I haven't had anything to eat or drink for forty-eight hours." So I offered him and he refused; and I thought: If you hadn't had anything to eat or drink for forty-eight hours, you don't refuse a drink or a sandwich. And as he was talking I realized that his American accent was disappearing. We looked at each other, and he knew that I knew that he wasn't

American, he was a German. I wondered how the hell I could lock him up. I tried to get him into the loo and he wouldn't go to the loo, and I tried to get him into the study, and I thought I could lock him in there. Eventually he sensed that I'd realized he was a bit dodgy and he said he must go. I said I'd give him a letter to give to someone who would give him the right papers to cross the frontier. He waited while I wrote a letter which was total gobbledegook and I gave it to him. I told him where to go, and as soon as he left I rang the military police and they caught him. It turned out that they had dropped German spies in the desert to try and cause dissension among the Arabs, to tell them that the war was over and the British were finished and the Germans were coming, and so on.'

Another tactic of fifth columnists was to try to distort news coming from the battlefront, as Richard Dimbleby noticed. 'In defeat, the rumours exaggerated grossly the extent of the enemy's success. In victory they exaggerated the extent of British progress, so that when we announced the capture of Derna, the people would say: "Only Derna? We heard the British were in Benghazi."'

In Alexandria, amid all the rumours, Miss Sale remembers that as the German advance into Egypt continued, the inhabitants of the city could hear the guns from Alamein night after night. Tension grew. 'Alexandria was a very cosmopolitan city with lots of Greeks and Italians – all the Mediterranean people; so you never knew who was for and who was against. During the end period when the Alamein fighting was getting too close to be funny, a wonderful cake shop in Alexandria made two cakes, one which said "Viva Mussolini" on the top, and the other "Long live Montgomery". These cakes were put up and down in the window as the battle raged.'

On one occasion it seemed that the Germans had reached the city. 'Over the tannoy where I was working one night, it said that if we heard the air-raid siren followed by another air-raid siren and no all-clear it would mean that the Germans had come into Alexandria, and those that could would go out street-fighting and others would just batten down in the houses. That night we heard one siren about 2a.m., followed by another; and we thought: that's it. We went on to the balcony and there was total silence. Then we heard some motorbikes and we were quite convinced they'd come in. We didn't discover until about three or four hours later that it was a try-out, to see who would go and help the British and who wouldn't. But it was a bit too near the truth to be funny.'

During this period of tension and uncertainty many foreigners packed up their possessions and moved out of Alexandria – some left Egypt altogether. The Arab population, though, remained, knowing that the outcome of the battles in North Africa either way would mean the continuation of foreign domination. Miss Sale recounts one incident which demonstrates well the fatalism of the Arabs, which tends to strike foreigners in the region so forcefully. 'At that time in Alexandria during the war we were being bombed most nights. On one occasion a land-mine came down in the middle of the road and it didn't blow up. The next-door gardener sat on it saying: "Keep away, keep away, this is a live bomb", until the army came and defused it. He was totally fatalistic.'

British troops in the convoys heading for the front line may similarly have felt that their fate lay in the hands of others. John Lewis joined the war there in May 1942 on the Gazala line in Libya, 350 miles west of Alexandria. 'We travelled by train and then by three-ton lorries or fifteen-hundredweight trucks into the desert. It was a mixture of rough going and very flat land, but all of it completely away from anything or anybody. Miles and miles of desert. As we went along we'd come across a knocked-out German tank, or maybe a knocked-out English tank or a few little white crosses where somebody had been killed. That was a little bit sobering. As you got a bit nearer to it you began to realize that you were going towards something that could be fairly unpleasant.'

Mr Lewis and his comrades saw plenty of action. 'The Gazala line was made up of a box for three battalions. They occupied this box which was surrounded by minefields and everything, but everything was below ground level. Trucks, lorries, even three-tonners; because being Durham miners they were able to dig pretty deep. Before the front line you went via a transit camp some miles back in the vicinity of the gun lines. They made us very welcome. We had a "bedroom" hewn out of the sand. It was big enough to have a single bed in it, chair, bedside table, holes cut in the wall to put things like books. Breakfast of eggs and bacon and so on was laid on – this was where the quartermaster was – that was before we went on to our respective battalions.'

This ability to create a different world under the sand was also remarked on by Gabriella Barker. She had arrived with her troupe at Mersa Matruh for a concert party. 'When we got underground it was incredible; just like fairyland. There was a band and champagne, nice lights, armchairs, a bar and lots and lots of charming men to receive us.'

While Mrs Barker was impressed by the charm of the British military, another female observer, a Frenchwoman, was struck by their politeness in the desert campaign – even though living conditions were hard. Eve Curie wrote in *Journey Among Warriors* about how the exchange of goods was an important part of daily life for soldiers in the desert. 'Every time we met somebody in the sand there was an immediate exchange of goods: water for food, army biscuits for petrol, or an extra tyre for a few rations of bully beef. Among those dusty primitive looking people the eternal British politeness survived. Such barterings took place with lots of "Are you quite sure you can spare this?", "Thank you, indeed, very much", "This is most kind of you", and wishes of good luck.'

Bartering and concert parties provided only a brief diversion from the job of soldiering, and of trying to keep body and soul together in a climate which produced wide ranges of temperature. William Stannard, like John Lewis, was on the Gazala line during 1942. He says that 'conditions in the desert were quite varied. You had to adjust to living in the desert. You had two blankets, a groundsheet and an overcoat. You needed the overcoat during the night because at times it was icy cold. You put your groundsheet down, another blanket down, and then the other blanket over the top of you – and invariably your coat on top of that. And if you were on sentry duty, which you would be for at least two hours, then you had your coat on, plus Balaclava, sweater and all sorts of warm clothing. In the front line all of you were on very meagre rations, just sufficient to sustain you; and while there might have been the odd moan or two, in general no one ever moaned about the food. When we were behind the line and had access to water, then we drank water. What the officers drank – well, it was their business. But we could only get water. On the whole we fared very well.'

A great source of sustenance, Mr Stannard says, was the ubiquitous British 'cuppa'. 'I can't remember a time when we didn't have tea and sugar, although there might have been the odd time. For the most part of life in the desert we were self-contained, which means that each truck had iron rations for four days, that's bully beef and hard tack biscuits, and tea and sugar. We used tinned milk, but we weren't fussy about that sort of thing. Wherever we stopped, wherever we were, we would always be foraging for the tea and the sugar, and we could drum it up in two minutes flat. As long as men in our regiment got a cup of tea, it was as good as a "fix", in modern-day parlance.'

On the Gazala line, part of the task of John Lewis's battalion was night patrolling to find out what progress the Italian working parties had made. 'We would travel by truck and then walk on a compass bearing; and the difficulty was finding the truck again. You had to backtrack by compass to the truck. We went by the North Star and by compass. We weren't disoriented, it was like being in a vast theatre, if you like; sometimes it was pitch-black, sometimes lighter – we were always worried about getting back to our truck.'

Eventually in June 1942, as the Axis armies closed in, the battalion was forced to retreat. 'We were not in disarray,' William Stannard remembers, 'we were a fighting unit, but we didn't have the backing of any tank strength. No tanks and no artillery, which you needed against German tanks. The fighting force that was hemmed in split into columns with the instructions to break out. Different columns were given different routes.' John Lewis and his comrades received the same order. 'It was a break-out on wheels – everything, lorries, armoured cars, Bren-gun carriers, ambulances, the lot, were all formed up and basically what we did was just burst our way through the German lines. We had quite a few casualties doing it.'

I asked Mr Lewis if they ever made contact with Arabs in the desert. 'We did see some Arabs when we were in the Gazala line. They would appear almost out of nowhere – you'd get maybe a group of ten or twelve, with a camel and that sort of thing, and they would be checked out; then they'd continue and a few days later they might come back again and then they'd go off towards the German lines; and in the same way they were let through the German lines. They weren't doing any harm to anybody but it was their desert, it wasn't our desert. The Bedouins were the ones who lived in that desert and we were just intruders as far as they were concerned. We had to search them, make sure they weren't carrying any weapons and that there weren't any Germans moving with them.'

In August 1942, with Allied reverses continuing and the German forces led by General Rommel making rapid progress, Field Marshal Alexander replaced Field Marshal Auchinleck in Middle East Command, and General Montgomery was appointed commander of the 8th Army. The fighting in the western desert was approaching its climax. The steady advance of the Axis forces had shortened the journey of British troops from Alexandria to the battlefront. John

Lewis remembers that 'Alexandria was only about an hour and half from the Alamein line, so when you'd had your leave in Alex they used to pick us all up from outside the Cecil Hotel. So you could be leaving Alex, the sea front, the sea glistening, the shops open – you could leave there at lunchtime and within an hour and a half you were going through the rear minefield gap of the Alamein line between Bofors guns on either side. You could hear the guns blasting away and it was going from one world to another.'

Mr Lewis remembers too the effect of the appointment of General Montgomery. 'He gave us back our morale, which had been dented a bit. Monty did a good job. He pulled the 8th Army together, gave them back their will to win. The whole of the Alamein line was known as the "devil's garden", it was absolutely crowded out with mines, booby-traps and trip-wires. It was a ghastly place to have to do any patrolling – one vast minefield. My company was in the south-west corner and the enemy were twelve hundred to fifteen hundred yards away; and there was a depression between us and the Italians – there were mostly Italians near us. This depression had to be patrolled every night to find out what was going on – we did twenty-two night patrols at Alamein, almost one a night. The big danger was the actual minefields. If it was moonlight you didn't let your shadow be thrown ahead of you because you couldn't see the trip-wires. It was all patrolling when we were there.' Montgomery stressed the need for good military intelligence. 'He wanted more information about what the Germans were doing than the Germans would get about what we were doing. We couldn't go out in the day – in my position at Alamein during the day no one moved out of their slit trench because they were overlooked. If you wanted to go to HQ which was over a rise, you had to wait until an Italian gun we called "Gucci" had fired and then run like hell and try and get over the top before it fired again. Food rations, water, everything was brought up at night. Chaps slept and ate in the slit trenches; they never took their clothes off, not for days on end.'

Mr Lewis recalls a contingent of Greek troops arriving at the line. 'They were absolutely mad, a rule unto themselves. They were Alexandrian Greeks and used to have food sent up from Alexandria. Our officers would be invited to marvellous meals with them and that eased tensions between us. We left them there when it was our turn to move up to the north.'

The crucial Battle of El Alamein, which began on 23 October and was the turning point of Allied fortunes in North Africa, will never be forgotten by those who took part in it. William Conner served with the Royal Irish Hussars. He describes Alamein as 'a terrific experience. It was quite a fantastic thing to see that number of tanks all suddenly going into battle. I believe there were three-quarters of a million mines spread out over the desert, a huge morass. The whole thing seemed terribly chaotic to be involved in. I remember hearing a wireless and going over to hear the news. To our amazement they were talking about a huge victory. How could this shambolic thing be a victory? We lost a lot of friends. At one point we lost fifteen tanks in about forty minutes. It was touch and go whether ours would survive, but we did.'

General Montgomery decided on 1 November that the moment had come to cut through the Axis lines and break Rommel's stranglehold. As he wrote to General Sir Alan Brooke on that day, 'I think he [Rommel] is now ripe for a real hard blow which may topple him off his perch. It is going in tonight and I am putting everything I can into it. If we succeed it will be the end of Rommel's army.' At one o'clock in the morning of 2 November the divisions drawn out of the line by Montgomery were launched at the Germans around Kidney Ridge. John Lewis was part of the assault group. 'My main memory of Alamein of that particular night was the fantastic gun barrage. It was due to go off at one o'clock in the morning. We didn't realize the number of guns that we'd got. We were on the white tapes – there was sort of plop-plop and two or three guns fired, and then the full weight of this barrage came on. It was absolutely fantastic – the whole of the night behind us was stabbed by gun flashes for three and a half hours. The whole of the time that we were advancing, once we'd crossed the tape. It was the biggest push at that time of the Second World War. What happened the next day I don't know because I got wounded just after we got to the first objective and I was taken back.'

Despite fierce German resistance and counter-attacks, the enemy's defence was broken. On 10 November, the German army was driven out of Egypt. Four days later, with Tobruk in Libya retaken, church bells were ringing in Britain to celebrate the success of the North African campaign.

Mr Lewis, meanwhile, had been taken from El Alamein 'back in the hospital train and ended up in the Fifteenth Scottish General Hospital. The whole of the entrance hall was a mass of stretchers

– the orderlies and the nurses had a hell of a job to put their feet between two stretchers to walk between people. Also, when they took us upstairs to the wards, they'd cleared the wards completely of all the chaps that were in there who were nothing to do with the Alamein attack. They cleared out the chaps with gippy tummy and the staff officers. We thought this was great, we could have the beds. But we were filthy dirty, we stank of cordite and dust and everything like that, but we were put in between beautiful clean sheets and there we were for the night. From there I went to a convalescent depot in Palestine.'

After all that happened in Egypt to Mr Lewis and hundreds of Britons like him, it is not surprising, perhaps, that his perception of the region ever since has been coloured by the memories of 1942. 'I have never wanted to go back to Egypt or anything like that,' he says candidly. In one respect the experience of British soldiers during the war was similar to that of other groups of expatriates working in the Gulf and elsewhere before and since: they were largely isolated from the local population. There was precious little opportunity for the two sides to get to know each other. Mr Lewis spoke of troops using guns to deter taxi drivers in Alexandria from robbing them and of searching Bedouins crossing the lines in the desert. Otherwise his only contact with Arabs was in a transit camp 'where the cinema was run by an Egyptian, and where a lot of Egyptians were available to launder our clothes. They were remarkably good. We called them "dhobis".'

In general, British troops only came into contact with Egyptians who were poor and uneducated – those who were prepared to do the dirty work for the foreigners. William Conner recalls that the two communities overcame the difficulties of communication by developing 'a sort of mongrel language'. Apart from the inevitable swear words, British troops picked up words like *bint* (girl), *felous* (money), *shufti* (look), and took some of them back to Britain to be incorporated into the body of British slang.

Humour was another bridge between British tommies and Egyptians. Mr Conner says there was 'a great sense of humour on both sides'. Valerie Sale, observing from the platform of civilian life in Egypt during the war, agrees. 'The Egyptians have a wonderful sense of humour. I think that's one reason they got on so well with all the British troops. Although they didn't have a common language they got on because of a shared sense of humour. And the Egyptians have a sense of the ridiculous, as the British do; whereas, many years later, they loathed the Russians – there was no rapport between them. The Egyptians love a good joke, and the humour is much the same as ours – not sarcastic, more banana skin'.

For all that the British troops and the lower-class Egyptians were able to find a means of communication, there was never a sense in which the foreigner felt anything but superior to the inhabitant of the host country. Because most of the Arabs with whom the British troops came into contact were poor and often ignorant, there was a tendency, inevitable but regrettable, to assume that this was the overwhelming characteristic of Arabs everywhere. William Conner, who got to know a wide range of Egyptians during the war and who has kept close links with Egypt ever since, believes that British troops 'got quite the wrong impression of that part of the world'. As an example he mentioned the workshops at Abbasiya where many thousands of Egyptians were employed each day. 'The British had the feeling that these people were representative of all the Egyptians, of all the Arabs. They didn't meet educated ones. There was constant ribaldry directed at the Egyptians in a totally superior way by all the troops at every opportunity.'

The Egyptians could not fail to be aware of the British attitude. Muhammad Hassanein Heikal, a leading Egyptian author and political commentator, writing more than twenty years after the end of the Second World War, made sharp comments about the presence of the British there at that time. 'About two or three million troops spent some time in Egypt but this still did not bring our two nations any closer. The ordinary soldiers mixed with the lowest elements: shoe-shiners, pimps, pickpockets, belly dancers and bartenders who formed their idea of the *Gippo*. On the other hand, officers met only the Circassian Turkish upper class, the circles connected with the royal family and centred on the Gezira Club – a cosmopolitan society isolated from the real Egypt. No British soldier ever entered an Egyptian home and our two nations never met.'

The experience of the Allied army in Egypt during the war, there can be no doubt about it, contributed to the racism towards Arabs that still exists in the West – the stereotype image of the 'filthy Arab'. Even among the British civilian population there was, more often than not, an attitude of condescension, if not contempt towards the local population. I asked Cherry Ballantine, the wife of a civilian pilot based in Cairo during the war, to characterize the British attitude to the Egyptians. 'I think honestly,' she said, 'it was rather patronizing. Looking back on it, it was insensitive and patronizing; but we saw so little of them this is more hearsay and more from reading books than anything I personally experienced because we hardly had any contact. We had servants who were wonderful people. They were very loyal, very honest and very clean. They considered themselves British; they liked working for the British.'

Mrs Ballantine remembers there being some intermarriage between the British and the Egyptians. She stumbled by chance on one instance of this. 'I had been to a tailor to have some clothes made for one of the little boys and he'd definitely cheated me. He'd taken my material, then not given me back what was left. You put up with behaviour like this a lot of the time and expected it; but eventually you got annoyed, and I thought I'd go and report this to the police. I knew it'd be no good because there was never anybody there who spoke English and my Arabic was purely kitchen. However, there was an absolutely charming Egyptian officer who spoke perfect English and whose wife was a Girton graduate. He came back and had a drink with me and said we'll now go and sort out the tailor. He told him he'd got to make two pairs of trousers for the little boys to make up for the material he'd taken.'

Mrs Ballantine's main occupation in Cairo was 'rearing children in difficult conditions. The heat was intense and we had no air-conditioning. We didn't even have ceiling fans. If you were lucky you could scrounge a table fan from the Americans out on a building project. When I was expecting my first baby the temperature went up to one hundred and twenty degrees one October. It was important that you could feed them yourself because there were no baby foods. Otherwise you had to feed them on buffalo milk, which was good if it was TB-free. We didn't have refrigerators – you had a huge zinc-lined ice-box. The ice-man used to come with a great lump of ice wrapped in a dirty old sack, and that was how you kept things cool. The other snag was that we had terrible flies – there were great piles of uncollected rubbish in open spaces, even in the good residential areas, and we used to have to put fly netting on all the windows. When we took the children out we used to put mosquito netting on their hat brims because you could get terrible eye diseases from the flies.'

Worries about personal health added to the anxieties felt by the British in Egypt as they followed progress in the war elsewhere. While

Cairo was never part of the theatre of war, it was dominated by military activity, with constant movement of troops and equipment to and from locations in the Middle East. Egyptians, still anxious to get full independence from Britain, knew there was nothing they could do while the British military had such a strong grip on the country. 'All Kinds of Equipment for British Officers and Soldiers,' declared a slogan under a British army cap in an advertisement for Alex. G. Avierino & Bros. published in *The Egyptian Who's Who* of 1944. Civilian influence was still considerable, too. A glance at the *Who's Who* shows a Mr James Baxter holding the post of Economic Councillor in the Finance Ministry. The Honorary Treasurer of the Royal Society for the Prevention of Cruelty to Animals in Egypt (founded 1894) was G. Sims Marshall Esq., and its members included T.W. Fitzpatrick Pasha. Captain E.C. Pilley was Secretary of the Gezira Club. There were also many British names among the lists of lawyers, chartered accountants and other prominent professions. Places of entertainment in the city included the Roxy Palace, the Royal and the Metropole cinemas.

On the surface, it might have seemed as though Britain had a secure hold on Egypt. But the reality was different. One event above all others during the Second World War – the humiliation of King Farouk and the country he nominally ruled by Sir Miles Lampson – had undermined any chance Britain might have had of staying in the country much beyond the end of the war. On hearing about the Lampson affair and how the army had been given no opportunity to defend the King, two young officers, General Neguib and Lieutenant Abdul Nasser, were enraged. Neguib wrote to the King, saying he was ashamed to wear his military uniform and wanted to resign. Nasser told a friend that he had 'almost exploded with rage', adding that army officers were now speaking of 'sacrificing their lives for their honour' at Lampson's behaviour. Neguib and Nasser never forgot the incident involving the British High Commissioner and the King, even after they had led the successful military coup of 1952 which swept the monarch aside.

10

CHANGING OF THE GUARD

Cairo in the summer of 1945, with the war in Europe at an end, had a morning-after-the-party feel to it. The heady days of gaiety which provided a distraction from the tension of the North Africa campaign were long gone. The Egyptian capital that summer was still teeming with Allied soldiers who were frustrated at being forced to wait to get home. The general shortage of air and sea transport was made worse for the troops stuck in the Middle East by the approaching end to the war in Japan. Many planes and ships were being diverted there to be ready to bring home released prisoners of war.

Among the frustrated soldiers were groups of civilians. My parents and my two brothers and my sister arrived in Cairo from Tehran that summer en route to England. My parents were heading for their first home leave for seven and a half years, during which time in Iran their three children had been born. They established themselves in the Continental Hotel, which was showing serious signs of wear and tear after six years of heavy and sustained custom during the war. 'It was a second-rate hotel by then,' my mother says. 'It was very badly run. In the five weeks we were there they never changed the sheets; and the room was full of flies – there were no screens on the windows. The food was terrible, there was nothing fresh. When we finally left Cairo we all had boils from unhealthy eating.'

Each morning my family would pack their cases, go to the military transport office in the city, be weighed (people as well as luggage) in the hope of finding seats on a flight to the United Kingdom. Each day they were told that their names were not yet on the list. For the rest of the time they walked, pushing my nine-month-old sister in a pram, around the city. 'There were masses of soldiers everywhere,' my mother recalls, 'especially around the Kasr el-Nil barracks next to the Nile. They were roaming the streets with nothing to do. The

Egyptians were very friendly to us – especially because we had children with us.'

Eventually places were found for the Butt family on the *Franconia*, a liner which had been taken over by the military. 'They managed to squeeze us in. My husband slept with the troops on a hammock down below. I and the children shared a cabin with other women, which meant my sleeping on the floor. It was a military ship, there were constant cabin inspections and lifeboat drills during the night. By the time I'd woken the boys and the baby and got them all up to the deck, the drill would be over. They told me I wouldn't have much of a chance if there was a real alert.'

Not all the British and other foreigners were keen to leave Egypt. Many families had lived in the country for decades and regarded it as their home. They can have had little idea of the changes that were around the corner, even though the mood after the war was changing fast. The anti-British rhetoric of the nationalists was getting more strident; and Britain's dominance of Egypt was beginning to be threatened.

The British had arrived with guns firing at a time of trouble in 1882 and had become well before the late 1940s, in the eyes of the mass of Egyptians, unpopular and unacceptable occupiers. Whatever friendship had developed between individual Britons and Egyptians, Britain's role as occupier was making life difficult for all its citizens in Egypt. Even British teachers felt disadvantaged because of their country's status when matched against Egyptian attitudes to other Europeans. The poet and novelist D.J. Enright spent three years up to 1950 teaching at Alexandria University. In *Interplay: a Kind of Commonplace Book* he remembers how the anti-Britain mood in Egypt served to emphasize the vulnerability felt by the British, in contrast to the confidence of their French colleagues. The French saw themselves and were accepted by the Egyptians as maintaining a tradition, started at the time of the brief Napoleonic occupation at the close of the eighteenth century, of satisfying the country's intellectual appetite. Furthermore, the French were given help and encouragement which enabled the best qualified to take jobs in Egypt. On the other hand, members of the English department in Alexandria University, Mr Enright wrote, were 'underprivileged intellectually, as well as financially. (The French government topped up their people's salaries while we lived on Egyptian wages.) There is a grain of truth in the odious insinuation that whereas France sent its leading intellectuals abroad, Britain dispatched its drunks and disorderlies – or, rather, left it to them to go.'

Mr Enright describes the relationship between the British staff and the Egyptians as 'a mixed affair, rarely passionate enough to qualify you as *odi et amo*. Some things you liked, others you needed to close your eyes to. There was a degree of violence in the air, which was exciting but alarming; there was a degree of kindliness too, of tolerance which shamed but solaced. For the French, Egypt was more of a symbol, historical and artistic; perhaps symbolic of themselves, at any rate a pleasingly exotic backdrop against which to play out their intellectuality. There were "Down with Britain" days; I never heard of a "Down with France" day. We were doing a humble job made difficult by sudden strikes ("It is Down with Britain day, sir, you must stay at home") and painful by the disappearance every now and then of some indigenous youth, wild-eyed and shabby, into prison or madhouse. The French teachers, so it seemed to us, catered exclusively for luscious Syrian or Greek girls, never agitating on the streets, speaking perfect French, *à la page* with the latest Parisian trends. Our colleagues were being fervid about *Les Chemins de la Liberté* while we were being pedestrian about *Silas Marner*. I can't imagine we were engaged with the same body of students.'

A very different experience of Egyptian university life at about the same time is recounted by Sir James Craig, a retired diplomat. He attended Cairo University as a student for a year, immersing himself in Arabic language and culture. He shared a flat with four Palestinians. 'Cairo was delightful. The life we led in the students' flat was rather dreary. But I had made a pledge with myself that I wouldn't get mixed up with the expatriate community which I kept faithfully for six months. That was in the interests of learning to speak Arabic quickly. Breakfast was *ful medames*, which you bought in those days for half a piastre, a penny farthing. It was half a round of Egyptian bread with some brown beans [the staple food for the mass of the Egyptian population] inside it. We came home at half past two for lunch, which was always rice and spinach, or rice and beans, or rice and peas. And in the evening we had that warmed up. Once a week I allowed myself to go to Groppi's and have a toasted ham sandwich with a milkshake, which was my only concession to European customs. But although it was dismal it was completely fascinating; I was living a completely Arab life in this very *baladi* [indigenous, native] quarter of Cairo. Palestinian students would come round and spend Friday evenings with us and we'd talk about the Palestine problem.'

The Palestine problem, born out of the creation of Israel in May 1948, hastened the revolution in Egypt. Because of Britain's role in the establishment of the Jewish state, resentment against the presence of British troops on Egyptian soil increased – even though the troops by this time were confined to the Suez Canal zone. Also, the Egyptian army had joined with other Arab armies in the war against newly created Israel. The humiliating failure of the Arabs to defeat Israel convinced young Egyptian army officers that the fault lay at the door of the inefficient and corrupt regime, and the equally ineffective and dissolute monarch.

With the Egyptian economy getting into a deeper and deeper mess, politicians sought other ways of winning public support. In October 1951 the government abrogated the 1936 Treaty with Britain – a move which the British rejected. Next, the prime minister ordered a state of emergency, and the cutting of fresh food supplies to the British garrison in the Suez Canal Zone. On top of these measures, Egyptians working with the British military were ordered out. The British army was heavily dependent on this corps of cheap local labour; and the days of good-natured banter between troops and poor Egyptians had gone. John McGirk, a military policeman with the British force, told me what he remembered of this period. The government, Mr McGirk said, 'sent storm troopers up to kill all the Arabs employed by the British army and air force. So all those – excuse me – wogs left their employment. So we had to do everything, like the toilets – do all our own washing, while those Arabs went off.'

The British base in the Canal Zone became the target of violence perpetrated by squads encouraged by the Cairo government. Mr McGirk remembers how patrols and guard duty were increased. Also, 'all the wives and kiddies were brought into the base from Ismailiya, into the barracks. So all us lads had to make our beds on the football pitch. On the Sunday I was guarding the YMCA bridge when General Erskine [Commander-in-Chief of British troops in Egypt] came by in his big Humber car and shook my hand. The day before, an Irish-American nun had been shot through the fence by an Arab. I was fuming. Suddenly while General Erskine was with us there we heard a bit of a noise, and all these bullets had gone into the board with YMCA written on it in cat's-eyes. "Ooh," the General says. "Getting a bit hot for me, Bob," he says. "Bye-bye." And I says:

"Bye-bye, sir", and he jumps into his car and drives off. So someone across the sweet-water canal near the police station had fired on us. So we were lucky there. A couple of days before that we had three grenades land in the middle of the YMCA bridge. Later they blew up the NAAFI; and there were riots in Ismailiya.'

Those riots, in January 1952, pushed Egypt towards revolution more certainly than any previous event. The British army, its eighty thousand troops pinned down in the Canal Zone by guerrilla and sabotage attacks, had started to take the offensive against suspects, who included the auxiliary police. On Friday 25 January, in pursuit of suspects, the British army surrounded the police station in Ismailiya. The British set an ultimatum for the men inside to surrender. But the Cairo government ordered them to stand their ground. When the deadline passed the British used force. In the ensuing battle, around fifty Egyptian policemen were killed and many were injured.

The following day, serious rioting broke out in Cairo, with the centre of the city being set on fire. In particular the crowds went for British targets and ones associated with Western affluence. It became known as Black Saturday. In *Tales of Empire* Derek Hopwood quotes an account of the day written by Dorothea Russell, wife of Thomas Russell (Russell Pasha), the retired head of the Cairo police. During the afternoon of that Saturday 'the town was blazing, the sky a blaze, a pall of smoke blowing away south. The most awful sight and terrifying. The sky red miles high! ... They burned the B.O.A.C. offices and Major Fanner's offices above. They burned the first floor of the great Immobilia block of flats and all the shops. The people above had the most narrow escape. While they were doing this another group was burning the Turf Club. Twelve people lost their lives there and we have four survivors here in the hospital.' Also destroyed was another symbol of British power, Shepheard's Hotel.

Eventually the Egyptian army was sent into Cairo to quell the trouble. As Peter Mansfield, in *The British in Egypt*, points out, 'the belated move to call in the army was prompted by the very real fear that the British troops might intervene from the Canal Zone. They could have been in the capital in two or three hours. No Egyptian in authority had forgotten that the Alexandria riots had been the chief justification for the British invasion seventy years before.'

In the face of such widespread and powerful street anger the government and the King appeared weak and helpless. King Farouk had become, to quote Mr Mansfield, 'a cartoon satire of middle-aged debauchery . . . Although intelligent and quick-witted, he lacked *gravitas*; his character was as light as his body was heavy.'

In the King's defence, Mr Mansfield also mentions how he had been a victim of 'unwise parental guidance and subsequent mistreatment at the hands of a domineering British ambassador'. Resentment at Sir Miles Lampson's humiliation of King Farouk in February 1942, when the British ambassador used the threat of military action against the palace to force a change of mind, was still felt by Egyptians. British families who were long settled in Egypt also cited the high-handed attitude of Sir Miles as a major cause of the revolution which brought down the monarchy. Valerie Sale says her father 'thought a lot of blame should be put on our ambassador of the time, who was not very popular. My father thought he'd committed quite a few boobs. Orientals are instinctively courteous, and they can't bear to lose face. Once an Oriental has lost face it takes an awful lot to get it back; and a lot of people at the embassy didn't understand the Oriental mind. Had King Farouk been properly handled he'd probably have been a very good king; instead of which he was totally ruined.'

In the aftermath of the July 1952 revolution, life did not change drastically for the dwindling British community in Egypt. After lengthy negotiations agreement was reached on the withdrawal of British troops from the country. The last contingent left at the end of March 1956. But by the end of that year, British forces had made another appearance – albeit brief and under very different circumstances – on Egyptian soil. Their presence was brought about by the Suez Canal crisis.

When President Nasser, who had emerged as leader from the ring of officers who engineered the 1952 coup, failed to secure Western financing for a project to dam the Nile at Aswan in Upper Egypt he decided to nationalize the Anglo-French Suez Canal Company. The revenue from the canal, he told a cheering crowd in Alexandria in July 1956, would finance the dam project. The British Prime Minister, Sir Anthony Eden, was sent into a rage by what he regarded as this impudent action and began what can only be described as an obsessive personal campaign to bring down President Nasser at any cost. That was certainly the view of the hapless British diplomats in Cairo. In the view of one of them, Sir Peter Wakefield, 'one of the problems was that the agenda in London appeared to differ from the agenda in Cairo. A few months before the balloon went up we were still actively working with the regime, particularly in the development

Viscount Buckmaster, wearing the dress of a Gulf Arab, prepares to set out on 'the last great camel caravan' in 1952.

Members of the 1952 caravan. Sheikh Said, the current ruler of Abu Dhabi, is on the extreme right.

Gerald Butt with his father's driver, Rushdi, at
Amman airport, 1955. King Hussein was about to
board a plane for Cairo.

The mosque in Isfahan in the 1940s.

Muhammad Hussein, houseboy in the
1940s to the Butts in Tehran.

Archie Butt and Angus Macqueen held the record in Tehran in the mid-1930s for regular patronage of cabarets.

The Butt family in Tehran, 1947, two years before the birth of the author.

Archie Butt, as a manager of the British Bank of the Middle East in Amman, greets King Hussein, 1954.

Glubb Pasha and King Hussein, November 1955, a few months before the King, reacting to the anti-British mood in Jordan, unceremoniously dismissed Glubb.

field. I remember bumping around the countryside in trucks talking about the irrigation help that we were going to give. It was a very constructive relationship'. At the same time, though, the embassy was getting reports of Sir Anthony Eden's obsessive desire to get rid of President Nasser. 'We felt at that time that Eden was going too far, that he had got almost a personal animosity against Nasser, and that he had departed from the statesman-like attitude which we would have expected from a man so experienced in foreign affairs. Clearly we found this upsetting and distressing. We didn't think that our interests were being helped by this.'

Despite the vicious war of words that developed between London and Cairo, life for the British in the Egyptian capital was largely unaffected. 'Cairo remained throughout,' Sir Peter says, 'remarkably calm. I say that because previously in some of the political crises and events there had been a lot of mob action which had led to deaths and must have been very disagreeable indeed. But during the whole of that time the Egyptian populace remained incredibly calm. It was clearly in the interests of the Nasser regime that it should be so, because they wanted to present to international opinion the example of a responsible country who were perfectly capable of taking over the running of the Suez Canal and whatever else it might be.'

Sir Peter knew of no personal animosity directed at individual Britons. 'The Gezira Club was still the centre of life, not just for the British but for the Egyptians and members of the international community. What also was good was the mixing of the different nationalities, and of foreigners with the locals. There was no feeling of "them" and "us" in social activities between the British and the Egyptians as far as I encountered.'

On the international diplomatic level, meanwhile, attempts to mediate in the dispute between Egypt and the previous owners of the Suez Canal Company made no headway. The possibility of Anglo-French military intervention grew. But still British diplomats in Cairo 'felt that a relationship with the Egyptian regime would be possible, though obviously more difficult and bumpier. But we could not see really what the purpose of a military intervention was. We had, after all, just left Suez militarily to relocate in Cyprus on the grounds that we could not spare the resources to maintain it in a hostile environment. It was not economic, politically or militarily. So if we came back in an even more hostile environment, what in the long run were we going to be able to accomplish?'

What neither the British Embassy in Cairo nor the British public knew was that the Eden government was secretly cooking up a plan with France and Israel to provide the excuse for an Anglo-French invasion of Egypt, the aim of which would be to bring down the Nasser regime. The plot was set in action. The pretext for a military strike was provided by an Israeli push towards the Suez Canal from the east. This naturally prompted a similar Egyptian move from the West. Britain then issued an ultimatum to both sides to pull back from the zone, in full confidence that Egypt would reject the demand, thus giving London and Paris the excuse they needed to send in troops.

On 31 October 1956, with the ultimatum rejected by Cairo, the first bombing raids on Egypt began. British diplomats in Cairo had no more warning than the Egyptian people about the start of air strikes. Sir Peter Wakefield remembers that he was driving to work from his house out near the Pyramids, crossing the Kasr el-Nil bridge over the Nile in the centre of the capital when an RAF attack on a military airfield on the edge of the city began. 'The sirens wailed, traffic ground to a halt and there was the usual milling mass of people. I had to get out of my car, and I suppose that being tall with blond hair I stood out like a sore thumb. I thought that the Egyptians would throw me over the parapet into the muddy waters of the river below. But in fact quite the contrary they treated me as the rest of them. Eventually, when the bombing was over, we were allowed into our cars and continued on our way.'

Diplomats, naturally, stuck to their posts. But most British civilians were evacuated before the crisis reached its climax and British forces landed at Port Said. Valerie Sale remembers those last moments in Egypt. 'We were told we had to go and meet in Cairo at the Semiramis Hotel and we'd be put on the next plane that was available. You weren't going with your family necessarily – you just had to go; it was shambolic. My father was locked up for two days in the Semiramis because of his position as British Consul in Upper Egypt. Egyptian friends used to go to the hotel and ask if they could help, lend him money, anything. There was no personal hostility – in fact a lot of them were very sad. An Egyptian minister friend of my father's said that when British troops landed in Suez he hoped we were coming to get rid of Nasser. All the old ones didn't want Nasser and his crew.'

While some opponents of the regime hoped the Suez crisis would see the removal of President Nasser, the overwhelming majority of Egyptians, along with Arabs throughout the Middle East, were solidly behind him and the actions he had taken over the Suez Canal. Egypt had been able to get its point of view across by means of Cairo Radio and its sister service beamed powerfully around the Middle East, the Voice of the Arabs. The British government was well aware of the impact of these broadcasts, and as the crisis developed sought ways of countering it. The BBC Arabic Service could be heard in the region, but only on short wave, while the Egyptians were putting their message across on easily located medium wave-frequencies. The British government found a solution on it own doorstep. Since the Second World War an Arabic-language service – the Near East Arab Broadcasting Station (known popularly in Arabic just as Sharq al-Adna – Near East) – had been broadcasting to the region on medium wave – first from Palestine, and then, after 1948, from Cyprus. In the 1950s Sharq al-Adna had become a very popular station, carrying high-quality music and entertainment – and advertisements. But the commercial aspect of the station was merely a cover for the fact that it was operated by MI6. Although, with its British managers and senior staff, this was an open secret in the region, Whitehall has always been coy in admitting its link with the station. The British government announced at the end of October 1956 that Sharq al-Adna was being 'requisitioned' and was being renamed the Voice of Britain. The station started directing crude anti-Nasser propaganda in Arabic at Egypt.

The broadcasts, written and recorded on gramophone discs in London and flown out to Cyprus for transmission, make chilling reading. For example, on 5 November the Voice of Britain directed the following message to Egyptian soldiers in Port Said. 'The first units of our paratroops have secured their targets. It will soon be dark. You have already discovered what our troops can do in the daytime. You have yet to find out what they can do by night. They know full well how to fight in the dark. How can you differentiate between friend and enemy by night? Our men, however, will be there. Soon, more of their colleagues will join them. The night shall be filled with troops. Soon, very soon, it will be dark, O soldiers in Port Said. Soon it will be dark. You are in a hopeless situation. Protect your lives. It is not your duty to die for your homeland. Your duty is to live and serve your homeland and return to your families and homes.'

The Arab staff of Sharq al-Adna walked out when the station was taken over, and so British Arabists from the diplomatic corps had to be sent in urgently to run the station. Donald Maitland was on his way out to Lebanon to run the Arabic-language course at the Middle East Centre for Arab Studies (MECAS) when he was diverted to Cyprus. 'It really was a nightmare,' Sir Donald Maitland says. 'There was an engineer there and the station was being kept on air simply by playing gramophone records. Of course they didn't know what they were, because they couldn't read the labels. And so our job was to organize things, and to receive material which came out from London and transmit it.' Looking at transcripts of broadcasts which he helped put on the air, Sir Donald says he is 'absolutely appalled. It really is unbelievable today that reasonable people could have drafted such material.'

The British Embassy in Cairo in November 1956 would have had little time to monitor the Voice of Britain or any other radio station. They were having to react to events as they unfolded, still largely ignorant of what the intentions of their masters in London were. Sir Peter Wakefield says he was 'in the dark about what was going to happen prior to the landing of British troops. It was quite an interesting shock to pick up the Reuter news agency tape from the machine saying that British troops had invaded. I trotted along the corridor with it to the ambassador. "Sir," I said, "you may be interested to know that we have invaded."'

With British troops on Egyptian soil, the British Embassy came under siege. The embassy also sheltered Britons and other foreigners in its building and grounds. 'We had a very efficient Head of Chancery,' Sir Peter says, 'and he organized the embassy along a mixture of military and Boy Scout lines. People slept all over the place. But we managed. Naturally we were very anxious. If law and order had broken down we might have met a bad end. But I think Nasser was keen that this shouldn't happen.' Within two weeks diplomats and others in the embassy had been allowed safely out of Egypt.

British citizens were having to flee from other countries in the Middle East – such was the outrage felt by the Arabs at the Anglo-French invasion of Egypt. My father was manager in the autumn of 1956 of a branch of the British Bank of the Middle East (BBME) in Aleppo in Syria. My brothers and sisters (who were at boarding school in England) had come out to Syria for the summer holidays. I was still too young for boarding school, so the plan was that I would stay in Aleppo when the others returned. In the event it was nothing of a holiday. We were confined most of the time to our flat as anti-British and anti-French demonstrations passed by on the street below. Two weeks later we had returned in haste to England, leaving my father in Aleppo. His brief diary entries for the period provide another perspective on the Suez crisis, showing how perplexed the ordinary Britons in the Middle East were both at the developments in the region and at the attitude of the government in London.

'Saturday, 1 September 1956. It was announced on the BBC tonight that British subjects were advised to leave Syria unless their work kept them there.

'Sunday, 9 September. The talks in Cairo between Nasser and the committee representing the London conference nations have completely failed, Nasser refusing to give an inch on the Suez Canal affair.

'Thursday, 13 September. Have been listening to the House of Commons debate on the Suez problem.

'Monday, 15 October. The Security Council debate on Suez ended with Russia vetoing the Western resolution, but some little progress has been made towards finding a basis for negotiation.

'Saturday, 27 October. All American citizens advised to leave Egypt, Jordan and Syria.

'Sunday, 28 October. Stayed indoors because of strike. Serious anti-French riots here – two French schools and French cultural office burnt out, and the Franciscan convent school close to our flat badly damaged by mob. Disturbances outside the flat for over an hour with soldiers firing repeatedly into the air. All quiet by afternoon. State of emergency declared and a curfew imposed.

'Monday, 29 October. News received last night of Israeli attack on Egypt in Sinai peninsula. Bank opened as usual, but Christian shops and bazaars stayed closed and after demonstrations by students and some firing all shops and banks closed. I was home before noon and brought Reitsma [his British accountant at the bank] to stay with me . . . All Americans have already left Aleppo. British subjects in Syria again advised to leave.

'Tuesday, 30 October. Situation more normal, but still military guards on banks etc. Curfew tonight from 10 p.m. News on the radio this morning that Britain and France have given Egypt a 12-hour ultimatum to allow forces to enter the Suez Canal area came as a shock to us. Reaction here unpredictable, but I feel we may have to leave shortly.

'Wednesday, 31 October. British and French have vetoed American resolution in Security Council that they should not take military action. World opinion is against us. Egyptians have refused to agree to British demands and will fight if troops are landed. Martial law declared throughout Syria – no civil planes allowed in or out. Pleased to get two letters from Muriel [my mother], and wonder when the next will come.

'Announcement tonight on radio that British and French have started bombing airfields.

'Thursday, 1 November. Bank still open for business – fairly heavy cash withdrawals. Position here becoming more difficult for us – all other British subjects have left Aleppo, except the Consul, with whom I keep in close touch by telephone. Allied bombing of military targets in Egypt continues. Syrian troops have left the town and only police guards remain – not much security against mob riots.

'Friday, 2 November. Bank open as usual this morning. Connolly [BBME manager in the capital, Damascus] phoned at 2 p.m. that Syria had broken off diplomatic relations with Britain. Phoned Hugh Pullen [the British Consul] who hadn't heard the news! – but later phoned back to confirm it. I decided that Reitsma and I would leave early tomorrow. Sent for George the bank driver – also for the three Syrian "B" officers to whom we gave the Treasury keys and a list of instructions, some of which I had already written out. Final instructions to servants, packing and little sleep. All our luggage will be left here – am only taking a suitcase. Surprised to get a letter from Muriel this morning – it had been opened by Syrian censor.

'Saturday, 3 November. Reitsma and I left Aleppo at 5 a.m. in the Bank car. Delayed half an hour at Syrian frontier and an hour at Turkish, but no trouble – and we arrived at Iskenderun 9.30 a.m. after crossing a mountain range. Very pleased to be safely out of Syria for the time being.'

The British military presence in Egypt in November 1956 was brief – under strong American and international pressure, the Eden government was forced, ignominiously, to order them out. By 22 December they had all left Egypt. But it took much longer for the diplomatic furore to die down. Britain, a fading power in the region before Suez, had in its bungled action in Egypt lost its role as a key influential player. Sir Peter Wakefield believes that the Suez affair did 'enormous damage to our prestige in the Middle East. It hurried forward the withdrawal of our influence and our military presence in the Gulf by a number of years.'

The Egyptian people are nothing if not forgiving. While relations between the governments in London and Cairo remained strained for some years, at street level Egyptians remained as friendly and as hospitable as ever to strangers, including the British. Arabs love families and they love children, and even the most politically hardened hearts melt in their presence. ('I remember Donald Maitland saying,' Lady Parsons told me, 'that if you haven't got a small child when you're travelling across the Middle East, just hire one.')

Sir Anthony and Lady Parsons and their children went back to Cairo when the British were resuming relations after the Suez débâcle. 'It took us two or three years to get back to embassy status in Egypt,' Sir Anthony remembers. 'After all, we'd invaded the country only a few years before. We had a long-standing reputation for imperialism and we could expect hostility. I remember in 1960 there was the annual military parade on Revolution Day and I thought I'd go and have a look, and take a chance on not being recognized as being an *Inglezi* [an Englishman]. Our daughter Emma was four and I thought it would be fun for her to see the parade. So I took her on my shoulders and pushed my way into this huge crowd with all this military hardware grinding past. Of course I was immediately recognized as an Englishman and I thought: 'This is where I get lynched.' But before I knew it Emma was taken off my shoulders and put on to the shoulders of an Arab spectator. She disappeared hundreds of yards down the crowd; they wanted to have their turn having her on their shoulders, and we were the heroes of the hour. If I'd have been on my own I wouldn't have had a very warm welcome.'

Lady Parsons also was impressed at the warmth of their welcome from the Egyptians. 'Arabs, much more than us, are able to distinguish between the official and the private. When we went back to Cairo there was official difficulty – but personally they were extremely nice to us. They didn't actually like to mention Suez. We don't remember anyone being unpleasant to us personally.'

His wife's comments reminded Sir Anthony of another aspect of life at this period. 'Our servant was told to take the names of all our guests and to listen to all our conversations. But he knew no English, and he listened so hard that he poured the wine all over the Turkish chargé d'affaires and drenched him. The servant was listening so ardently to his conversation he forgot to stop pouring the wine.'

Also in the aftermath of Suez another British diplomat received a surprisingly warm welcome in Egypt. Alan Munro, newly married in Beirut, arrived with his wife, Grania, in Alexandria at the start of a leisurely cruise back to England. They planned to spend a week in Egypt. 'Having arrived in Alexandria we took a taxi to the old railway station and found that, because it was still only six years after Suez and Britain still had no diplomatic relations with Egypt, there were very few British visitors to Egypt at all. When we arrived at the station steps we found a very smart gentleman in a tarboosh and with a frogged uniform who greeted us: "Are you Mr and Mrs Munro? Would you like to come with me." Somewhat aware of our having had the temerity to come to Egypt at that time we followed him up the steps on to the station concourse, where he took us to sit at a table surrounded by other gentlemen in similar uniforms and he bade us sit down. They offered us coffee and I pointed out that it was all very kind but we had a train to catch to Cairo. But he said that the train could wait. Then the most elegant of those around our table got up and made a little speech to us saying: "I am the station- master of Alexandria station and on behalf of the Egyptian railways I wish to welcome you to Egypt as we believe you are the first British visitors to come to Egypt for many a year and you are most welcome." We were overcome with emotion to have these august figures greet us with such ceremony – so characteristic of that joyful spirit that runs through Egypt. No matter how its politics run, there is still a very strong bond between us all. Having greeted us in this way – the train was of course substantially delayed – they took us down to the platform, where a whole lot of other passengers were wondering what on earth had happened. They ushered us into a private compartment and sent us off happy as could be.'

One other anecdote illustrates the mixed feelings that Egyptians have had towards the British since the occupation of the country in 1882. It concerns, appropriately, a bust of General William Earle, a British military commander who took part in the occupation of Alexandria that year. The bust was placed in the garden in front of St Mark's Church in the city. During anti-British riots at the time of Suez in 1956 the bust was attacked and it disappeared. The assumption was that demonstrators had made off with it. In 1994, the Archdeacon of the Church at the time, Howard Levett, asked, out of curiosity, the Egyptian gardener – whose father had also worked for the church – if he happened to know about the fate of the statue. 'Oh, yes,' he replied, 'my father buried it to keep it safe.' Expecting a negative answer, Father Levett asked if he happened to know where it was buried. 'Yes, over there behind the vestry,' replied the gardener. And there, indeed, it was, safely snatched from danger by a loyal gardener and saved for posterity. The guard has changed in Egypt. But the character of the Egyptian people is the same.

Part 4

PALESTINE, JORDAN AND LEBANON

11

PALESTINE: HEAVEN AND HELL

It is striking how many Britons can recall in detail their first impressions of Palestine. Maybe it is because the label which is so often attached to this area of the Middle East – the Holy Land – has evoked images in the minds of Westerners since the time of the Crusades. Travellers have always arrived with high expectations and with their senses attuned to the religious significance of the experience. But not all those first memories have had a religious theme. Charis Waddy arrived in 1919 as a small child; her father had been a chaplain during the First World War and had reached Jerusalem in 1917 with General Allenby's army which defeated the Turks. After the war her father stayed on as a teacher at St George's School. Two years later his family joined him. 'We came by train from Port Said,' Miss Waddy says, 'and my first impression was waking up in that train when it stopped at Gaza. There was the most extraordinary growling outside the window. It was a camel.'

Frequently, though, the first memories of Palestine have been closely associated with the rich religious significance of the region. Joyce Frecheville, now in her mid-nineties, took up a job as secretary to the Anglican Bishop in 1928. 'I arrived out there by night and took the one train that travelled to Jerusalem. The next day the Bishop took me to one of the old high places near what was Bethel and where Jacob had his dream. There were a lot of large white stones there, very like pillows. Up from this high place, to my astonishment, I looked north and there was Mount Hermon with snow on it. It looked so far on the map, and yet there it was in the clouds, visible from near Jerusalem. Then you looked east and the land dipped down to the Jordan valley below sea level; and there was Jordan on the other side and what we call the mountains of Moab. Looking south the hills rose a bit to Hebron, then you looked west and the hills were going down gradually to the coastal plain and the Mediterranean, which was almost within sight. When you read the Bible, so many things happened there you think it's a large place but it's tiny.'

The first experience of the Holy Land for Kenneth Cragg (now Bishop Cragg) came ten years later, in 1939. He reached Jerusalem in a shared taxi from Haifa. 'We crested the hill to the north of Jerusalem. The view from there is not quite as vivid as that approaching from the east when you come from Bethany over the crest of the Mount of Olives and the whole Temple area bursts into view. This could be the place where Jesus wept over Jerusalem, according to the Gospel. The northern approach in '39 was somewhat the same, though not quite so dramatic. I remember the vista of the domes and the towers and the flat roofs, and the thrill of seeing them. It's really an entrancing experience, that first sight of Jerusalem. And I remember on that northern hill singling out the two towers of St George's Cathedral, very English-looking, very Edwardian, rather like Magdalen College tower in Oxford, though of course very recent.'

Something else that made an early impression on Kenneth Cragg was a ritual peculiar to the Old City. 'One thing that always embarrassed me was a tradition of those days: when ecclesiastics came down the roofed-in, narrow streets you'd have a chap who would go in front banging a kind of heavy wand in front of this patriarch or whoever it was. And it always embarrassed me when I went down with the Anglican Bishop. I think we've got rid of it now, at least I hope we have. But it was a kind of "Clear out of the way!"'

Gawain Bell (now Sir Gawain) was released from the Sudan Political Service at the start of the Second World War in order to take up a post in Palestine. By this time, Palestine was beginning to dissolve into chaos. Arab–Jewish, Arab–British and Jewish–British violence was starting to dominate life in the territory. Mr Bell's first impressions were radically different from those of a churchman like Kenneth Cragg. 'I suppose my introduction to Palestine,' Sir Gawain says, 'was joining a train at Port Said and then travelling slowly up the line as far as Haifa. All the way along there were the effects of Jewish terrorism, the telegraph lines were down and the posts were lying on the ground. When we got to Lydd there were two trains upside down beside the track. However, we gradually got through to Haifa, and from Haifa I was then told I'd be posted to Tiberias. Alec Kirkbride was my boss. He drove me over to Tiberias; and in just the same way, the road was again littered with broken telegraph posts and wire lying all over the place and bridges blown up. We went, of course, with a largish escort. When I got to Tiberias I was introduced to the two District Officers who were to work under me – one an Arab and the other a Jew. But they didn't have any communication one with the other except through me. They didn't speak. Within a very short time, ten days or less, the mayor of Tiberias was shot dead in the street; and very soon after that the Arab District Officer was also shot, and he disappeared. His successor arrived and immediately had a heart attack.'

When Charis Waddy had first arrived in 1919, such major unrest was still a long way off. Jewish immigration had started; and in the twenties and thirties there were periodic bouts of serious trouble. But in general, by comparison with later years, it was a period of peace and innocence. 'We lived in a large cool house in St George's Close, next door to the cathedral. We loved it. There was a constant stream of people in and out, to and fro.'

As far as education was concerned, Miss Waddy says, 'we had people to teach us for a lot of the time. Then I went to the Jerusalem Girls' College – this one and St George's, the boys' school, were among the few places where all the communities were educated together. Ninety-five per cent were Arab, but we had everybody – Arabs, Jews, Armenians, Russians. I was the only English girl at that point. The British community in Palestine was quite large – when we first got there it was still occupied territory and there were quite a lot of army people and many connected with the administration as it was being set up. There were lively services in St George's on Sunday mornings. One of our friends was a doctor working on a programme to combat malaria; when we went to Palestine malaria was a constant obsession – you had to be terribly careful.'

I asked Miss Waddy about social life. 'There was lots of tennis, also plays and concerts. The Governor, Sir Ronald Storrs, was a real musician, and he was involved. On the Jewish side there was a lot of music. My youngest brother, aged about seven, took the part of Peter Pan in a performance which was put on – my sister had a good voice and used to sing in concerts. There were also picnics, drives out seeing the countryside. There was one famous one which we were not on. The Bishop had taken a couple of carloads for a picnic one evening at the Dead Sea and didn't know that an eclipse of the moon was due. The road was extremely steep and winding and they had to stay where they were until the moon came out again because they had no means of moving in the dark.'

Travelling around Palestine, Miss Waddy's 'father went on horseback through villages – he travelled a lot to visit the families of his students. When we got a car we saw quite a few different places.'

The Waddy family 'left Jerusalem in 1926. My father worked in London. I went to boarding school and then to Oxford, where I read Arabic and Hebrew, which no woman had done before. After that, in 1934, I was offered a post under the government of Palestine to teach in a training college for women teachers. It was one of a number of advances in the education of women right across the Muslim world; already the Turkish authorities had women doctors – Egypt was well ahead. This college in Jerusalem had girls picked from different parts of the country. The idea was to train them, then send them home to start a school. It was a very varied set of Arab girls – one of my colleagues and I used to conduct a crocodile of veiled Muslim girls through the streets of Jerusalem to a primary school by the Old City for them to give practice lessons in Arabic, and I, very boldly, afterwards would tell them how they ought to have done it. It was a very pioneering piece of work, and one of our ex-students became the first woman cabinet minister in Jordan.'

Even with the periodic outbursts of violence a mood of peace and calm prevailed for the most part over St George's Cathedral in the late twenties and thirties when Joyce Frecheville was working for the Bishop. 'You came in through an open gateway. There was the Cathedral, the Bishop's house on the right, cloisters around, and through an archway you got to the pilgrims' hostel. I had a room in that archway. I woke up one night and heard heavy breathing outside. There were seats just outside the window, and I thought I must investigate; so I put my head out of the window in the dark and said: "Meen?" "Who [is there]?" "Ana," came the reply, "Me", which wasn't exactly enlightening. It turned out to be the policeman who was supposed to be on duty but was having a nice little doze. This was in a time of trouble, but life was much more informal and less dangerous in a way.'

The congregation at St George's in the late twenties and thirties reflected the tendency of the British to stick to their own community. 'There were a lot of English people coming to church, and there were always these pilgrims and a constant stream of visitors. I'm sorry to say there was a separate church at the foot of the Street of the Prophets which was Arabic-speaking. Most of us didn't speak Arabic, unfortunately. It's characteristic of the British abroad, I'm afraid. You mixed very much socially with educated people, and our main contact with Palestinians was with the servants.'

One of the servants at the Cathedral was the gardener, who was also the night-watchman. Shortly after Miss Frecheville arrived his daughter was married and she was invited to the wedding. 'It was in a village near Nebih Samuel. They hired a camel to bring the bride, and as the bride arrived they sang things about her. Then they had a feast. We would have liked to be like all the people eating with their hands, but we were put in a separate room; and to our astonishment we were eating off the St George's Hostel plates with its knives and forks. But I was told that this sort of thing happened a lot – that English residents in Jerusalem might go to a friend's dinner party and to their astonishment they would find they were eating off their own plates. The servants knew each other and they wanted to make the best thing of the occasion. Speaking generally, I think the British and the Palestinians liked each other.'

Miss Frecheville remembers that the Bishop used to travel around Palestine by car. 'Once he got held up between Jerusalem and Jericho. There are steep valleys and rocks, and the habit of the thieves was to hide behind big boulders, having put something in the road to stop the car. Then the brigands came out from the boulders and the Bishop was held up. His Arabic-speaking chauffeur explained who he was. I don't think he lost anything. But in connection with that in the time of the troubles there was attached to the mandatory government a chief social worker by the name of Miss Nixon. She was quite a character. She travelled about a lot and on one occasion when she was travelling she came across stones across the road and she knew there were people hiding behind the boulders. She got out of the car and said in a loud voice in Arabic: "Oh, I do need a strong man to come and take these stones away." And from behind the boulders came strong men and removed the things for her.'

As the years passed, the trouble and uncertainty in Palestine intensified as Jewish immigration and acquisition of Arab land increased. At the same time, Arab resentment towards the new arrivals was building up. Even the peace around the Cathedral Close was shattered from time to time. 'Occasionally,' Miss Frecheville told me, 'we heard a shot. I know one of the middle-aged spinsters who sang like me in the choir was coming to the Cathedral one day and there was a Jew at one end of the road and an Arab the other and they were shooting at each other past her. She was in the middle of the area but luckily they were bad shots and she wasn't hurt.'

Being on the alert for trouble was increasingly the order of the day for civilians throughout Palestine. Derek Cooper arrived in Haifa to work out a three-year contract with a British company building Haifa harbour. 'There were a few flare-ups,' he recalls, 'and we expatriates all had to join the reserves of the Palestine Police, which consisted of Arabs and Jews in equal numbers with British officer commanders. We took part in one or two affairs. Jaffa was always a bad spot. There was general rioting and stone-throwing on a couple of occasions and we had to make baton charges. But there were no deaths at that time.'

The company building the harbour employed both Arabs and Jews, the latter mostly doing office work. 'There wasn't much trouble between Arabs and Jews in those days,' Mr Cooper says. And in between work he and his colleagues enjoyed life without fear of trouble. 'There was very good bathing along the coast, and riding along the beach. There was the Haifa Club for the British. Very colonial, I suppose, but very amusing. I was young then. We had dances and cocktail parties. It was very British. Some English wives came to the club and various entertainers came in from time to time. I got a tremendous rocket for taking in a girl who was riding in the Wall of Death near the Nasser Hotel. She was South African and very attractive. We had become acquainted, so I invited her to the club. But you weren't supposed to bring in artistes. I was sent for by Mr Sharp, the head of the company I was working for.'

While Mr Cooper and other Britons were doing jobs of work in Palestine, younger generations from the various communities were growing up in an atmosphere of increasing hostility in the territory. Vera Shamma had the benefit of spanning two communities, British and Palestinian. Her father, like Charis Waddy's, came into Palestine with General Allenby's forces. He stayed on after the war and got a job in the civil government in Haifa. Mrs Shamma's Palestinian mother, who spoke good English, was taken on as a telephone operator in the District Commissioner's Office, where the couple met. They married in 1921 ('My mother was one of the first Arab women to marry an Englishman,' Mrs Shamma says) and settled in Haifa. Vera, as a girl, was sent to the English High School, which was run by the Church Missionary Society. 'We had English teachers mostly: the headmistress was called Miss Emery and we had a Miss Morgan – all very "Churchy" types of people. We had a full curriculum of English studies, history, geography and so on; scripture was very important. In the history lessons we learnt English history and about the English way of life. We wanted to know about England – there were English people all around us. We had Arab and Jewish girls together in the school, we did scripture together. It made no difference then being an Arab or a Jew or a Christian, I had a lot of Jewish friends.'

For recreation, Mrs Shamma says, the family 'had a beautiful beach to go to, picnics up Mount Carmel, we used to go in the car to Mount Tiberias picking wild flowers in the spring. At school we performed Shakespeare, there was a choir, and we played tennis, and rounders and netball. It was really an English school but we studied Arabic as well. Every second summer we'd go to England on holiday – we'd go down to Port Said by train and take a P & O liner to Britain. It would take about seven days, and we'd stop at Malta and Gibraltar. It was all very nice – we'd come home to my English grandmother's house in Darlington.'

Another perspective on British schooling and social life in Haifa at this time comes from Abla Odell. She is Palestinian, and married to an Englishman. But her childhood was spent in an Arab family environment. She remembers being strongly aware of the British influence in every aspect of life outside the home. 'The police were British, the government, taxation, everything. Even in my school, which was a French convent, the students were told that the main language in Palestine was English. English first, French second and Arabic third. My Arabic was poor. There were British families we knew. But they had their own lives; even in our school there was a British wing – part of the school was only for the English. They made you feel they were superior to the rest. But we liked the British, we looked up to them. However, most of my friends were Palestinians. The British had their own clubs with cricket and so on. But because it was our country, we didn't need the social life of the British.' Mrs Odell remembers Palestine as 'a very well organized country. We Palestinians didn't feel any animosity to the English until we had to leave Palestine. And then we blamed the British government.'

The major flight of Palestinians from their land came in the turmoil following the creation of Israel in 1948. Before that, all the inhabitants of Palestine experienced the anxious years of the Second World War. 'We had air-raid shelters in Haifa,' Vera Shamma recalls,

171

'but our house was above the city, on Mount Carmel, so we could see it all happening below. We used to sit on the balcony and watch the air raids. The German planes used to come over from Lebanon – Lebanon was occupied by the Vichy French – to bomb Haifa harbour and the refineries; and we thought we were quite safe up there. It was very exciting to see the guns shooting the planes, to see the tracer fire whizzing through. One plane came down, it came right over our house. It was crashing, and it came down in the mountains behind us. That was only for a short time until Lebanon was taken over again by the Allies.'

The level of intercommunal violence in Palestine dropped during the war years, and Mrs Shamma remembers it as a time of parties and dancing. She recalls with nostalgia the music and films of the day, 'Vera Lynn singing "We'll Meet Again"; Deanna Durbin was the film star of the time and I used to like to sing her songs. But mostly it was the war songs. We used to go to tea-dances with my brothers. My brothers collected records – it was all Glenn Miller music and jazz, the jitterbug. There was one café we used to go to called the Café Verna, and on a Sunday we would go to church first, then my father would take us out to lunch, at Spinney's Restaurant in the German Colony; and then we'd go to Verna's Café for a tea-dance. In the evening we'd go out to another place called the Casino where they would have dancing music and a cabaret – not really a Casino. Saturday was spent on the beach – we had a good social life. I had a lot of friends from school, and I had a boyfriend from the army. I haven't heard from him since – his name was Al Rae and he was a pianist with the Billy Cotton Band. He was stationed in Haifa. He used to come and visit and he'd play the piano and I would sing with him. Then we parted; he was posted on. He was a nice young man, I don't know what happened to him. We had a lovely social life in those days until the troubles started in 1947 – then we began to realize the distinctions between Arabs and Jews. Before that we mixed freely, it was one big happy family.'

The task of trying to stop intercommunal violence in Palestine – the task assigned to the Palestine Police and the British army – was getting harder as the months passed. Donald Cartwright, a former member of the police force, says that with the pressure mounting to let more and more Jews into Palestine, in the wake of the Nazi genocide in Europe, 'it was a situation that could not be resolved. The police could not win. Both sides accused us of bias. Any tricky stuff, the

British were always blamed.' Terry Shand, another ex-Palestine Police officer, remembers the difficulty of controlling the highly motivated and increasingly well armed and trained Jewish fighters. 'The Jews had an unofficial army, the Haganah. We were a force of four thousand and were very stretched on the ground to deal with the type of terrorism which their people were carrying out against us – the blowing up of railway stations, police stations, military areas, and so on. Even in the last year of being in Palestine we lost one hundred and twenty of our men – which is a very large number for the force we had at the time. I can only say that I believe our people treated the people of Palestine fairly, squarely and right through the middle of the line. And this is borne out as we go back today. They invite us into their homes.'

Sir Gawain Bell, who was in Tiberias as the Second World War was getting under way, also believes that both the police and the army did as good a job as they could, given the obvious difficulty of fighting a war against terrorists among a civilian population. 'Whenever the army went out I went with them because I felt that, just conceivably, speaking Arabic, I could be of some use. The army, I think, behaved very well; I never knew of any case where a woman was interfered with. But sometimes they were overenthusiastic and sometimes too they shot a cordon-breaker dead, which wasn't perhaps always necessary; and on those occasions I could be of some use talking to the *mukhtar* [Arab village or community chief] or whoever necessary.'

The British army and the Palestine Police certainly had their critics. But Mrs Shamma is one of those to retain good memories of the police force. 'They were very strong. They were everywhere, and very well respected. There were Arab, Jewish and British members. A lot of young men who were friends of my brothers were in the police. They used to hold parties and dances, and there were lots of associations connected with the Palestine Police. It was a brilliant force, very respected.'

The police found themselves targets of attacks on many occasion. 'One incident springs to mind,' Mrs Shamma said. 'There was an Arab inspector – Inspector Shahaba. I was coming out of school – I was about twelve or thirteen – and the inspector was in his car waiting to pick up his daughter from school. Suddenly I saw a man come and shoot the Inspector. I just stood and looked and saw this man shoot Inspector Shahaba in the head and run off. All the girls were screaming: "There's a shooting." I remember it so clearly. An ambulance came, police came, and fortunately he didn't die. That was about 1938 or 1939. Other incidents you heard of. For example, a bus going up Mount Carmel being held up by terrorists – and we'd say: "Terrorists? What does that mean? Why should a man with a gun get on a bus and hold it up?" And then we'd carry on with our daily life.'

Among former members of the Palestine Police, memories of those violent days are particularly clear. I visited Ivor Heaton, in retirement in Plympton in Devon, and he brought old photos and memorabilia from his Palestine days. As he showed me one of the photos he told me about his colleague, Bob Faulkner. 'He was killed by terrorists there,' he said, pointing to the photo of a street in Haifa. 'On that corner there was a café. I'd been in there once or twice. We'd had egg and chips there. He was killed while I was on Mount Carmel. We all went to the funeral.'

Then Mr Heaton told me the story of Bob Pringle. 'He was blinded when the Central Police Station was blown up. He used to be a source of amusement to us. When he went on patrol in the grounds of the police station he used to arm himself to the teeth, a ".45" on each hip and a tommy-gun ready and loaded. We used to laugh at him. When he got blinded he was down in his billet in the Central Police Station and happened to be looking out of the window. On the edge of the pavement there was a high barbed-wire fence, at least eight or nine feet. This lorry came along with a ramp on it, and a barrel of explosive on the ramp. As the lorry passed, they released this barrel, this bomb, over the fence, where it exploded. Bob Pringle, looking out of the window, caught the blast and it blinded him.'

On another occasion Mr Heaton was in a police camp when it came under attack from Jewish terrorists. 'On the south side of the camp there was a perimeter fence, and there were orange groves. Parked there was an armoured car – a post for the sentries. One night at around 1 a.m. in the morning we were wakened by loud bangs and the glass in the windows breaking. The camp was chock-a-block with vehicles. The orange grove was good cover, and terrorists had somehow driven in, hidden bombs among the vehicles and driven out, almost under the nose of the sentries. They said they hadn't seen anything, or if they had they weren't telling. We stayed around about half an hour and then we went back to bed.'

Sometimes the terrorists themselves were killed during an attack – as happened, Mr Heaton told me, when the railway workshops in Haifa were their target. 'Several of us were on duty in the morgue at the hospital to make sure that all the bodies of the terrorists were brought in. The bodies were just dumped anywhere. I couldn't help feeling a touch of sympathy because during the day old ladies came in to try to identify the bodies. At one point there were three old ladies and a young man with them. And they were pointing as they recognized each one. It was quite a sad time. While I was there one of the terrorists must have died in the ward. A couple of Arabs came in with a body on a trolley and just dumped him off.'

There were occasions, too, when the police were called on to search out the terrorists. Mr Heaton remembers once being sent into a Jewish neighbourhood to look for arms. 'We just went in and we had to ransack these houses. I don't remember finding any weapons. But we didn't get complaints.'

Many of the Britons who joined the Palestine Police did so on little more than a whim and with little idea of what might be in store. Ivor Heaton 'was in the King's Own Royal Regiment, and the Palestine Police came round recruiting. A friend said: "Shall we join up?"' I said: "Why not."' Terry Shand says he joined the force 'and came to a country I knew nothing about'. Donald Cartwright, on the other hand, had 'always wanted to be a policeman. I worked for the railways during the war and so wasn't called up, and the police wouldn't take me because I was in a reserved occupation. One of my friends noticed an advertisement in the *Daily Telegraph* for the Palestine Police. Eleven pounds a month and all fares. Three-year contract. I was duly interviewed in Millbank and sailed in March 1943.' Mr Cartwright was sent to Hebron, where he studied Arabic and got to know and like his Arab colleagues. 'Hebron was the only place where Palestine Police officers pounded the beat, exactly as they did in the British force. So I did this with two Arab officers. I got to know them well and got to know their families. We would go on patrol for four or five days and would sleep with our colleagues in village guest-houses. The village would feed us.'

Mr Heaton learned some Arabic in Palestine. He can still count to twenty and recite his force identification number in the language. He also has not forgotten the taste of Arab coffee. 'When we were on patrol and we passed a café, they'd invite us in. An Arab showed us how to make the coffee. Put the coffee into the little pot with about as much sugar as coffee. Then boil it. It was beautiful, thick, black and sweet.'

One of Mr Shand's memories of Palestine is of dancing. 'I was twenty-one and loved dancing. By 1946 and '47 the Jewish terror organizations were strong. And they didn't want Jewish girls dancing with the British. I remember one evening going to a dance with a friend who spoke fluent Hebrew. He said: "Go and dance with that girl over there." I said: "But if I ask her in English she'll say no." So for ten minutes he started to teach me what to say in Hebrew. "Pardon me. Would you dance with me?" I went over to the table and said it. And there was tremendous consternation. There was one word – instead of "dance" with me, I'd said "sleep" with me. I followed her father into the toilet and explained. I actually went over and she did dance with me. My colleague's Hebrew was perfect. But a week later he was shot dead.'

Britons were undoubtedly on safer ground courting people of their own race. In 1946 Mr Cartwright remembers being told about 'a girl called Joan Watson working at the 16th Airborne Hospital on the Mount of Olives just outside Jerusalem. After leave I was posted to the police station responsible for the hospital, and we met." Later they married.

'I know why I went out with you,' Joan Cartwright said, as the couple reminisced during a Palestine Police reunion in Sussex in 1994, 'it was because you could take me to Hebron. No army were allowed to got to Hebron, but the Palestine Police could go.'

'I used to take you walking, too,' said Mr Cartwright. 'That was the start of it.'

Mrs Cartwright recalled that she was 'working for the Green Alexanders, the Imperial Military Nursing Service. It was more difficult than a hospital in England. But they were a good crowd of lads. We worked hard, but were appreciated, I think. There were a lot of army, and Palestine Police and RAF. They used to look after the ladies. As I say, it was hard work, but I wouldn't have missed it for anything.'

The sense of camaraderie among former members of the Palestine Police and those associated with it is striking. Reunions are frequently held, and a newsletter keeps members, who live in many places around the world, in contact with each other. 'The force was fantastic,' Mr Shand says, 'because we had this fantastic comradeship. We lived together, we borrowed each other's ties, played sport together, played against the army and military forces. We lived a life that was so totally different from that in any other force in existence at the time. And because of this we consider our association of old comrades to be as strong today as it was forty-five years ago. We also had a feeling that our people provided all the other forces with personnel – Singapore, Malaysia, Australia. We provided the last remnants of the empire with the men that we had had – wherever there were troubles.'

In May 1948, the work of the Palestine Police stopped with the ending of the Mandate and the creation of Israel. In the three months before that, life for the police was even tougher than ever. Mr Cartwright was working in the Secretariat in Jerusalem, and to get to work had to cross 'two front lines, Arab and Jewish. And we were fired on. So they sent us in an armoured car. Then even that got too dangerous, so we slept in the Secretariat. This was going on from February, so that was a bit tricky.'

Finally, the withdrawal date, 18 May, arrived. 'It is the one colony,' Mr Cartwright says, 'where we didn't hand over to anyone. We just left it. When we left on 18 May there were thirty-two of us in Jerusalem, including the British High Commissioner. We were getting on a Dakota aircraft. But the Dakota only takes thirty, and everyone else was a director of this and a director of that. So myself and the other acting cipher officer were told to get into the High Commissioner's Rolls-Royce and take it down to Haifa and get on the boat. But as our convoy went through, fighting [between Arabs and Jews] started. There was fighting all the way. When we got to Haifa, the Arab part of the town was deserted, all the Arabs had been driven out and had gone over the border into Lebanon. We stayed in the Windsor Hotel and were vetted by the Haganah, the Jewish army. We stayed two or three days until the withdrawal officer got us on to a boat home.'

Finding an objective assessment of Britain's role in Palestine is impossible. Too many passions were aroused during that time to enable cool judgement to prevail. It is probably true to say that the British tended to have more sympathy with the Arabs than with the Jews, and those Britons who served in Palestine have tended to espouse the Arab rather than the Israeli cause. But such generalizations are dangerous – they do not allow for the way in which human emotions can be touched by particular incidents. Joyce Frecheville, back in the late 1920s, said that she, like her colleagues, felt that her sympathy lay with the Palestinian people. But an incident witnessed during a shared taxi ride from Nazareth to Jerusalem opened up her mind. During the course of the journey 'a great argument broke out. I couldn't speak Arabic, but I gathered that one of the passengers was a Jew. They didn't want to arrive in Jerusalem with a Jew on board. Again I didn't know, but that day things were happening in Jerusalem, one of the critical events. It had inflamed the passions of the Arab and so this man's suitcase was thrown into the road. They said he couldn't go on. I just sat there and I was used as a kind of pawn because I was British. I wanted to get to Jerusalem, so I just sat there and in due course the man was taken on again and we went on a bit further. Then the same sort of thing happened several times. It was the beginning of bitterness and conflict between the Jew and the Arab.' The way in which that particular Jewish man had been treated in the taxi made Miss Frecheville realize that two sides of the story needed to be understood. 'Up to then I was passionately pro-Arab; but after that I found myself getting to know a very fine Jewish family and that opened my eyes to the other side of things.'

It is precisely because there were two irreconcilable sides that the British finally washed their hands of the problem. For Vera Shamma and her family – as for thousands of others – the events of the late forties represent nothing less than a disaster. 'We were evacuated with about thirty-six hours' notice. We went to Egypt by train. We left the house as it was, we just took our clothes; this was after the King David Hotel in Jerusalem [used as headquarters by the British military] was blown up. They decided the Britishers had to leave and we left.

'My father came with us too. He had never intended to leave – he had built this house on the mountain and he'd always meant to stay in Palestine; we never thought we were going to leave. It all changed over night. It was very sad, very shocking – I couldn't believe it. I remember saying: "Do we have to leave, does it mean us?" My father said: "Yes we do, but maybe we can come back, but now we've got to go, it's a government order, a military order, for the safety of the British." Britons were being killed, two soldiers had been found hung on a tree and another two people had been shot, and people were being kidnapped. So all Britishers had to leave until it was decided what would happen to the Mandate of Palestine.'

I asked Mrs Shamma about the state of mind of her parents – her

British father and Palestinian mother. 'They were both shocked – they didn't know what was going to happen, whether they would be able to come back or not. It was obvious that a war was building up with some of the Arabs leaving to go to the neighbouring countries and Haifa being zoned off into Arab areas and Jewish areas. It was so different from the Haifa we knew – it became a really frightening part of the world. As children we were really frightened – we didn't know what was going to happen to us and our parents were also upset.'

Vera Shamma and her family went to England. 'Then at Christmas in 1947 my parents decided they must go back and see what had happened. We managed to go back by boat and arrived in Haifa. The city was in a turmoil, there were bombs going off everywhere, fires all over. It was like a military area, but we managed to get up to our house. There was a Jewish man with his family already living in our house, they had taken it over. We said: "This is our home", and he said: "We're living in it now and we'd like to stay here." We managed to get all our furniture out and pack it for shipping to England and my father managed to sell him the house. That was the time he realized that we couldn't live there any more. The British government were leaving in May 1948 and giving up the Mandate to Israel. He gave up the idea of living there. For both my mother and my father this was the end of their dream. We left for the last time by boat and saw Haifa burning and bombs going off. It was very difficult to get to the harbour and get to that boat. Sailing out of Haifa harbour seeing the city practically in flames was heartbreaking and I haven't seen it since. I don't want to go back, I want to hang on to my memories.'

Memories of Jewish suffering – as much as that of Palestinians – during this traumatic period in Palestine still haunt some of the Britons who were there. Britain has been much criticised for its pre-1948 policy of restricting the flow of immigration to Palestine, even of refugees from Nazi Europe. George Gilson, who was in the Palestine Police, married a Jewish girl and lives in Israel. His eyes filled with tears as he recalled one incident. 'I was stationed in Haifa Port one day when one of the refugee boats came in, captured by the British on the high seas. People were walking ashore with no clothes, just a blanket on them – starved. And it hit me.'

179

12

JORDAN: BRITISH ROOTS

During my subliminal transition from infant to child I must have realized suddenly at some blindingly important point that we – my family – were different from most of the people round about us. This was Jordan in the mid-fifties, and I was emerging as a small boy into a small British expatriate society. But the passage of forty years has, sadly, filtered out the memory of such significant moments of earliest childhood. Such meagre drips of recollection that survive have merged into a cloudy pool. I recall, for example, without any thread of significant connection, going on family picnics in wooded hills among seas of anemones; travelling by car past the railway station in Amman (it must have been the Hejaz railway, which T.E. Lawrence helped to sabotage in the battles against the Turks) up towards the airport where my father played cricket; walking round the Roman ruins at Jerash; being laid up with measles at the same time as my sister, and a Jordanian doctor towering over me at my bedside; watching petrified as our servant gave a beating to an Arab boy he had found committing some misdemeanour or other; and watching my mother with groups of ladies at sewing mornings. They were sewing 'for the poor refugees', I was told. But that meant nothing at the time. Many years passed before I realized who the refugees were and began to understand the reasons for the tragedy of the Palestinian refugees. Many of the refugees, no doubt, were living in shelters near to my closed world which was firmly linked to Britain by airmail letters from my brothers at boarding school and other members of the family, by the tissue-thin airmail edition of *The Times*, which I would see my father reading, and by the perennial football or cricket scores on the radio.

I had no idea either, as a child, of the significance of much that was going on around me in Jordan, so I find difficulty in pinpointing when certain events happened. There are exceptions. With the help of reference books I can see that King Hussein married the Sharifa Dina Abdel-Hamid on 1 April 1955. I remember that day well because of the fireworks. Saleh, our servant, took me up on to the flat roof of our house in the evening to watch them while my mother went to part of the wedding celebrations. She has a clear memory of the occasion. 'We were very excited to get the invitations. The men were invited to the official signing of the documents and we, the ladies, were asked to the party side of it. It was such a state of excitement. Everyone was going to an expensive dress shop in town which got clothes from Paris; the cheapest frock in that shop was 500 dinars. So I made mine from Damascus brocade, a long dress. I got my booking at the hairdresser in early and was nearly lynched when I arrived there on the morning of the wedding as it was full of women who hadn't made a booking. They thought the people were doing my hair just because I was English.'

On the way through the centre of Amman towards the palace 'the streets were full of people cheering and shouting. Our driver for that night took the wrong turning and ended up in amongst the crowds off the official route. The crowds were peering into the car. I had on this low-cut dress and I felt they didn't like women like that. Somebody must have told the police because two policemen arrived and got on to the running-boards of the car and got us out to the main road again. The crowd was jeering at us. We went up the hill towards the palace and the car had a puncture. We got out and my dress was blowing about. At that point young King Feisal of Iraq came down the hill with cars behind him – he'd been visiting King Hussein. He passed by, and then his entourage drew to a halt and an Iraqi officer came and saluted and said: "His Majesty wants you to use one of his cars to take you to the palace." So we drove up in one of his cars.' My mother and her lady companions passed the traditional Circassian guards at the palace gates. 'There were fireworks all along the front of the palace – banks of Catherine wheels, a blaze of colour. We went into a hallway which was full of ladies and stood there for a long time. Some of the Egyptian ladies were dripping in jewels, over the back as well as the front, one with emeralds hanging down her back. Then the couple arrived and as they went up the stairs, the King, Princess Dina and the Queen Mother leaned over the balcony, showering gold Turkish coins on to the crowd of us below. I had to peel off my long kid gloves and we were all down trying to pick up these tiny coins – I had three and I wanted four for my four children. The diplomatic ladies went up first and were presented to the King and the Queen. They looked lovely: he had a nice uniform and she had a beautiful dress – very pretty. You had to curtsey to the King and then the Queen and then walk backwards to the edge of the room. I was afraid of tripping on my dress.'

After everyone had been presented to the royal couple and had congratulated them the guests went into the room where the wedding cake was ready to be cut. 'There were about four enormous tiered cakes, sponge cakes. I had an evening bag and a handkerchief. I was ready for souvenirs, and I put my piece of cake into the handkerchief and took it home. The couple came into the room and stood by the cake for photos. Later we all went off to another palace and there was a concert. The Queen Mother and the royal party walked to the front chairs and we were near the back. The concert of Egyptian music went on and on – they had special guest singers and an orchestra over from Egypt. All the ladies were talking, and servants brought coffee and tiny glasses of lemonade. I arrived home at about six o'clock in the morning.'

King Hussein married Princess Dina two years after assuming his constitutional powers. His accession to the throne as a young man had been brought about by an assassination and an abdication in the space of only a few years. The target of the assassination was his grandfather, King Abdullah. The British had made him Emir of Transjordan in 1919, and in 1946 he had become King of the Hashemite Kingdom of Jordan. He was assassinated in July 1951 at the Aqsa mosque in Jerusalem, one of the most sacred sites in Islam. His grandson Prince Hussein witnessed the killing and escaped death himself only because a medal he was wearing prevented a bullet entering his chest. The assassination of King Abdullah came three years after the creation of Israel and what the Arabs have always referred to simply as al-Nahda, 'the disaster': the first war against the Jewish state in which the Arab armies were defeated and more Arab land lost to Israel. King Abdullah had had meetings with Jewish leaders, trying, without success, to reach accommodation with them in the hope of avoiding military confrontation. The King eventually paid with his life for his attempts at bridge-building.

The atmosphere was as gloomy in Amman in the aftermath of 1948 as it was in any Arab city. British influence was still strong, but Anglo-Jordanian relations were suffering from the shock of the creation of Israel and the subsequent Arab-Israeli war. Peter

Wakefield (now Sir Peter) was a young diplomat at the British Legation in Amman at this time. Relations between Britain and Jordan, he says, 'had taken a deep setback because of the equivocal attitude of our government towards Israel. I arrived just after the Jordanian and other Arab armies had been defeated. It was an uneasy and rather depressing period.'

The Minister at the British Legation was Sir Alec Kirkbride. Sir Peter Wakefield remembers that Sir Alec 'had been one of T.E. Lawrence's officers and had taken Emir Abdullah to Amman in 1919 and said: "Here you are, here's your capital." And it was a pretty one-horse capital at that time. Subsequently Sir Alec had come back as Minister and was on very close terms with King Abdullah. Things were discussed over tea once a week and things were decided. Sir Alec was a little puzzled to find a young diplomatic officer working for him, because he wasn't really sure what political advice he needed. He felt he knew it all and I was too young to know anything.'

News of the assassination of King Abdullah, Sir Peter says, 'came as a great shock, combined with disbelief. Then there was the question of who did it. It was very unpleasant and disturbing to find that the plotting had been done by charming people we knew; and we had no perception that they would have perpetrated such a crime.' The perpetrators were tried and sentenced to death.

King Abdullah was succeeded by his son Prince Talal, who was abroad undergoing treatment for mental illness at the time of the killing. 'He was an extremely friendly and very nice man with a charming wife,' Sir Peter recalls. 'The terrible tragedy, though, is that as the days wore on his behaviour became more and more erratic and dangerous. It was difficult to know what to do, because a doctor doesn't particularly like signing a certificate saying: "The King is mad." Eventually, though, a group of doctors did sign a certificate and he was restrained and went to Turkey, where he lived out the rest of his life.'

Next in line was fifteen-year-old Prince Hussein, who was attending Victoria College, a British-run boarding school in Alexandria in Egypt. A decision was taken that he should complete his education away from the Middle East, where enemies of the royal family might still lurk, until he came of age to assume his responsibilities as king. Father Kenneth Campbell, who taught at a Roman Catholic school in Amman in the late forties and early fifties, had known Prince

Hussein 'when he was eleven and used to play around with the other boys. Some years later, when his grandfather was killed, they decided to send him to Harrow in England. I had to tell this boy what Harrow was like, even though I'd never seen Harrow.'

Prince Hussein's cousin Prince Feisal of Iraq was also a pupil at Harrow. While there was the comfort of seeing one familiar face when he arrived, the shock to Prince Hussein of being thrust suddenly into the peculiar world of the British public school was considerable. In *Uneasy Lies the Head*, King Hussein wrote that 'it may seem a trifling reason for being a fish out of water, but Feisal and I were about the only two boys at Harrow who did not have surnames. English schoolboys are sticklers for protocol (much more rigid than we are in our palaces in Amman!) and they could not accustom themselves to switching from Smith minor or Brown major to just "Hussein" – so they very rarely called me anything at all.' But there were compensations for the privileged stranger at Harrow. His great joy there, according to his biographer James Lunt in *Hussein of Jordan*, 'was his car, a Rover given to him by a friend of his father's, although boys at Harrow were forbidden to have cars during term-time. His housemaster was therefore not let into the secret, and matters were better kept that way.' So the car was kept in a garage a discreet distance from the school.

Prince Hussein's education in Britain ended with a course at the Royal Military Academy, Sandhurst. This was logical enough, given that knowledge of the military (and how to keep it on your side) is a necessary qualification of every Arab leader.

The Jordanian armed forces, at the time when Prince Hussein was coming of age, were still strongly influenced by Britain. And the story of the development of the army in Jordan is dominated by one Englishman, John Bagot Glubb, Glubb Pasha. He joined what was known as the Arab Legion – a British-officer-led force of Bedouin camel police – in 1930. He took over as commander of the Legion in 1939, and completed the process of upgrading the force from a gendarmerie to a fully trained army. Gawain Bell (now Sir Gawain) first met Glubb Pasha at this period. 'I saw him when I first went to Beersheba to take the job of reorganizing the camel gendarmerie there. "I want someone with Kordofan ideas [with experience of the Kordofan campaign against nationalists in Sudan], who knows one end of a camel from another, and who speaks to Bedu as gentleman to gentleman." I took to him at once. Here was an absolutely dedicated chap but with a sense of humour. "Come over into Transjordan and go round the camel posts," he said. "I'll send you round with a fellow called Lash [Brigadier Norman Lash]." I got a lot out of that.'

The Beersheba camel gendarmerie post had been destroyed in an attack by Jewish terrorists, and the policemen had all fled with their arms. British troops had taken over the town, and Gawain Bell's assignment was to rebuild the camel corps. 'My first job was to get out and meet the sheikhs and try and find out exactly what was happening. I did a good number of camel journeys all up and down Beersheba subdistrict. I'd ridden several thousand miles on a camel in the Sudan. Gradually people showed signs of friendship and the camelry soldiers gradually started to come in. They said they'd had to run away otherwise they'd have been killed. So we re-enlisted the greater number of those, and gradually reformed this into a very useful body of chaps. By the autumn of '39 we had got the camelry posts re-established, got wireless sets put in them, plus a couple of cars with desert tyres. We were then just beginning to re-establish government authority.'

Gawain Bell lived in a building that had once been a railway station, and turned what had been intended as a garage into a reception room to entertain Arab sheikhs, with rugs and cushions around the walls. 'I used to go down and invite the sheikhs from the district to lunch to emphasize that the government writ was re-established. They were always entertaining me. Later in the year, when the Australians came, I was worried because they were a rumbustious lot and I thought they'd be chasing the girls all over the place. I thought it was a good idea to get senior officers and sheikhs to lunch – not that one could talk to the other, but at least they could see each other; and we really had very little trouble.'

Gawain Bell also thought up forms of recreation to bring the Australians and the Bedouin closer together. 'We instituted a couple of race meetings because most Australians know something about a horse and the Bedu certainly knew about horses. We advertised the races quite a bit and the British High Commissioner came and it was quite a success. An enormous number of Australians came from camps in Gaza and the Bedu came in great number. We had camel races and horse races and so on – and I think that it possibly did some good. There's a quite amusing story in this connection: we ran a tote, which was pretty well unknown to the Bedu – they'd never had anything to do with a tote before, but of course the Australians had. In one of the races there was a young Bedu man who'd come from a long way away to watch the races and he had a friend there and he asked the friend: "What's this tote business?" and the friend explained: "You take a number on a horse and you pay whatever it is and with any luck, if the horse wins, you get not only your money back but more, possibly quite a lot more." And this simple fellow said; "But what horse is going to win?" And his friend said: "Well, you silly ass, you must watch and see." Anyway he took a ticket and, lo and behold, his own horse, which was a rank outsider, won. His friend said: "Go back to the tote with your ticket and see what you get." He presented it, and to his absolute astonishment the man in the tote started paying out pound notes to him – in the end they paid him twenty pounds. The young man was so overcome that he fainted.'

Sir Gawain Bell remembers with great pleasure his time with the Arab Legion. Recruiting men for the force was no problem. 'There was a tremendous flow of Bedu out of the desert who wanted to join Glubb Pasha, and we had no difficulties from that respect.' But after carrying out assignments for Glubb Pasha in Transjordan, Syria and Iraq, Mr Bell began to be impatient and wondered whether he was ever going to get command. 'Glubb told me I needed more experience, because I only had a territorial commission. So I did all sorts of jobs from Amman, and then I said to him; "I haven't seen much action. Don't you think I ought to go off to the western desert for a bit?" He said: "What a good idea", and got in touch with the British army. "We've got a fellow here," he told them. "Would you take him for six weeks so that he could learn about war a little bit?" And they said: "Yes, with pleasure, we will."' But the plan was vetoed by the British High Commissioner and Mr Bell stayed in Transjordan.

I asked Sir Gawain about the process of turning Bedouin warriors into Arab Legion soldiers. 'We had to westernize them. If these tribesmen from out of the desert, who were largely illiterate, were going to become modern soldiers they had to be able, for instance, to write a message; and they had to be able to read a map. That was all entirely new to them. They were very brave, they were all right at the mechanical things, they learnt very quickly about motor cars and weapons. But writing with a pen was very much more difficult. And this really was one of our problems, to try and turn these desert warriors into modern soldiers, wearing modern clothes. Until I first joined the Legion they all wore this long garment right down to their ankles. They didn't wear boots, they wore sandals. And they were festooned about with bandoliers and cummerbunds and all kinds of lovely-looking things, which were good for their morale but really weren't wanted in a modern war. So we had first of all to introduce them to battledress; and they didn't like battledress because it was tight, and the trousers were very uncomfortable for them.'

The provision of footwear also created problems. 'They hated the army boots they were issued with, and in many cases the men, having got ones the right size, with their daggers cut off the top so that the wind could blow through and their feet could be more comfortable than in these wretched things. All that took a bit of time. We were trying to westernize them the whole time; and a number of British officers who came to us couldn't understand this.'

There were other aspects of Western life that the Bedu had trouble accepting. 'They were very shy about relieving themselves, and they were accustomed to walk off into the desert and find a bush or a hole in the ground and make use of that. But when we went into camps where we were training, for instance in the Jordan valley, here were all these beautiful latrines which had been built; and to persuade them to go into the latrines was very difficult. For some months they loathed going into the latrines, a line of twenty men all sitting there, they couldn't understand it at all. And they would slip away down into the wadi or behind a tree. So keeping the camp clean was very difficult, and lots of these medical people came round and said: "This is impossible, these fellows can't behave like this."'

I asked Sir Gawain what the latrine arrangements were for the British officers. 'If one was with the Bedu one did exactly what they did, one wandered off into the desert or found a bush. But if you were travelling in the settled areas and going to the police posts, for instance, and spending a night, it was different. In every police post there was a very unsavoury latrine which was, I suppose, occasionally used. But the post commanders were not much interested in unsavoury latrines, they didn't much like going in anyway, it wasn't the sort of thing they cared for; and so if one went to a post, after a little while one would say to the post commander: "Do you have a latrine here?" He'd say: "Yes, yes of course we have a latrine." But it was so foul you knew that you couldn't go into it. And you'd say: "Do you think you could do something about it?"

Now, they had prisoners in most posts and the commander would summon them and they'd get a hose and sluice down. They'd have a brush and this-that-and-the-other – there'd be a great deal of shouting. Finally the soldier in charge would salute and say to the corporal that the latrine was ready for the visitor, and the corporal would then come to me and say: "The latrine is now ready." This would have been perhaps forty minutes after one had originally said to the chap that one would like to go to the latrine.'

Spending so long with Arab troops and officers of the Arab Legion enabled Gawain Bell to build up friendships which revealed, under the tough exterior of the desert warrior, surprising tenderness. Sir Gawain remembers in particular a squadron commander called Ghazi al-Harbi. 'He was quite illiterate, so commanding a squadron was very difficult. He used to say to me: "You're taking all this too seriously, and you're too thin. I can see that you don't eat enough." Then he used to say: "Could I have leave to go to Damascus for a week?" and I'd say: "Ghazi, you had leave a month ago, what about the other chaps, it's their turn for leave now." It would come out in a rather shy way that he had a new wife in Damascus, and he told me I didn't know anything about having a new wife and being in love with her. "One wants to see a great deal of her. You're a bachelor, you don't seem to know anything at all. Just you wait," he said, "when the time comes you'll find someone you want to marry and you'll appreciate the fact that she wants you to be fatter. She will say to you: 'Eat a little more, eat this little bit for my sake', and when she says: 'for my sake', you will eat it." I asked whether he told his new wife about how we lived, and about the Arab Legion and our training. "Certainly not," he said. "It's the last thing I would tell her, it's a military secret. I don't tell her anything at all. All I have to say to her is: 'How sweet you are.'"'

Sir Gawain Bell, like so many other Britons, is still deeply impressed by the memory of Arab friendship and hospitality during his days in Palestine and Transjordan in the wartime years. Two decades later Alan Munro (now Sir Alan) found, as a young diplomat, that the tradition of hospitality among the Bedouin in Jordan had not changed. 'Their hospitality was remarkable, and I had to learn not to admire any item too generously lest it be given to me. I found myself presented with an Arab stallion at one point which I had been rash enough to admire. I had the greatest difficulty in returning it to its owner because it would have been a dreadful indignity for him to have accepted it back, great though his need was for it.'

Sir Alan told me what he remembered of the ritual of eating with the Jordanian Bedouin. 'I had to learn how to eat with the right hand and learn what parts of the beast to go for. We would be sitting in one of their camel or goat-hair dark tents with a screen across the middle. The women would be within the screened portion and the men would have their meal in the male side of the tent. We would have a great brass dish brought in with a most succulent lamb or young kid on it surrounded by rice and we would be given the invitation by the sheikh to plunge our hands into this fairly sticky and certainly quite warm on the fingers collation. When we had eaten our fill, sitting cross-legged, which takes a bit of practice, we would rise up and others would take our place. You could be quite sure that not a scrap would be left. When the tribe, both male and female on their respective sides of the partition, had finished their meal, we would be served water from the nearby well, normally delightfully cool, to go with it, and if somebody had been marketing in the nearby town there would be some fruit to follow. All of it would be accompanied by anecdotes and more anecdotes, all of which would help to build up one's store of Arabic. I used to ask about the war, because then it was only 1959 and within living memory of the First World War and the Lawrence period. These were the tribesmen who had been the principal allies of Lawrence and the other British officers who had participated with the sons of the old Sharif of Mecca in that well-known campaign to move north up from the holy cities to push the Turks out of the Jordan Valley all the way up beyond Damascus. A number of the older men around us had participated in those campaigns. I did notice that they remembered more clearly some of the other British officers who had obviously not been so self-publicizing nor had had such remarkable literary gifts as Lawrence in projecting his own activities.'

No doubt today, if sufficient numbers of Bedouin could still be found, they would sit around and talk about the days of Glubb Pasha. My childhood memories of him have nothing to do with the desert, but with the Glubb house in Amman. There were lots of animals and birds, and my mother remembers a gazelle which wandered about chewing the chairs. When the Glubb family went away from Jordan for a holiday we were given the care of a Siamese cat called Anna.

My mother tells me, too, that the Glubb family were regularly seen at the Anglican Church in Amman. Again, that is not something that I recall – although I do remember attending Mrs Blackburn's Sunday School classes and also finding to my delight that I was small enough to squeeze through the gap between the end of the seats and the wall in church, and thus could effect my exit when boredom set in during services without being pursued by an adult. Outside I would find our driver and my adored hero, Rushdi.

That Glubb Pasha was a churchgoer was confirmed by Bishop John Brown, who then was a young priest working under the Reverend Donald Blackburn. 'Glubb Pasha was a very committed churchman and was a churchwarden. Their house was not far from the church, and he never missed. He came with an armoured car and his Bedouin guards. The guards surrounded the building and were inside, too. I grew up as a very young priest with the strange experience of having a churchwarden who had to be guarded when he came into church and who came with a bodyguard. It affected the whole of our lives – we had this experience of being eye-searched at the very least by very strong, beak-nosed Bedouin guards. Glubb was a good man and a surprisingly gentle man with civilians.'

I remember Glubb Pasha's name coming up at a later point during anti-British disturbances in Amman. These broke out in December 1955 when Britain was trying to persuade Jordan to join the pro-Western Baghdad Pact. Egypt, under the strongly anti-Western leadership of President Nasser, was leading opposition to the pact, and public opinion in Jordan and elsewhere was hostile to it. My flimsy and fleeting memories are of angry chants from crowds, of groups of demonstrators passing close to our house, of the sound of shooting, of anxiety on the faces of my parents, of my mother urging my father to call Glubb Pasha for help, and of a live broadcast of a football match from England. My father's diary entries help to inject order into what happened at this time.

'Sunday, 18 December 1955. Cloudy and dull, occasional drizzle . . . I had a telephone call from the Embassy at 9 saying we were advised to stay at home today, and a little later all shops were closed and troops and armoured vehicles appeared in the streets. There were demonstrations against Jordan joining the Baghdad Pact and stone-throwing – but not in front of the Bank [the British Bank of the Middle East, BBME] this time. We heard shooting at intervals. I closed the Bank at 11, and was safely home by 11.30. Muriel [my mother] made Xmas puddings today and prepared the cake. The streets quite empty this afternoon.

'Monday, 19 December. Same but warmer. I went to the Bank as usual, but crowds soon gathered and demonstrated against the Baghdad Pact, and at 10 a.m. we closed the Bank and put everything moveable in the Treasury. Shortly after, a mob attacked the Bank with stones, and the office was soon littered with broken glass and stones. Luckily the staff escaped injury by sheltering behind cupboards etc. I got home safely later. There was a lot of firing today, and it has been a shock to Muriel and Gerald.'

Meanwhile, as a Foreign Office document of the period reveals, the British Embassy in Amman was wondering how to advise its nationals. 'As soon as reports were received this morning of the likelihood of trouble in Amman,' the Ambassador reported to London on 19 December, 'we warned the RAF and British civil community to keep to their houses as far as possible. In view of the increased scale of the disturbances today I have considered whether to advise members of the community to withdraw or at least send their families to the RAF camp for protection. After consultation with Arab Legion Headquarters and the RAF Station Commander, however, I have decided against doing this at present. It would, I think, be likely to cause more alarm than the situation warrants; it would be likely to cause a bad impression on the local authorities . . .' The next day a report to the Foreign Office listed among violent incidents directed at British targets the stabbing of a British army sergeant and the fact that 'a crowd broke the windows and the BBME'.

Meanwhile, my parents, for my sake, tried to prepare for Christmas as if nothing was happening.

'Tuesday, 20 December. Fine and sunny, warm. There was a general strike today and we all stayed at home. More demonstrations and some shooting . . . We cut a branch off one of our fir trees for a Christmas tree and Muriel has decorated it. But it doesn't seem much like Christmas for either of us. The King dissolved Parliament yesterday and the unpopular Govt of Majali who wanted to sign the Baghdad Pact and who has only been in office for a week resigned today.'

The formation of a new cabinet calmed the atmosphere. Christmas came and went. On 3 January 1956 my father was called to the British Embassy to be told, as he recorded in his diary, that further anti-British demonstrations were expected 'which may extend to our houses. An evacuation scheme has been evolved which won't work in practice, I fear.'

Looking at the diary entries, it seems that many of my fragments of memory of this time may have been drawn from the trouble four days later – certainly the memory of the football match broadcast was.

'Saturday, 7 January. General strike declared, and this morning crowds of students demonstrated against the Baghdad Pact and in favour of free elections. We saw bands of them near here. This afternoon large crowds began to appear and it was obvious that this was the mob and not just students, and with no soldiers in town they quickly got out of hand. The Bank was heavily stoned and many buildings set on fire or damaged, and some shops entered and sacked. I phoned Glubb and the Embassy; troops were soon sent to the Bank and later entered the town in force and restored order. Curfew was imposed at 9 p.m. until further notice ... Football broadcast was Bristol Rovers v Manchester United (Division 1 leaders) in the Cup and Rovers won 4–0. I only heard snatches being busy at the telephone. Today's events have shattered Muriel and she will have a nervous breakdown if this goes on much longer.' On 11 January, leaving my father behind, my mother and I travelled in an Arab Legion car through the wrecked town centre to the airport, where eventually we were put on a flight to Britain.

Bishop Brown has good cause to remember this period, too. He saw plenty of the rioting at very close quarters during the Baghdad Pact troubles and the tension leading up to the Suez crisis of November 1956. 'I frequently had to drive, at least once a week, between Amman and Jerusalem on business and was quite frequently caught up in riots, sometimes dangerous ones, with buildings on fire, especially in Jericho, which was always a difficult place to drive through. Going to Jerusalem on the old road down through Salt, across the Jordan Valley and Jericho and then across the mountains to Jerusalem, for all those weeks surrounding the crisis there were constant riots, there was always the light of fires in the sky as you drove. I vividly remember driving up the mountain from the Jordan Valley back to Amman from Jerusalem and seeing Amman on fire – there were so many fires it looked as if the whole city was on fire in the dark.'

One of the factors contributing to the Suez crisis inasmuch as it fired the determination of the British Prime Minister, Sir Anthony

Eden, to get rid of President Nasser of Egypt, was the sudden dismissal of Glubb Pasha. The pressure from Egypt and from Arab nationalists generally on King Hussein, having rejected the idea of the Baghdad Pact, to distance himself further from the West was considerable. The King's decision to dismiss the British commander of the Arab Legion was conveyed to Glubb Pasha on 1 March 1956. As shocked at the news as Glubb himself was the British Ambassador to Jordan, Charles Duke. 'I was received by King Hussein this evening,' he reported to the Foreign Office, 'and asked him why he had taken this sudden and drastic action.' King Hussein started by saying that he wanted cordial relations between Jordan and Britain to continue. Mr Duke interjected, stating his view that the King had 'delivered a sharp blow at us'. King Hussein said he had discovered what he regarded as some 'grave deficiencies of equipment and stores' in the Arab Legion had noticed 'serious discontent among officers'. He ended by saying he felt 'bound to do what he considered essential for the preservation of the honour of the Kingdom, and if he had not acted as he had he feared a much worse situation might have developed'. Mr Duke, for his part, wondered why the King had not discussed matters with Glubb Pasha first, adding 'that it hardly seemed worthy treatment to dismiss him suddenly like a pilfering household servant . . .'

Having read this dispatch, an enraged Sir Anthony Eden wrote in black ink on Number 10 Downing Street notepaper a message for Mr Duke to take to the King which predicted that 'resentment in Britain at this action will be widespread and deep. I cannot foretell its final consequences upon relations between our two countries.' In a separate message to Mr Duke, the Prime Minister wrote: 'You have spoken well to the King . . . If Glubb has to go, should we not try to preserve the fiction that he has gone to Cyprus on leave until we work on the King, if the story of his dismissal has not broken?'

At two minutes past four in the morning of 2 March Mr Duke cabled the Foreign Office saying: 'I fear that there is no chance of getting the King to modify his views before Glubb's departure.' Later that morning Glubb Pasha arrived in Cyprus. He was, according to a British diplomat who met him at Nicosia airport, 'clearly very cut up, but spoke most calmly'.

The abrupt departure of Glubb Pasha had negative repercussions for a while on Anglo-Jordanian relations. It also had direct bearings on another relationship – that between John Brown and his wife-to-be, Rosemary. 'Glubb's dismissal,' Bishop Brown told me, 'was a surprise and sad for me because that was the very night my fiancée was coming out from England for us to be married. Glubb was to give her away at our wedding in Jerusalem. He was dismissed that same night, and flew in the opposite direction from my fiancée coming out from England.'

Jerusalem, where John Brown got married, was where he had his first experience of living in the Middle East. He arrived, as an Anglican layman, in 1954 and taught at St George's School. His subjects were history, English and religious education. 'The students were extremely bright and very anxious to learn. They were Arabs, Muslims, and Christians of different denominations and Armenians. They were all intelligent, very brittle, politically articulate, extremely anti-Zionist. We were always having political arguments; but the only problem one had with Arab boys was that they all wanted desperately to get into Western universities and they would learn whole books by heart, it was their way of passing exams. Our job as an English boarding school was to give some education and not just learning, because it was so easy for them to learn by heart without understanding what they were writing and saying.'

I wondered if it was strange to be teaching a class of Arabs about British history, about the Tudors and Stuarts, for example. 'Yes it was. I taught the juniors Greek mythology, and that was even stranger. The real interest in the history class was over the French Revolution, and that did capture their imagination.'

I asked Bishop Brown whether, after a life working as an Anglican churchman in the Middle East, he considered himself a missionary in the normal sense of the word. 'Not really. I have never in the whole of my life in the Middle East openly or publicly sought the conversion of a Muslim to Christianity – the Muslim has a coherent faith and it's extremely dangerous for a Muslim to convert to Christianity. Even in the sophisticated Middle Eastern countries like Egypt and Jordan, I always took the view that it was not part of my job to bring about the death of a good Muslim simply because he converted to Christianity. On two occasions I had to deal with Arab converts who came to me for protection. These men were in real danger. One of them was a soldier and I got protection for him from Glubb. I am a missionary in the sense that I have a message to proclaim and I call myself a missionary bishop. I will always be ready to declare my own faith and to speak about it.'

I have often wondered whether or not it is presumptuous of

Anglicans to establish themselves in a region where there are indigenous Christians and where Christ lived and preached. I raised the point with Bishop Brown. 'The wife of Bishop Kafity [a Palestinian Anglican] of Jerusalem,' he said, 'was asked once by an American how long her family had been Christian, and she replied: "About two thousand years." We have to remember that Palestinian Christians have been around since the beginning, and they and the Syrian Christians began it all and we're the Johnny-come-latelys. It might be presumptuous of Western Christians to come into an Arab environment – I do detect a reluctance on the part of Arabs to concede that Western Christianity has anything to give the Arab world.'

Despite the sensitivity of Arab Christians to the subject, British missionaries have continued to come to the Middle East. Bishop Kenneth Cragg says the missionaries have 'varied according to their own doctrinal positions. There were elements I remember who used to be interested very much in what used to be called in the old language soul-winning and evangelism, and the concern was with the individual, with the possibility of confession and baptism. In practical terms for many the role amounted to education, to a lesser extent hospitals. These were generally thought of as places to offer means of evangelism. If you had patients in your hospital then you could preach. Similarly if you had pupils in your schools. The English medium was very much sought after and the assumption that English education would be worth having for various reasons meant that there was no dearth of students from other faiths; and so it was often seen as a means to an end, though for some as an end in itself. Then there would be a few who were engaged in direct evangelism, but increasingly in the Islamic context that became extremely difficult for various legal and physical reasons. Just to go into a village and start preaching in the open air was extremely problematic. In some areas there was increasingly a sense that religions had to relate to each other as institutions rather than a rather forlorn effort to bring this man or that man into the Christian faith as a person. There came to many, I think, the sense that there should be a mission to Islam, with certain dimensions about God and faith and society, with distinctively Christian compassion, non-violence, a sense of the love of God embodied in the symbol of the Cross. "Father, forgive them." This has a different quality to the belligerence that so often characterized Islam.'

Canon John Wilkinson, who first went to Jerusalem in the mid-fifties, also saw the role of the Anglican Church in the Holy Land as that of bridge-builder. 'We tried to get to know the sister churches, the Greeks, the Latins, the Uniat churches, and try and teach them things that we as British people knew. That was a continuing ministry to the churches, and on the whole I think that the missionaries did a good job – not trying to convert people, but a necessary social job.'

In the early 1960s, John Wilkinson was back in Jerusalem, setting up a theological centre for Anglicans at St George's. 'I started the work in the college. Unfortunately, while the British thought they were still in charge of things in 1961 and felt a great responsibility for the Arab people among whom they dwelt, they hadn't much money. So the college was not well finished, nor was it able to provide enough scholarships to fill it. In the main we had only about four students, two of whom were Egyptians. The Egyptians are not typical of Arabs when it comes to humour. Whereas all around us there were people who didn't like humour and were accustomed to speaking in abstract nouns, the Egyptians were used to speaking in jokes. My wife is an Egyptologist and we were entertained by an archaeological inspector whose brother was in what must have been the jokes department of the Cairo police. He told us some of the jokes. For example, just after the '67 war [when the Arabs suffered a humiliating defeat at the hands of Israel], one of the jokes went: There was a woman whose child was very ill and she took him to the doctor. She put the child on the ground and it started crawling backwards, and the doctor said: "Congratulations, madam, your child will be an Egyptian officer."'

On another occasion 'some Ethiopian monks came to study things that we weren't qualified to teach. We took them to the Trappist monastery in Latroun, which was still occupied by monks who didn't speak – only the guest master spoke. He had a habit of going to the dormitory to show it to guests. He would open the door and say: "This is where we sleep", and people would ask if they slept all night and he would reply: "No, only for two hours." When he told all this to the Ethiopian monks, they said: "Oh, you sleep, do you?" They, apparently, stand all night in prayer on their sticks.'

Canon Wilkinson mentioned the Arab–Israeli war of June 1967. During this conflict and other times of trouble he developed an enviable ability to shut his thoughts off from the events around him and concentrate on scholarship. 'I realized very early on that there were very few people in Jerusalem who knew Latin and Greek as well as I did. I realized that one of the contributions that I might be able to make was to translate pilgrim texts. I went on translating, and I've now translated all the pilgrim texts from the Crusader period. That's what I did when the wars came. There were three wars during my time there so I had quite a lot of free time.'

The Arab-Israeli war was as disastrous for Jordan as for Syria and Egypt. The Jordanians lost control of East Jerusalem and the West Bank. They also had to cope with a new influx of Palestinian refugees. The Palestinian presence within Jordan became so big and strong that it threatened to undermine the state. Also, guerrilla attacks launched by Palestinians based inside Jordan against Israeli targets to the west of the River Jordan were bringing swift and tough retaliation from the Jewish state. In September 1970, King Hussein ordered his army to take the offensive against the PLO forces. A bloody civil war erupted. Sister Magnificat, a Roman Catholic nun, was working in a hospital in Amman when the fighting broke out. 'Looking back it seems just like an awful nightmare. The civil war was the culmination of a whole year of troubles. The PLO had been getting bigger and bigger and the refugee camps were recruiting grounds. Conditions in the camps were grim. The guerrillas could go in there flashing their uniforms and their Kalashnikovs and the boys just flocked to them. Over the years the numbers increased and they gained footholds here and there, including one about a quarter of a mile from the hospital. They set up a camp on waste ground which grew, and by the time the civil war began in 1970 they'd even got anti-aircraft guns there. There was a lot of unrest in the refugee camps because it looked as if nothing was being done.'

Sister Magnificat says she will never forget the date the battles started, 17 September, the beginning of a period called ever since by Palestinians 'Black September'. 'We knew something was coming because there was a feeling in the air. I sent the driver into town to buy as much food as he could because we still had to feed the patients. Then the army started attacking all the guerrilla camps – just a little way up behind the hospital was a camp which the army blew to bits and the occupants came down to the hospital and surrendered to us and asked if we would take them in and hand them over to someone who was good.' The convent where the nuns lived was on the roof of the building. As the hospital got caught in cross-fire, the upper floors had to be abandoned. 'We had to move all the patients down to the ground floor and we put them into the rooms down there and we slept on mattresses and chairs in one room. The hospital was damaged but no one was hurt. In no time at all the army came and took over the building and we became a military hospital. The tanks came down the road and they'd stop outside the hospital and start shelling this refugee camp a quarter of a mile down the road, and the camp would return fire. Because they weren't too accurate the shells landed on the hospital and in the hospital grounds.'

Sister Magnificat witnessed some horrifying scenes during the fighting. 'One man brought in had lost both legs but didn't know it; another man had lost his arm; and others also were very badly wounded. In the first days we received casualties we had nothing to give them; they were on the floor in a room downstairs and one man bled to death. There was nothing we could do; we couldn't give him blood because we had none to give. There were other very bad experiences, and yet in the bad conditions in which we worked not one of our patients turned septic. God was looking after us. The army also picked up the guerrillas who were injured and brought them to us as well, so we kept them all together. We had eight at one point in one of these double rooms. The war sometimes divided families; on one occasion there was a soldier on the front steps and a guerrilla was brought in and it happened to be his brother. They met on the steps – each thought he was doing the right thing in the war.'

Sister Magnificat also told me about two incidents which vividly demonstrate both the courage and sense of humour that one finds so often when Britons have been in danger in the Middle East. 'I went on to the roof once,' she said, 'because they'd hit our water tank and water was running down the road. I couldn't bear the thought of losing our water like that. There were three tanks together. The third one was hit and if I'd left it the water in all the tanks would have sunk to the same level. The only thing to do was to close the valves between the tanks so we didn't lose any more water. I asked a couple of boys who worked in the hospital but they wouldn't go on the roof, neither would the soldiers. So I borrowed a tin hat from one of the soldiers and I made him stand just inside the doors to watch in case I was hit. Then I went out and turned it off. A few days later I went up to the convent, very daringly, to get a kettle we needed downstairs. I went on to the roof and ran round into the convent and got it. As I came out on to the roof again I looked over to the hillside where there was a partly built house. I saw a head in the window but I couldn't tell whether he was facing me or the other way. I didn't know whether he was for or against and whether he could see me. I plucked up courage and ran out and he fired at me. I jumped and ran round to the door as fast as I could. Jumping, I dropped the lid of the kettle, and I did not go back for the lid of the kettle. When it all quietened down and we went up I found the bullet holes in the wall where he'd missed me. At the time it was quite frightening but looking back it's something to laugh at. It all lasted about ten days, ten horrific days.'

The battles ended in victory for King Hussein's army. The PLO were forced to withdraw their men and weapons and regroup in Lebanon. King Hussein had withstood his toughest test thus far.

The monarchy in Jordan had adapted skilfully and tactfully to the changing circumstances in the region, which explains why it has survived while others, like that in Iraq, did not. It is, therefore, a Jordanianized British institution – the Emirate of Transjordan, the seed of the current monarchy, having been planted by Britain. As an institution nurtured by the British, I believe that the monarchy in Jordan is one of the most enduring and most successful British legacies in the Middle East.

The Jordanian monarchy was certainly well steeped in British culture and tradition when I was a child in Amman in the 1950s. Like me, Crown Prince Hassan, brother of King Hussein, attended the British community school, which was headed by a certain Miss Webster. I still have an acceptance note for my fifth birthday party signed simply 'from Hassan' and have kept the huge gold-coloured box which contained Barker & Dobson chocolates which he brought as a present that day. Prince Hassan was accompanied at my party by his English nanny, as my mother recalls. 'Prince Hassan was at school with you and I knew his nanny, Miss Goodman, a Norland nanny. She brought him each day and never let him out of her sight. I asked how he was enjoying school. Apparently he loved it, so I invited him to your party. She said his parents were keen that he should mix with English children before he went to Harrow. He was excited and pleased at being asked. He was very polite, and when he said goodbye she straightened his tie and he came to me and shook hands and took his going-away present. His manners were perfect.'

13

LEBANON: THE 'SCHOOL FOR SPIES'

In the summer of 1957 I spent many hours on the balcony of our house at the end of rue Bliss in Beirut just watching. There was always plenty going on, ships heading towards the port or trams stopping and starting at the terminus just up the street. As darkness fell, groups of young people would wander down from the American University towards the sea front, where families paraded slowly and gracefully up and down. Sometimes they would stop a while to buy a coffee or soft drink and watch a fisherman with a long and curving rod standing patiently on the rocks. From the balcony you could hear the rhythmic clicking made by the sellers of charcoal-cooked sweetcorn banging metal tongs against the wooden carts as they pushed their way in among the crowds.

It was clear, even to a seven-year-old, that Beirut was a city that was loud and full of energy. The sound of car horns never let up, and huge American limousines would screech round the corner in front of our house and down to the sea day and night. I knew, too, that there was plenty going on for the adults. My parents, it seemed, were out at official or private functions most nights. There was lots to choose from. Looking at *Lebanon This Week* of 22 July 1957 I see there was the choice of watching the London Old Vic productions of *The Merchant of Venice* or *Antony and Cleopatra* at the Baalbek International Festival. In Beirut itself a list of places to eat and drink included the Caves du Roy and the Whisky A Go-Go bars, the Blue Bird and the Genève patisseries, and the Eden-Roc and Lucullus restaurants. Most of these had become victims of the civil war by the time I went back to live in Beirut as an adult many years later. But Alan Munro, a young diplomat attending an Arabic language course in Lebanon at about the time I was there as a child, remembers it all. 'Beirut was an extraordinary mix of high society, low society, fashion and fun. They did know how to enjoy themselves, and they offered a great deal of enjoyment of a very stylish kind to the rest of the world. We became quite wise in the ways of making our money reach far. There was a restaurant called the Lucullus where we language students discovered that if you started with the marvellous cold hors-d'oeuvre dish, the *meze*, you could exist simply on that for the rest of the week. We devised a way of having our *meze* and then having ourselves suddenly called away and managed to survive very adequately. There was a great deal to enjoy. Later I did a spell in the embassy in Beirut, living in the very lovely Greek Orthodox quarter in an old coach-house in a splendid nineteenth-century, sugar- dome palace and it was a very attractive and stylish way in which to start one's diplomatic work overseas.'

Sir James Craig's memories of Beirut in the fifties are also coloured by the style and dynamism of the city. 'The inhabitants of Beirut were so full of energy, wit, initiative and vivacity that I found the whole thing fascinating. Whether I would today, I'm not so sure. But in those days I was quite happy to go to three cocktail parties and a dinner most nights of the week, dinner starting at half past eleven and finishing at one in the morning. Beirut is an almost unique place for a diplomat to work in. In most places in the Middle East the problem is getting information. In some countries people are afraid to talk because there's a highly developed secret police system. In other countries people are unwilling to talk because they don't particularly like foreigners and are suspicious of diplomats anyway. In Beirut everyone wanted to talk and they poured out their hearts and the gossip to you. Whereas in country "A" the problem was to find even one version of some incident you'd heard about, in Beirut you got ten or a dozen versions of it, and the problem came in assessing which was right or which had elements of the truth in it, adding them all together and dividing by ten. In those days Beirut was cosmopolitan. Life was international, vigorous and alert.'

Beirut was the centre of the Middle East, the hub of the region's business life and an international crossroads for travellers. Every country and group in the region had its representation there. Given the maelstrom of activity it is hardly surprising that it became a centre for gossip and intrigue. Glencairn Balfour-Paul remembers 'the famous attempted coup by what was known as the PPS, the Partie Populaire Syrienne, which played quite a part in Middle East political thinking for a time. Anyhow, we didn't know anything about this, but I was woken up one morning at six o'clock by a

Lebanese member of the staff to say there was a coup going on. So I jumped into a car and drove round to see what was going on – I was Political Officer in the embassy then and obviously there was something extraordinary going on, there were soldiers everywhere and firing and so on. So I drove round to wake the Ambassador up – it was before his normal getting- up time, so he wasn't best pleased. Anyhow, I explained things, and in due course we went to the office and later in the day – this is one of the entertaining things about Arabs, they always tend to blame somebody other than themselves for whatever goes wrong – the then Minister of the Interior, I think it was, announced that this plot had been engineered by the British Embassy and he had himself seen the British Ambassador standing on the roof of the embassy at dawn signalling to a British warship offshore. Well, I knew where the British Ambassador was at dawn and there was certainly no British warship nearer, I should think, than Malta. Anyway it was all dealt with – a few people executed, and so on.'

With so many groups represented in Beirut, diplomats had to be on their guard, as Sir James Craig recalls. 'Our great foes in those days were considered to be first of all the Iron Curtain countries and particularly the Soviet Embassy, so we had to maintain all the usual security measures, no careless talk, watch out that nobody unauthorized got into your flat and bugged it and so on. Our second perceived enemy in those days was the Egyptian Intelligence Service, the EIS. I think now that its efficiency and its hostility were probably a little exaggerated, but in those days of Nasser, relations between Britain and Egypt were not good, so we were supposed to watch out for them. But it didn't affect our lives – social or political – very much. My three years in Beirut were very stimulating.'

Beirut's reputation as a centre of intrigue and espionage was enhanced when Kim Philby, working as a journalist in the Lebanese capital, suddenly disappeared and turned up in Moscow. He had managed to escape just before his cover was blown and he was revealed to have been an agent of the Soviet Union. Mr Balfour-Paul knew Mr Philby. 'He was a close friend of mine, and my one moment of world fame was when I was the man he was dining with the night he absconded. But I knew half of him and it was a very attractive half. He was a very good friend. And I remember a letter that some American friends of mine in Beirut received from his wife in Moscow with a postscript written in Kim Philby's hand saying: "If only you knew what hell it is when your personal affections clash with your political convictions." He was a marvellously entertaining friend, and a very helpful one to me as Information Officer in the embassy because he knew much more about what was going on in the Middle East than all the other journalists put together and would dictate his pieces for *The Economist* straight off without looking at them again until his wife typed them out and sent them. Not many people could do that.'

All the retired British diplomats quoted thus far in this chapter learned Arabic in Lebanon at the Middle East Centre for Arab Studies, known universally as MECAS. It was situated in the village of Shemlan in the mountains overlooking Beirut. The centre was set up by the British army, with Foreign Office co-operation, in Jerusalem in 1944. The idea was to take people who might be needed in the Middle East after the war and teach them not only the language, but also something of the history, religion and culture. The centre was moved to Lebanon in 1946, where it remained until 1978, when, with the Lebanese civil war under way, it was forced to close.

Julian Walker, another retired British diplomat, attended MECAS in the early fifties, when the attitude to study was serious, but relaxed compared with the way it became later. 'We had a nice pastor who directed the studies; it was fairly pressurized in that you had to try and learn fifty words of the language a day. You went through the MECAS grammar, and you went through tests every month. But there was still enough time to get morning sunshine and go down and paint and things of that sort. Later on, MECAS got to be a really hard-working sausage machine, but it wasn't so in our time. We lived in an old building at the bottom of the village. The roof was rather inclined to leak and the washing facilities were a bit primitive, but there weren't very many of us. We were a mixed group, RAF people, Army people going out to Aden, a few oil company representatives. There weren't so many members of foreign diplomatic services at that time.'

I asked Mr Walker about the relationship between the language students and the villagers in Shemlan. 'It was very good, with Elias the barber, who used to rush out of his shop with his shotgun in the middle of haircuts to shoot at sparrows which he didn't think much of, and with all the other people running the stores. Of course we practised Arabic, but it was Lebanese Arabic, and when you got down to the Trucial Oman they mocked our Arabic and I was very shy about using my Arabic there, so reverted to a few very basic words.'

Mr Balfour-Paul, who attended MECAS after the course had been restructured, thought he was speaking good modern Lebanese Arabic, until he was rudely disabused of the fact during a party in Beirut. 'I was never a brilliant Arabist of the James Craig type. But once, at a dinner party with some Lebanese members of parliament, there was a power cut and all the lights went out and we wandered around the big room talking in the dark. I joined a group. And suddenly the lights came on again, and one of the Lebanese ministers turned round and said: "Who was that talking?" And it turned out to be me, and he said: "I thought you were an Iraqi Bedu." That was how my Arabic was said by the Lebanese to be like.'

Sir James Craig, among the cream of Arabists in the British diplomatic corps and a former teacher at MECAS, would not like to think of the centre as a sausage machine; nor would he accept that graduates in the main sounded like Iraqi Bedu. Mr Craig, as he was in the mid-fifties, was one of those involved in restructuring MECAS. When he arrived there in 1955 he found it had 'an unsystematic approach to teaching. The teachers were good pedagogues. My predecessor did sterling work, but was not an Arabist. What happened was that students were put in a room and the teacher told them to get on with it. What we did, Donald Maitland the director and I, was to systematize the whole thing. It was important to recognize from the very start that in so short a course there was a limit to the number of words which could be learnt by the students. We were going to restrict the vocabulary to three thousand words. So Maitland and I sat down and went through the dictionary word by word ticking off the words we thought should be in our three thousand. I can't tell you how dreary it was.' The words were then divided into ten sections, which were matched with reading and grammar exercises. A new competitive spirit developed at MECAS as students strived to gain the eighty per cent pass mark to move on to the next section of the course. 'I'd come from university,' Sir James Craig says, 'where the problem was always to make people work, and I discovered to my surprise at MECAS that the students were most eager to work and be tested.' Sir James also remembers camaraderie developing between students and villagers. 'Many of the villagers could speak English. The village taxi driver, for example, George Hitti. But I was able to say to them: "I know you speak English, but you are forbidden to speak it to the students." So if the student engaged George's taxi and addressed him in English, he would say in Arabic: "I don't understand you." The same with renting a house. It was clumsy to begin with. But there's no doubt that the biggest aid to learning a language is compulsion.'

When I came back to Beirut as an adult in 1980, MECAS had closed down. But it was still talked about, and by Arabs invariably called the 'British spy school'. I asked Sir James about this title. 'At first it was a piece of nonsense, but it became irritating when some Lebanese politicians took up the cry. It was, of course, nonsense. If you were wanting to train your spies, the last thing you would do is take them to a foreign country and engage as their instructors a group of Palestinians who, because of history, were extremely hostile to British foreign policy. No doubt there were from time to time among the Foreign Office students some who came from what you might call the other side of the house. But mixed up with them were the armed forces, the oil men, the bankers and the businessmen. What set the story going afresh in the sixties was when George Blake, a spy for the Russians, happened to be studying Arabic at Shemlan when he was uncovered, taken home, tried and sent to prison. That irrationally revived all the rumours.'

Sir Alan Munro also calls the spy-school label nonsense. 'It makes for a good joke and a bond when one is in the Arab world nowadays. This was an allegation that was manufactured by the fairly venomous, at times, Voice of the Arabs radio station in Cairo. The epithet stuck; it suited everybody's book that it should be regarded as such, partly because there was in the Arab world so much that went on that was regarded as being the consequence of activity by the British intelligence service – a myth that dies very hard. Because of this idea MECAS was dubbed the spy school and the name stuck. In fact it was the most effective training machine for the Arabic language and we had students from all round the world.'

Mr Balfour-Paul was at MECAS when an Egyptian magazine published an article 'about what it called the famous spy school in Shemlan. There was a picture with the article, I remember vividly, of the young men stalking through the trees in a suspicious manner carrying pieces of paper in their hands. The caption said these were young spies being taught to deliver secret messages in obscure places. Actually of course it was the young men studying their word lists at night – they had to learn fifty new words every night including, mysteriously to me, such things as the word for having six fingers on the right hand. An Arabic word which you wouldn't have thought was essential for anybody.' Mr Balfour-Paul chuckled. 'But I remember when I was in the embassy in Beirut in those idyllic days of the foreign service I had as my assistant information officer a man who subsequently became permanent under-secretary in the Foreign Office, Patrick Wright. He came bustling into my office one morning saying he'd just been visited by an Imam from Tripoli in northern Lebanon who had six fingers on the right hand and he was able to use the word. He thought this was the greatest triumph that MECAS had ever had.'

Diplomatic life in Beirut in the pre-civil war era of the fifties and sixties appeared to be, as Mr Balfour-Paul suggested, idyllic. I asked Sir Alan Munro for his memories of embassy life in 1960. 'My ambassador at that time was very much an ambassador of the old school: Ponsonby Moore Crosthwaite. He was a man of great taste and much respected within Lebanon. He arranged to take over a very beautiful semi-ruined Druze manor house up in the mountains not far from Shemlan to use as a weekend house and he put a lot of his own good taste into its restoration. At the weekend sometimes he would invite me, his third secretary, to spend a couple of days up there with him and with whoever he had as guests. I remember on one or two occasions his very good friend Freya Stark would be there and we made a very happy threesome, and the time would be delightfully spent – it sounds idyllic now – in walks with Freya Stark over the stony hillsides. She would proceed in flowing cotton long dresses which of course snagged on every bramble and gorse bush that you could find and she'd be wearing of course her traditional wide-brimmed hats. She took us around villages and around hillsides and always she had their instant history at her fingertips – where Lady Hester Stanhope would have lived, and village tribal groupings, and so on – a fascinating, wonderful companion to have. At the end of the day we'd play interminable games of Scrabble which somehow Freya Stark always won and that seemed entirely appropriate.'

Sir Alan met his wife Grania in the British Embassy in Beirut, where she also worked. Their liaison was not much to the liking of the head of mission. 'When we decided to get married I went as one duly did in those days to ask my ambassador for his permission to marry. As a confirmed bachelor he said: "Must you?"; but I managed to carry my point and he agreed that we could get married. But when it came to the matter of having a little time off for a honeymoon he wasn't too keen on this, and in the end he settled for three days. That gave us just enough time for a very brief trip to Rhodes before scuttling back to Beirut to resume our tasks under his watchful eye. He was a great stickler for proper use of the English language and I think indeed much of my own affection for the English language stems from that hard training that one received from him. One would put up one of one's immature drafts on some subject or other – it might have been the question of Palestinian refugees or some other political issue – and he would look at it and send his secretary back to my office down the corridor bearing my draft with a lot of red ink on it and a copy of *Fowler's Modern English Usage*. There would be a note in the margin saying: "I find two litotes and an anacoluthon in this draft. Get rid of them."'

Most of the correspondence between British embassies in the Middle East and London has undoubtedly concerned weighty matters of politics and international affairs. Sometimes, though, much more mundane affairs have to be discussed, with the men and women in the field phrasing their message in the most tactful way possible in order to secure the co-operation of the bosses in Whitehall. For example, in July 1955 the British Consul General in Jerusalem cabled the Foreign Office on the subject of a planned visit to Britain by the Arab governor of the city, Hassan Bey Katib, and his wife. The Consul General clearly had no confidence in the ability of Foreign Office officials to handle the visit sensitively. 'It is important,' the cable read, 'that some effort should be made to pay Hassan Bey some attention and to ease his path in the unfamiliar world he is proposing to visit. He is profoundly sympathetic to us, and I doubt whether there is a more devout admirer of Britain in the whole of the Middle East . . . Hassan Bey has never been in England, nor so far as I know in any Western capital, and I fear his courteous and self-effacing character will not let him easily adapt himself to the rush and bustle of life in London. It would be unfortunate if, for lack of a little guidance and help, his faith in our way of life should be diminished.' Sadly the Public Record Office archive does not record how Hassan Bey coped with the rush and bustle of London, nor whether the Foreign Office read sufficiently between the lines of the cable to accord him the sensitive guiding hand that the Consul General felt was needed.

Cable traffic between embassies in the Middle East and the Foreign Office has also been tinged now and then with humour. In April 1957, with the anti-British uproar in the Middle East after the Suez débâcle subsiding, the British Embassy in Amman reported that the wives and families of US diplomats had returned to Jordan. British Embassy dependants were already back. The author of a cable thought it worthwhile pointing this out, aware too, it seems, that even one's bosses like to be flattered. 'It is mortifying,' the cable read, 'for the U.S. Embassy to have seen our wives and families return, as they did thanks to your decision four months ago, during which period there have been no dangerous anti-foreign incidents at all.' To which a hand-written note has been added at a later date: 'One marvels at the prescience of the Levant Department.'

Many of the Arabists in the diplomatic service who came out of the MECAS fold in the fifties and sixties found themselves posted to the Gulf states. While physical conditions were tough, life was enjoyable in another way because they were involved much more in practical action than in routine desk work. As recently as the fifties, for example, a young British diplomat could be called up to lead a military expedition. Viscount Buckmaster had the honour of performing this role for the last time. 'In 1952 I led a small group of sailors from one of the visiting Royal Navy ships and Trucial Oman levies. I led them into the palm groves north of a little village called Rams, which lies about five or six miles north of the most northerly of the Trucial States, Ras al-Khaimah. The object of it all was to remove a man who had defied the ruler by shooting up all passing vehicles. It was the last occasion on which an armed group was called into action in this way. In the nineteenth century, of course, it was very common, there was a great deal of outlawing and so on. But this was the only one in recent years.' I asked Viscount Buckmaster if he had personally been at the front of the armed force. 'Yes, I was. It was quite harmless, we didn't shoot anyone, we didn't do any harm. But we managed to overcome the rebels and took the leader back to Sharjah, where he was incarcerated.'

On another occasion, in the sixties, a British diplomat was required to engineer what might be called a gentlemanly *coup d'état*. This was in Abu Dhabi in 1966, when Sheikh Shakhbut, the ruler who was unwilling to spend oil revenue to develop his emirate, was deposed. The diplomat carrying out this role was Mr Balfour-Paul.

'I knew Sheikh Shakhbut very well and liked him a lot. But during an interim between two Political Residents – Sir William Luce and his successor – the present Ruler of Abu Dhabi, Sheikh Zaid, came to me after visiting London. He told me that he and his family wished to have a change of ruler because of Shakhbut's notorious meanness or wisdom, depending on whether you think that spending vast sums of money on welfare was for the benefit of the people or not. But anyhow, Sheikh Zaid decided he must go, and all his family wanted him to go. He wasn't prepared to do it himself because they were all very frightened of Shakhbut. So I had to go down and visit the Ruler in his isolated fort in what then was desert and tell him we wished him to retire with dignity and so on. He got very, very angry indeed and shut all the doors and sent his retainers up into the roof with their muskets, and they were carrying ammunition up and down stairs – it was quite a dramatic time. I was quite glad to get out of the palace after an hour or two, and it took several hours in the afternoon to eventually persuade him as decently as we could to come out. We had some Trucial Oman Scouts hidden around the palace, but they were not to intervene unless the balloon went up. Appeals were made to his retainers to come out and some of them came without shots being fired. In the end he emerged, there was a guard of honour, and it was all done with as much dignity as possible.

'Shakhbut remained curiously friendly towards the British even after that. He always came to the Queen's Birthday Party. It was rather moving really that he bore no grudges, which is another great Arab characteristic – however much one quarrelled politically, at the personal level they remained quite extraordinarily friendly, everywhere in the Arab world.'

Even when British diplomats weren't leading military expeditions or deposing rulers, life in the early days in the Gulf had a wonderfully free feel to it. Sir James Craig remembers life in the Trucial States in the late sixties. 'It was almost like a colonial service job. In those days these emirates were not colonies, nor legally protectorates. But they had a special relationship with Britain under which we were responsible for foreign affairs and defence. Since they were at that time both poor and undeveloped, economically and technically, the British representative, who was known as the Political Agent – the title being an inheritance of the old Indian Empire – in fact had a great deal of influence on internal affairs. He worked very closely with the rulers. The British government supplied a small development budget. When I got there, oil had been discovered in Abu Dhabi, but nowhere else. But it had only been discovered. The necessary facilities for producing it and exporting it had not yet been built. So life was little changed. Some things had happened. In Dubai there was a small water scheme, so we had water from the mains. Not everywhere. There was a small telephone system, but no roads. Not an inch of tarmac. We went everywhere by Land Rover. These were possibly the three happiest years of my life, because you were doing things. Most people's lives, certainly most people's lives in the Foreign Office, consist of reading telegrams, letters, assessing, judging, advising, but very seldom doing something. I found in the emirates that I did things. I might notice, for example, on one of my trips to the mountains a number of Bedouin who looked rather sick or who had obvious eye complaints. So I would come back, call a contractor and sketch a small medical station on the back of an envelope and ask him to quote me a price. Six months later I could visit this clinic, install a doctor in it and see the Bedouin men and women coming to get treatment. At the end of each day you really felt that you'd done something.'

For rest and recreation there were plenty of opportunities for camping or bathing on some of the finest beaches in the world. Also, Sir James says, 'the British Political Agency had its own dhow of which we were very proud. It was the only dhow operating from Dubai which had its own flush lavatory. You had to pump. But still it flushed. Most of the others had a kind of primitive thunder-box on the stern of the boat. Lots of people went camping. In those days it was all very romantic. The chief of police was a Scotsman who had his own hawks for hunting.'

British diplomacy in the Middle East this century has also had plenty of awkward moments which have come back to haunt diplomats in subsequent years. For example, the secret Sykes-Picot agreement with France and Russia during the First World War which led eventually to the establishment of nation states tied to Europe in territory where Britain had promised the Arabs independence. Few Britons remember Sykes-Picot; but most Arabs do. The Balfour Declaration promising a homeland for the Jews in Palestine caused years of heartache for British officials, soldiers and policemen in Palestine as they tried to match irreconcilable Arab and Jewish demands.

The merits of the Balfour Declaration are still contested; but few defenders will be found today of Britain's role in Suez – least of all among the diplomatic corps. Diplomats are servants of their government and are required sometimes to lie, spy and perform other nefarious activities at the behest of their masters.

The performance of Sir Miles Lampson, the Ambassador to Egypt during the Second World War, in arriving at King Farouk's palace at the head of a column of tanks to threaten the Egyptian monarch, was an extraordinary enough act of diplomacy. But the Suez crisis was British diplomacy's darkest hour. The connivance of Britain and France with Israel to find a pretext to launch a military strike at Egypt to bring down President Nasser was shameful. But more shameful was the way in which the affair left British diplomats in Cairo and elsewhere in the Middle East ignorant of what the Eden government's intention really was. Peter Wakefield was one of the British diplomats in Cairo as the Suez crisis developed. 'We were pawns,' Sir Peter told me. 'One likes to think that what one says as a diplomat is true for one's country, that one is not sent abroad to lie for one's country. Therefore when we are shown to have been very "economical with the truth", in the modern phrase, it is upsetting for us personally and I think it's very harmful to our diplomacy in general. I considered resigning over Suez, and the thing that saved me from doing it was the fact I was locked up in Cairo and by the time I got home to the Foreign Office the policy had changed and therefore one was not resigning over a policy that one disagreed with, because the policy was no longer there. So one was persuaded that it would be very silly to withdraw one's services when so much needed to be done to repair the damage.'

Donald Maitland, one of the most distinguished Arabists in the Foreign Office, was drafted in to help run the ill-reputed Arabic-language propaganda radio station the Voice of Britain during the Suez crisis. When I interviewed Sir Donald in 1994 for a BBC programme about Suez I asked him if he felt he had been put in an invidious position by being told to work for the Voice of Britain. 'I think this is an important issue. When I joined the foreign service after the Second World War, like all new entrants, I was given to read a lecture by Harold Nicolson about the role of its members. He described loyalty as one of the qualities which were required. He said there may be times when you are called upon to do things with which you disagree. Your conscience may be offended. As a loyal member of the service you should carry out your instructions to the best of your ability. But if, when that episode is over, you still feel you cannot continue to serve the government, then that will be the moment to resign. That was very much in my mind after Suez. My feeling was that it was better to remain in the service and do what I could to mitigate the damage which had been done to our interests through this deplorable affair, and also, to the extent that I can, to influence ministers in future in such a way that this folly will never be repeated.'

The occasions when British diplomats in the Middle East have had to wrestle with their consciences over policy dictated by Whitehall or 10 Downing Street are few compared with those when they have had to face raw danger. Even during the Suez crisis diplomats were forced to remain sheltered in the British Embassy in Cairo. But the environment was even more hostile when British diplomats in Baghdad remained trapped in their embassy during the Rashid Ali uprising described in an earlier chapter. On occasions diplomats have been killed. For example, Lord Moyne, the British Minister Resident in the Middle East, was murdered in Cairo by a Jewish terrorist group in November 1944.

Moments of danger in British diplomatic missions have normally been reported through the mouths of diplomats, usually in retirement. My sister, Rosemary Foxcroft, was a secretary in the British Embassy in the Libyan capital, Tripoli, at the time of the Arab-Israeli war in June 1967. The Arabs' anger at their humiliating defeat by the Western-backed state of Israel was compounded by accusations – false accusations – made by President Nasser that British and American aircraft carriers had provided support to the Israelis. 'When the Middle East war began,' my sister told me, 'the Libyan members of staff said rumours were going round town that anti-British demonstrations were planned. So the huge embassy door was shut and all of a sudden we felt trapped. The light, the breeze and the view of the sea had all gone. And it was like that for days. Soon we heard the sound of chanting outside and rocks being thrown. We could peak out through the shutters and see the mob waving angrily and throwing stones. On the fourth day we went up to the roof and burned all the secret files in incinerators. And amid all the smoke from the burning papers rocks and stones kept landing on the roof around us.'

Word reached the embassy that the British mission in the eastern Libyan city of Benghazi had been stormed and broken into by an angry crowd. 'The news made us tense. It was pretty grim being trapped as we were. But there was a lot of joking. Only one person couldn't stand the pressure and flipped.'

But despite the anxiety and tension an exterior face of calm was maintained by the embassy staff – but only just. 'We had to man the telephones all the time, and on one occasion when one of the girls picked up the phone there was a call from a newspaper in London wanting to know what was happening, and so on. "It's chaos here, pandemonium, we don't know what's going on," she started to say. At which point one of the diplomats grabbed the phone and said: "Everything's fine, all under control, no problems." An extraordinary case of stiff upper lip.' In the end, the crisis abated without the embassy staff coming to harm.

Of all groups of Britons working in the Middle East this century diplomats have probably had to make more adjustments than any others to adapt to their country's changing role in the region. In the first half of the century Britain was drawing the maps, installing the governments and providing military assistance to a string of countries. By the beginning of the 1970s, there was only the odd patch of territory where open British influence remained, notably Oman. Britain's economic interests, on the other hand, were as strong as ever, and tens of thousands of Britons continued to follow in the footsteps of the pioneers.

The fashionable way to assess Britain's hour in the Middle East would be to dismiss it as the last spasm of a dying imperial lion – an era that has produced lots of amusing and interesting anecdotes and can now, with embarrassed relief, be forgotten. Or there is the view of romantics like T.E. Lawrence and Wilfred Thesiger, who have written contemptuously of the arrival of twentieth-century materialism in the Arab world and of the foreigners who brought it. In consequence, in their view, the purity of the region has been spoiled. 'Inevitable, of course,' T.E. Lawrence wrote, 'that these impurities should come. As pools shrink they stench.' But these assessments are unfair to those who gave service in the Middle East, ordinary people who, in good faith, went to the region to do jobs of work and whose stories fill the pages of this book. It is equally unreasonable and patronizing of Westerners to try to deny the Arabs access to products of the modern world simply to keep alive a romantic myth.

Even the architects of policy that seems crude or antiquated should not be judged too harshly today when standards are very different from the way they were in the first half of the twentieth century. Mr Balfour-Paul, now in retirement, experienced at the sharp end of British diplomacy the decline of British power and influence in the Middle East. 'I'm an ex-brutal imperialist myself. If we hadn't believed that we were in the Middle East and elsewhere to benefit our subject peoples we wouldn't have done it. I'm a very ambivalent imperialist now. I think, like everything else in the world, it's part good, part bad. I think we were there trying to do good. One of the troubles was that the man in the field has a very different approach to the problems from the man who makes policies in London, who has to take into account global interests and strategies, whereas the man in the field has a much more parochial view of the problems and of what ought to be done. So there was never a hundred per cent agreement between those in the field and in London.'

As for assessing the British legacy in the Middle East, Mr Balfour-Paul told me about an incident in Iraq (a country created by Britain and run by the British for many years) in 1970 when the Baathist regime foiled a coup attempt. 'They extracted the necessary information by the usual means from those they caught, they collected seventy people and got any more information they wanted. They then shot them all summarily, put the corpses on to a lorry and distributed them about the town, kicking them off in front of their own houses and saying to their families: "Take your dog." I was so nauseated by this behaviour that I really couldn't address a Baathist for a few days. And I went, under cover, to see the leader of the opposition – a very nice, gentle, bourgeois character. I told him how nauseated I'd been by this behaviour of the government. And he said to me: "What are you complaining about? If we'd been in power, we'd have done exactly the same thing." Now this was the most gentle gentleman Iraqi. And I liked the Iraqis, I found them enormously vivid, volatile and interesting people. But violence is perhaps in their nature. So what we left in Iraq is hardly measurable today. The Iraqis thought that we were just misusing our power for our own benefit. Of course we wanted the control of Iraq and our own interests, but at the same time we wanted to make the Iraqis, like any other Arabs that we had power over, friendly with us and happy and contented and developed. I don't think there's anything disreputable about wanting both things – that's to say one's own national interests and the interests of the people one was dealing with. I'm not as ashamed of imperialism today as all that – I think it was perfectly legitimate – it's what all good empires have done. On the other hand I can't claim that we've left a tremendous legacy behind – though it may be slightly more than in our self-critical way we assume.'

There is a legacy: a respect for the rule of law and a sense of organization. In some Middle Eastern countries the legacy is stronger than in others, but even Arabs who demonstrated against British rule concede that this is what Britain left behind. Akil Wahby, a retired UN administrator, joined anti-British demonstrations in Cairo in the 1940s. Today he reflects on the era when the British governed Egypt: 'I'm sorry to say this, but it was a very well organized government.' Mr Wahby laughs. 'There was very good discipline and very good respect of the law and the police.'

Sari Nasser, a Palestinian-born professor at the University of Jordan, took part in anti-British protests in Jerusalem in the 1940s. He still blames Britain for the fate which befell the Palestinians in 1948. But, he says: 'I must admit that the British also introduced a lot of positive things. We learnt quite a lot, for instance, about administration and discipline. These were positive things.'